The Postcolonial City
and its Subjects

ROUTLEDGE RESEARCH IN POSTCOLONIAL LITERATURES

Edited in collaboration with the Centre for Colonial and Postcolonial Studies, University of Kent at Canterbury, this series presents a wide range of research into postcolonial literatures by specialists in the field. Volumes will concentrate on writers and writing originating in previously (or presently) colonized areas, and will include material from non-anglophone as well as anglophone colonies and literatures. Series editors: Donna Landry and Caroline Rooney.

The Postcolonial City and its Subjects

London, Nairobi, Bombay

Rashmi Varma

Routledge
Taylor & Francis Group
NEW YORK AND LONDON

First published 2012
by Routledge
711 Third Avenue, New York, NY 10017

Simultaneously published in the UK
by Routledge
2 Park Square, Milton Park, Abingdon, Oxon OX14 4RN

Routledge is an imprint of the Taylor & Francis Group, an informa business

Typeset in Baskerville by IBT Global.
Printed and bound in the United States of America on acid-free paper by IBT Global.

Library of Congress Cataloging-in-Publication Data
Varma, Rashmi.
  The postcolonial city and its subjects : London, Nairobi, Bombay / Rashmi Varma.
    p. cm. — (Routledge research in postcolonial literatures ; v. 34)
  Includes bibliographical references and index.
  1. Cities and towns in literature.   2. Literature, Modern–20th century–History and criticism.
3. Literature, Modern–21st century–History and criticism.   4. Postcolonialism in literature.
I. Title.
  PN56.C55V37 2011
  809'.93321732–dc23
  2011028498

ISBN13: 978-0-415-88039-8 (hbk)
ISBN13: 978-0-203-82781-9 (ebk)

For my beloved mother
Priyadarshini Varma
for her love and her laughter
for her courage and her spirit
for being there for me even when she is not

My city --
    is like a long debate...
    the streets—are illogical pronouncements
    and the alleys are such—
    as if a long-winded argument
    is being dragged first here and then there.

                        Amrita Pritam

Contents

Permissions

Figure 1   A wall in Southall reproduced at *The Southall Story* exhibition at the Royal Festival Hall, South Bank Centre, London. (Photograph by Rashmi Varma. Copyright by Dennis Morris, www.DennisMorris.com).

Preface

An exhibition on *Global Cities* at London's Tate Modern Museum (July–August 2007) included the following ten cities: London, Los Angeles, Sao Paulo, Mexico City, Johannesburg, Cairo, Mumbai, Istanbul, Tokyo and Shanghai. Of these, only three, London, Tokyo and Los Angeles, are in the so-called First World, a striking fact about the twenty-first century in which the key sites of rapid and mega-scale urbanization are not the erstwhile metropolitan centres of New York, London and Paris, but are located in the postcolonial or the Third World. Peppered with staggering bits of information about Mumbai's exponential population growth (that will result in 50 million people in the city by 2050) and the astounding levels of unemployment in Johannesburg (about one in five households in the city has no income), questions about what *explains* the spectacular and uneven dominance of these cities and/or urbanization in the twenty-first century remained largely unaddressed in the presentation.[1]

The Tate Modern exhibition, however, presented a striking contrast to the theoretical and literary narratives in which I had first noticed the marginality of the postcolonial cities I knew first-hand, at odds with the facts of urbanization in the twentieth and twenty-first centuries. Within my reading universe as well, from T. S. Eliot's *The Waste Land*, seen as the paradigmatic modernist poem of the fragmentation of urban Europe in the aftermath of the twentieth century's First World War, to Zadie Smith's celebration of a multicultural London at the turn of the new millennium in *White Teeth*, the twentieth- and twenty-first-century city in the "West" had indeed been a key site for narrativizing experience, or the "atrophy of experience" as Walter Benjamin put it, in modernity.[2] In particular, modernism and postmodernism's vexed relationship to the city has been the subject of some of the most trenchant thinking about the meaning of modernity as not just the consciousness of a temporal break from the past but also of a profound spatial re-orientation, indeed of a radical dis-orientation.

In these cultural and theoretical elaborations, postcolonial cities appear largely in margin notes, as spaces of radical alterity and backwardness, or as the predictable product of the nightmarish teleology of capitalist development.[3] I found both this marginality and this appropriation of postcolonial cities within narratives of modernity puzzling and discomfiting. Growing up in Indian cities such as New Delhi and Patna (the latter, I do realize, is hardly on any cosmopolitan traveler's itinerary in India—even the *Lonely Planet Guide* condemns it as a hell-hole of a city, to be avoided at all costs!), I have long been familiar with an obsessively articulated ambivalence towards (western) modernity that shaped both my own cultural and political sensibilities as well as those of the cities I lived in. These cities, while physically "outside"of the West, were always also deeply imbricated in it. New Delhi, the city of my birth and early childhood was independent India's capital and the center of its "national" modernity, even as it harbored refugees of the Partition violence who still gave it, in the 1970s, a lingering Punjabi/regional flavor. It was where it was possible to escape into a nationally ordained cosmopolitanism ("unity within diversity") without leaving home in Patna, where I had spent most of my teenage years, too far behind.[4]

Patna, once the capital of ancient empires and of a robust mid-twentieth-century nationalism, was by the time of my arrival there in the late seventies already a "failed" city.[5] It was reeling under corruption, municipal breakdown and the social upheavals unleashed by the "total revolution" of students, peasants and trade unionists against Indira Gandhi's regime in the early seventies. In spite of these contradictions, and sometimes even because of them, we who lived in Patna always thought of ourselves as modern. We were definitely more modern than the provincials who surrounded us from even smaller towns and villages of Bihar, the state of which Patna is the capital city, though perhaps less modern than Bombayites or the relatives who had made their way to the suburbs in America or England. Schooled by the Sisters of Notre Dame at the elite girls' convent school in the city, I spent my free time devouring English novels borrowed from the modest school library or the local British Council library (that shut down a few years ago, for want of subscribers). My schoolmates and I learnt that we were certainly less modern than the characters we read about in English literature, no matter if they were nineteenth-century heroines in the English countryside! From here, some of us counted days when we, too, would fly out of our city, modernity's purported elsewhere, to experience wider horizons in the nation's capital, its modern center.

It is this context of postcolonial education and urban culture, with all its contestable claims to modernity and its own complicated dialogue with narratives that rendered the world in terms of centers and peripheries (Patna was peripheral to Delhi but central to other peripheries in the "backward" state of Bihar) that produced for me the question that led to this book. This is the question of how and why the city in postcolonial literature in particular and postcolonial discourse more generally has been the concentrated site for theorizing, indeed for narrating and thus generating, the postcolonial subject. The postcolonial city, while retaining its national identity, has become both the terrain and the instrument for the struggles—over identities, resources and rights—unfolding in a globalizing, neo-imperialist, world order. The question of the postcolonial subject and the postcolonial city as a space of contestations linked simultaneously to national identity and globalizing forces provokes a series of other related questions that this book aims to engage: How are we to read the historical processes and political and cultural formations that lie within the folds of postcolonial cities? And what about the spaces that are not yet cities, or that were once cities, or that will never be cities? How can I try to apprehend that the cities I have lived in and those that I have only imagined, dreamt and read about, shape two of the fundamental questions of our time—those of citizenship, entailing the question of belonging in an increasingly deracinated while simultaneously racialized world, and of justice, the dream of an even and equitable, though not flattened, world space, the "global city" of our times and of our futures? And finally, how is the postcolonial city both the arena and the subject of our assertions of humanity against the onslaught of ever-contracting spaces for self-expression and collective solidarity in a neo-liberal world order? These are some of the questions I hope to address in this book, if not to answer, with any semblance of satisfaction.

Acknowledgments

This book has taken far too long to finish and accumulated far too many debts in the process of writing and thinking. I would like to thank the anonymous reviewers for Routledge, the editorial board, and especially Erica Wetter and Elizabeth Levine for enabling this book to see the light of day.

Although it reads nothing like the dissertation that first explored the idea of the postcolonial city in modernist and postcolonial literature, first I must thank my teachers at the University of Illinois at Chicago, where I began writing the thesis—David Spurr, Sandra Bartky, Nancy Cirillo, Jamie Daniel, Judith Gardiner, John Huntington, Ned Lukacher, Charles Mills and Peg Strobel. They provided the best mix of intellectual probity and friendly guidance. I was also immensely lucky to have a fabulous cohort of graduate students. Among them special mention needs to be made of Gwynne Gertz, Anne Flanagan, Mike Perkovich, Jeff Purdue, Vainis Aleksa, Julie Lindquist, Laura Bentz and Sue-im Lee. Their sense of humor and comradeship was a source of constant support, delight and insight. Thanks are also due to the Julia Stukel Award in Women's Studies at UIC, the University Fellowship and the National Women's Studies Association's Pergamon Prize for the Best Dissertation Proposal in Women's Studies for encouragement and financial help.

My life in Chicago, where I began writing on the postcolonial city, was deeply enriched by friends and comrades outside my university and departmental existence. In particular, the India Alert family (Manji, Brajesh, Atsi, Sanjoy, Rachana, Yaseen, Amrita, Sanjay, Naim Saab, Catherine and Shyamala) sustained me in more ways than I can list. Bindu Desai's love, erudition and passion for justice fired me up and still does. Shobha Srinivasan's endless supply of kamikazes and laughter helped me get through the low points in Chicago and then again in North Carolina, while the Mamdani household of Meenal and Bashir in Oak Park provided a terrific *adda* in the truest sense of the word, where politics, food, friendship and wine came together in beautiful ways.

The thesis was completed during my time in Burlington, Vermont. A big thank you to Robyn Warhol, Nancy Welch, Joni Seager, Laura Ring, Sheheryar Hasnain, Margot Harrison and Kari Winter. Robyn, Nancy and Laura in particular not only opened up endless horizons of feminist thinking, but also guided me towards embarking on my life as an academic in my own right.

It was in Chapel Hill, North Carolina, then, that I arrived as a newly minted Ph.D. and an Assistant Professor. I am extremely grateful for John McGowan's fine mentoring and friendship that helped me get through the early career years with confidence. Pam Cooper, Erin Carlston, Tyler Curtain, Maria Deguzman and Jill Casid were also exemplary colleagues and dear friends. The Progressive Faculty Network at UNC-Chapel Hill was an incredibly committed and politically astute group. I was lucky to have been a part of it in the especially challenging times after 9/11. Political engagement became an excuse for friendship. Catherine Lutz, Elin O'Hara Slavick, Sherryl Kleinman, Sarah Shields, Steve Wing, Frieda Behets, Karen Booth and Elyse Crystal are the most amazing comrades and friends one could wish for. Judy Farquhar opened doors when she invited me to join the writing group that she was part of with Jane Danielwicz, Kathryn Burns, Joy Kasson, Laurie Langbauer and Megan Matchinske. I learnt again how to write and I owe a tremendous debt of gratitude to them. Friends across the road at Duke were integral to my life in North Carolina and I would like to thank Ranjana Khanna, Srinivas Aravamudan, Ajantha Subramanian, Vincent Brown, Mandakini Dubey, Diane Nelson, Miriam Cooke and Laurel Frederickson. Other friends who supported me in more ways than one through those years in Chapel Hill include Arturo Escobar, Durba Chattaraj, Liz Mason-Deese, Michal Osterweil, Mark Hayward, Jessica Wolfe, Sanjoy Baruah, Maya Jerath, Yumna Siddiqi, Rajika Bhandari, Charlie Kurzman, Deborah Barrett, Bob Podolsky, Chad Haines, Yasmin Saikia and Shantanu Phukan. Yumna in particular read numerous drafts of the manuscript and pushed me to finish the book. Burns, Maria, Karen and Elyse were my emotional anchors without whom I would have been adrift. Finally, for inspiration, Mab Segrest and Stan Goff—salutations!

In December of 2003 I moved to London, where I would finish writing this book, a place that also literally provides a resting place for the long argument I had been having with the idea of the postcolonial city. I would like to thank Paru Raman for inviting me to SOAS and to Ide Corley to UC Dublin to present some of this work. Adjusting to life in London was made profoundly fulfilling by the friendships of Chetan Bhatt, Steve Cross, Sharad Chari, Shabnum Tejani, Paolo Novak, Giuseppe Caruso, Gita Sahgal, Cassandra Balchin, Sohail Warraich, Ardashir Vakil, Phiroze Vasunia, Miriam Leonard, Ramesh Fonseca. Denise Ray, Asad Ali Khan, Suma Athreye, Sanjay Jain, Kamalini Ramdas, Sharun Mukand, Anandi Mani, as well as our family in Reading—Vibhu, Svetla and their daughter Tavisha. Our niece Shruti Sinha in particular added much charm and joy to life in London while she was here. In the final days of writing, the help, affection and support of Ethel De Silva has been incalculable.

At Warwick, I have had the most amazing and incomparable group of colleagues, interlocutors, friends and comrades. In particular I owe thanks to Peter Mack, Maureen Freely, Emma Francis, John Fletcher, Jane Poyner, Sharae Deckard, Pablo Mukherjee, Sarah Hodges, David Hardiman, David Arnold, Srila Roy, Karen O'Brien and Neil Lazarus. Benita Parry has been a powerful source of inspiration and an amazing friend. My Ph.D. students Sumana Ray, Sorcha Gunne and Norbert Bugeja have taught me a lot, and showed incredible patience as I tried to finish my own work.

There are of course also friends and family in other places who have provided help and friendship long distance. Among these I count Amitava Kumar, Shuchi Kapila, Sanjay Joshi, Sanjam Ahluwalia, Rakesh Chandra, Ron Herring, Robert Jensen and Ananya Kabir, as well as our brother and sister-in-law in Milan (Prabhat Sinha and Susmita Sinha) and my loving family in Rome (Shantanu, Sharmishtha, Shashank and Shamini Mathur).

But in the end I must return "home" and thank the friends who have inspired me and loved me through these long years. Aslam Khan, Tom Kocherry, Dilip Simeon, Madhu Sarin, Somnath Sen, Upamanyu Hazarika, Manish Puri, Nisha Gupta, Archana Garodia Gupta, Manisha Priyam, Srirupa Roy and Lalit Vachani, as well as the Patna gang of Anunaya and Smriti, Vibhoo and Leena, Anuj and Arika, have all been more hospitable and welcoming of me than I deserve. In recent years I have also experienced the sheer joy of re-connecting with old friends and teachers from my school, Notre Dame Academy, Patna, and from my college, Lady Shri Ram, in Delhi. Those are among the oldest and most meaningful debts that are also gifts.

I have also been blessed with so many loving families and my final thanks go to them. My Allahabad family in all its various extensions has made me feel connected, always, to the happier times of childhood. My maternal family, especially my late grandparents Shiva Mohan and Shanti Nandkeolyar, but also my aunts and uncles and the extended family, have loved me and been proud of my achievements. My parents-in-law, Anjani Kumar Sinha and Ashalata Sinha, have always supported me in both life and work, as have my sisters and brothers-in-law Bhawana and Sanjeev Sinha, Manisha and Sanjeev Sinha, and their wonderful children Aditya, Rathin, Akanksha and Ira. My father Arun Kumar has been the rock of my life, allowing me to float and rise, and has been there at the most critical moments. The love of my sister Ratna, my brother Chaitanya and my brother-in-law Rajesh is far too immense to express in words. My darling nephew Manas has been the source of real joy in my life and I look to his future with hope and love. But above all, and because thanking him is so inadequate, this book also belongs to my beloved partner, husband, friend and comrade Subir Sinha. If it weren't for his abiding and deep love, patience and intellectual brilliance, as well as for his fine cooking and love of music, his endless enthusiasm for ideas and conversation, his passion for cricket so that it was a perpetual background (on Cricinfo or on Skysports) to all writing done in the home, and for being an amazing Baba to our daughter Lila, this book would never have been finished.

It is one of the greatest sorrows of my life that my beloved mother Priyadarshini Varma is not physically around to see and hold this book. But I know that wherever she is, she is here in spirit, smiling at what is also her achievement. And now there is Lila Priyadarshini, who has entered my life and made me experience love, beauty and joy as never before. In her everything lives on.

Introduction
A Postcolonial Itinerary

> To dissect the urban process in all of its fullness is to lay bare the roots
> of consciousness formation in the material realities of daily life.
> —David Harvey, *Consciousness and the Urban Experience*

This book then is about twentieth- and twenty-first-century formations and
fictions of the postcolonial city and the constitution of new subjects within
it. It offers a reading of both historical and contemporary debates on urbanism through the filter of postcolonial fictions and the cultural fields surrounding them. In particular, the book presents a representational history
of London, Nairobi and Bombay in the twentieth and twenty-first centuries
and engages three key theoretical frameworks—the city within postcolonial
theory and culture (its troubled salience in the construction of postcolonial public spheres and identities, from local, rural, ethnic/"tribal" and
regional, to "national", cosmopolitan and transnational subjects/positions);
postcolonial fictions as constituting a new world literary space and as a site
of articulation of contending narratives of urban space, global culture and
postcolonial development; and postcolonial feminist citizenship as a universal political project challenging current neo-liberal and post-neo-liberal
contractions and eviscerations of public spaces and rights. *The Postcolonial
City and Its Subjects* weaves together these material and discursive threads
in order to present an analysis and theory of the representational space of
the postcolonial city and its subjects.[1]

The book argues that postcolonial cities produce a proliferation of subjects and collectivities difficult to categorize within the terms deployed in
modernist as well as postmodernist discourses. It provides ways of thinking about citizenship as a material and symbolic *relation of belonging* articulated in the postcolonial city that is riddled simultaneously with imperial
legacies and nationalist re-inscriptions of spatial practices, as well as with
the complexity of representing "difference" within the city, situated as it is
within a global capitalist order. As such, a key concept that this book elaborates is that of the postcolonial city as a *conjunctural* space that produces
a critical combination of historical events, material bodies, structural
forces and representational economies which propels new constellations
of domination and resistance, centers and peripheries, and the formation
of new political subjects.[2] In the account that follows, I argue that what is
specifically postcolonial about the postcolonial city as conjuncture is its

particular elaboration within an imperial and a neo-imperial world system that is crossed over by a specific, unfinished and sometimes distorted anti-colonial and nationalist project.

The book begins by interrogating the centrality of the city within theorizations of modernity, and argues that the "standard urban narratives" of modernism did not account for women's and colonized people's relationship to, and appropriations of, the modernist city. As such, the book engages the complex representational history of the modernist city.[3] Indeed, within these standard urban narratives, the city became the site for staging the incommensurability of gender identity and the public sphere, an incommensurability that was typically represented and understood as urban "crises". Throughout the chapters, I employ the figure of "unhomely women" to elaborate new forms of political identity and to disarticulate the city as the site of masculinist and colonial publics, enforced by the historic privileging of Enlightenment-derived understandings of citizenship based on abstract principles. At the same time, the book also attempts to make a case for a universalism that is not indebted to the Enlightenment exclusively; instead, the disjunctures of the Enlightenment projects of humanism and citizenship, as re-articulated in anti-colonial and nationalist movements, provide the space for the formulation of a postcolonial feminist citizenship. In particular, the book focuses on the question of women's labor that has underpinned the modern city, whether through prostitution, sweatshop labor, reproductive practices, or the ideological work that women perform in literary narratives. I foreground the simultaneous reconfiguration and subversion of women's "proper" place in the city, and of their proper work, as central to thinking and theorizing postcolonial feminist citizenship.

But the book works against the grain of the search for an authentic postcolonial feminist subject; it focuses instead on feminist practices and collectivities as being worked out or negotiated in the conjunctural location of the postcolonial city in which rural, urban, national and trans-national are simultaneous geographies just as imperial and anti-imperial histories are concurrent events. In other words, the book proposes a definition of postcolonial feminist citizenship that is drawn from the gendered labor of obtaining the right to inhabit the city as a political subject, and to be represented as such in the cultural work of postcolonial fictions.

In the following sections I outline the key theoretical frameworks that have been influential in, or indeed constitutive of, the theorizations of the postcolonial city. It is in the gaps and elisions of these frameworks that the book locates the postcolonial city. In doing so, it undertakes the theoretical task of providing a critical framework for reading the postcolonial city as not just an absence but as a key site for understanding contemporary articulations of urban power and feminist citizenship.

Modernist City

The modernist city's inextricable embeddedness within the capitalist system meant that the very experience and representation of modernity is filtered through the frame of an already globalizing *imperial* world system. As such, the modernist city is the formal and ideological *precursor* of the postcolonial city. Thus, rather than understanding the postcolonial city as an imitation of the modernist city, one could read it in terms of an imperial genealogy that can also be placed within the project of resistance to imperialism.

Georg Simmel's apprehension of "the sensory foundations of psychic life" in the city where there was a growing "multiplicity of economic, occupational and social life" points to the ways in which urban life was becoming entrenched within an intensifying and expanding capitalist economy since the nineteenth century, producing the individual as a detached, calculating self, alienated from his or her environment in the city.[4] On Simmel's analysis, the metropolis itself was the diabolical incarnation of money form. Benjamin developed many of the ideas in Simmel's work and deployed Marx's theory of commodity fetishism to understand the monumental changes in experience and subjectivity in the modernist city. For Benjamin, the modernist city could best be understood in terms of commodification, a process that was engulfing everyday life and experience under capitalism. The modernist city was distilled as a set of spectacular arrangements of commodities in the ever-expanding arcades of the marketplace, where "the commodity luxuriates and enters, like cancerous tissue, into the most irregular combinations", and in the everyday spaces of the home and of intimate life.[5] What was hidden from view in these seductive arrangements of commodities was the real world of gritty and often unseemly human labor, and nasty relations of social and economic exploitation. Even as labor assumed the form of things and fashionable images (that involved the continuous production of the new) in the marketplace, the modernist city of fashion and glamour could *barely* conceal the dark underside of modern urban life—of lives lived in slums, brothels and factories. The contradiction between the real and the image, between the glitter and the grime, between labor and commodity, produced what came to be theorized as the fragmented consciousness of modern subjectivity.[6]

And yet it was in the city itself that everyday acts of resistance, surprising social improvisations and unexpected constellations of mundane acts were to reveal the fault-lines of a capitalist culture that had made the city its (natural) home. As "the locale of freedom", the city provided an arena for self-fashioning.[7] The latent revolutionary potential in the chance encounter on anonymous streets, in the surprising juxtaposition of commodities and human consciousness, and in the ultimate inability of capitalism to colonize and assimilate human experience were aspects of urban life that were evoked in particular in the work of the Surrealists. For other theorists of capitalist modernity such as Benjamin, the urban street became the "dwelling place of the collective" and the site of new possibilities that emerged from the very same logics of commodification and fragmentation constitutive of capitalism.[8]

But there was hardly a consensus on the place of the city in modern culture. The dominant response to modern urbanity, seen as a veritable crisis of space and consciousness, consisted of either appeals to what Raymond Williams referred to as "unlocalized accounts" of an "organic community", or as denigrations of the modern subject's alienation and fragmentation in the city.[9] Conservative critiques of modernity such as those found in Martin Heidegger and Bachelard rendered urban space as "the deracinated home of post-industrial society", even as Left-wing thinkers like Friedrich Engels (especially in his 1845 classic *The Condition of the Working Class in England*, and his 1872 *The Housing Question*) and writers like Charles Dickens, Emile Zola and Honoré de Balzac in the nineteenth century had also derided the alienation, the material depredation and the consequent dehumanization of the working classes in the newly industrializing European cities.[10] Others such as Regis Debray saw the twentieth-century city as a reactionary space of bourgeoisification, and therefore inconsequential in the larger history of anti-colonial resistance.[11] Anti-colonial theorists such as Frantz Fanon have also been read as privileging the rural and the peasant as the exemplary site and figure of anti-colonial resistance. Mike Davis furthers this line of argument by questioning the salience of the city in anti-colonial narratives, arguing that colonial cities were both "demographically rather insignificant" and not "the most important centers of native resistance".[12] For Davis, the urban crisis in the global South is very much a mid-twentieth-century and later phenomenon, coterminous with de-colonization and subsequent developments in the global economy. But as I argue throughout this book, the spatial power that cities exerted in the colonial project is not reducible to the demographic power of sheer numbers. The chapters on early-twentieth-century London and mid-twentieth-century Nairobi also, if only implicitly, counter the disproportionate prominence given to global capitalism in Davis's account of the rise of the significance of cities in the Third World at the expense of the historical trajectories of accumulation via colonial rule.

While drawing upon Raymond Williams's *The Country and the City*, which chronicled the ways in which "the decisive transformations, in the relations between country and city" since the Industrial Revolution shaped English literature, *The Postcolonial City* seeks to bring to the surface a question that lies submerged in Williams's work. That question concerns the city's emergence as a powerful signifier (a) of relations of colonial rule and (b) of urbanism (the ideology that privileges cities as loci of cultural and economic development) as key to the colonial project, and indeed to the very production of the country-city dichotomy by the colonial-capitalist state (see Chapter 2).[13] In her critique of Williams, Gauri Viswanathan argues that

> in describing imperialism as one of the "last models" of city and country, Williams obfuscates imperialism's relation to British economic production, and by extension, its cultural formations, by suggesting that British influence existed outward rather than that the periphery had a functional role in determining internal developments.[14]

Underscoring Viswanathan's point, a key argument of this book concerns troubling such ultimately static models of center and periphery that would render the metropolitan city of the colonial world as the exemplary model of modernist urbanity everywhere. Such a modular view would run counter to the ways in which notions of center and periphery are scattered, twisted and reconstituted by contestations with, and transformations of, the imperial project, and the centrality of the city within it. After all, we know from the historical record that modernity's norms crucially shaped the forms of cities in the colonized world, even as the peripheral modernity of the colonized city leaked into Europe's metropoles. Thus, it is important to call into question, even as one takes critical inspiration from, Marxist and materialist theories of modernist urbanism and make a case for the necessity of a wholly adequate account of the postcolonial city. Largely absent from both the Marxist accounts of the city and the "standard urban narratives" of literary modernism (see Chapter 1 for an extended explication of this concept) has been an engaged discussion of the material production of the spaces of modernity and of subjects within them as articulated in *the colonial project*. The lineages of the city in Left theory, in which the modernist city is the product of capitalist development, thus must also take into account colonialism as a constitutive elaboration, however subsumed within the larger narrative of capitalism.[15]

Postmodern Forms

If literary modernism spelled out the complex connection between modernity and urban life by locating the modern subject's alienation and fragmentation in the capitalist city, materialist theories of postmodern culture have also entailed attempts to re-formulate the relationship between subjects and urban space, especially in the context of late capitalism and economic globalization.[16] A key idea in such a re-formulation has been cast as the impossibility of retrieving authentic subjects within city spaces. This has led to urban sites being delineated as spaces of hybridity, of heterotopias and of newer, more diasporic subjectivities. Guy Debord's "society of spectacle", theorized in the late 1960s, now seems to provide a prescient reading of the postmodern city in which surfaces and images present new forms and arenas of increasingly flexible capital accumulation.[17] Intricately interwoven with tectonic shifts in global capitalism—from the early 1970s crises within capitalism to the late 1990s full-blown neo-liberal globalization to the early-twenty-first-century's intimations of a global financial collapse—has been the sweeping transformation of urban spaces.[18] Cities, comprising complex networks of capital and culture, have emerged as the model for postmodernist characteristics of time-space compression, de-centering, and flexible boundaries, as the contemporary global economy transforms, in Manuel Castells's formulation, the city's "space of places" into the "space of (informational) flows".[19]

Within these readings of global shifts and transformations, there is a sense of optimism as much as there is doom and gloom about the future of cities. Whereas some progressive critics have lamented what Michael Sorkin calls "the end of public space", referring to the veritable exhaustion of the idea of public places under the neo-liberal order that has engulfed and privatized the entire globe in some form or another, others have added their voices to a growing critical consensus that cities are now especially salient sites for analyzing "the making of modern citizens", indeed for understanding current renegotiations of "citizenship, democracy, and national belonging".[20] The dizzying pace and unexpected constellations of urbanization since the late-twentieth century are seen as having opened up new possibilities for citizenship detached from older notions of locality and nationality.

An understanding of the city as the space of new subjectivities and political identities can be traced back to the important work of Left theorists from the 1960s onwards (especially in and around 1968), for whom the urban street provided an authentic site of progressive politics and revolutionary social change. Henri Lefebvre's idea of the "right to the city" prefigured the sense that the contradictions within, and of, urban space would spearhead new kinds of class formations emerging from democratic and radical claims to citizenship. Lefebvre's foregrounding of bodily and experiential *difference* within struggles for a right to the city were to become immensely valuable within feminist and anti-racist urban struggles.

Likewise Castells saw the capitalist city as expressive of fundamental social relations, and theorized how urban struggles would ultimately displace old-style class struggle, producing what would come to be known as "new social movements" that would articulate "city, community and power".[21] David Harvey deployed analyses of the crises of late capitalism—overinvestment, devaluation of capital, the formation of fictitious capital—in order to counter-intuitively project a more hopeful, concrete, Utopian urban space emerging from a dialectical Marxism that could effectively grasp the contradictions generated by and in the late-capitalist/postmodernist city. On his view, urban space is both a unit of capital accumulation and constitutes a renewed site for class struggle. Equally importantly, Harvey's Marxist urbanism has been insistent that gender, race and discourses of power need to be integrated within analyses of late-capitalist urbanity.

Amidst these new materialist conceptualizations of urban space and citizenship, a new kind of world space is heralded, one that condenses all the contradictions of postmodernity and late capitalism—the global city. The global city troubles older binaries of nation and city, of local and global, and indeed of citizens and non-citizens. Engen F. Isin writes:

> Global city-regions give us not only the geographic metaphors with which we think about the social world, but also the concrete sites in which to investigate the complex relays of post-modernization and globalization that engender spaces for new identities and projects which modernization either contained or prohibited, and generate new citizenship rights and obligations.[22]

The global city literature, like postmodern theory in general, emphasizes diversity, fragmentation and difference, with overlapping networks of flows that replace the older binary of core-periphery. North and the South are represented here as simultaneously nestled together within global cities, analyzed more in terms of "regions" than city center and peripheral country. In fact, the recent surge in the "global city" literature emphasizes the passing of national sovereignty and older forms of citizenship in the city.[23] Global cities are seen as sites of not only new regimes of accumulation and modes of regulation; global cities theory emphasizes an erosion of modernization and nation-based trajectories of development, stemming from a supposed disappearance of religion, tradition and particularistic identities. They are thus seen as presaging new forms of flexible citizenship (for new classes of global elites) and of informal citizenship networks (for asylum seekers, refugees, etc.) that provide openings for challenging existing inequities of globalization. In global cities, previously marginalized groups—refugees, sex workers, informal laborers—can now claim rights as groups rather than as individuals, thus opening up citizenship to new political articulations and contestations.

At the same time, the purportedly open global city, a city without borders, engenders a different economy of inclusions and exclusions, based on new hierarchies and institutions of governance, while precipitating a de-linking of material places and virtual flows. Paradoxically, IBM's slogan of "solutions for a small planet", with its emphasis on the increasing contraction of places, represents the degree to which the unevenness of economic development, as well as the national site upon which political struggles are waged, is glossed over within the commodified celebration of "global cities", an idea which has the danger of in effect erasing the still persistent boundedness and materiality of these spaces.[24] Arjun Appadurai and James Holston express this tension by arguing that "for most of the modern era, the nation and not the city has been the principal domain of citizenship", that in fact the triumph of the nation-state over the city has been fundamental to the project of nation-building.[25] Such a formulation reflects the ways in which contemporary postmodern and Left analyses of the city continue to read a binary oppositionality between the city and nation. The tension between the city and the nation as categories of belonging and as complexes of cultural, technological and political power opens up the question of whether the city belongs to the nation proper, especially as *capital* city, or whether the city is more of a node in the network of global *capital*.

The recent mythic evocation of place in global cities like New York City through the sacralization of Ground Zero, the entrenched national identities of cities like Tokyo and London, the new metropolitan forms of cities such as Dubai and other petroleum cities in the Gulf, and the particular forms of urbanization in the US South, as evoked in the high-tech "urban" architecture of the Research Triangle Park in "rural" North Carolina where I lived in the late 1990s and early 2000s, all suggest that by no means can we settle on the meanings of cities and the making of modern citizens just yet. Questions about the rights and responsibilities of women, workers, aliens, immigrants and asylum seekers in cities become ever more urgent even as they are contested, repressed and ultimately contained by new policies and discourses of the "war on terror", national security and bio-technologies.

A critical examination of some of the claims that underwrite the theory on global cities is necessary to open up space for thinking about the postcolonial city. In particular, the task before *The Postcolonial City* is to read the two, nation and city, as interlocking and mutually constitutive spaces where a project of postcolonial feminist citizenship can be articulated.

"Zone of Occult Instability"

One of the sharpest evocations of the coming postcolonial city and its unacknowledged centrality to the material and discursive formations of colonial urban modernity is to be found in Frantz Fanon's writings. In the following sections of the Introduction and the book as a whole, I seek to establish Fanon's searing portrait and deft analysis of the colonial city as a template on which I will seek to build the book's central argument about the postcolonial city as conjuncture. Whereas Fanon's writings refer specifically to the Algerian situation, they provide us with a theoretical and critical vocabulary and tool with which to understand and unravel the historical and political context of the postcolonial city today.

In an essay titled "Concerning Violence", Fanon, the Martinican/Algerian revolutionary writer describes the colonial world in the following terms:

> The colonial world is a world cut in two . . . The settlers' town is a strongly built town, all made of stone and steel. It is a brightly lit town; the streets are covered with asphalt, and the garbage cans swallow all the leavings, unseen, unknown and hardly thought about . . . The

settlers' town is a well-fed town, an easy-going town; its belly is always full of good things.

The town belonging to the colonized people, or at least the native town, the Negro village, the medina, the reservation, is a place of ill fame . . . The native town is a hungry town, starved of bread, of meat, of shoes, of coal, of light. The native town is a crouching village, a town on its knees, a town wallowing in the mire.[26]

The highly poeticized and polemicized description of the contrast between the two cities in terms of both visual and material difference can be mapped on the spatial distance between the colonizer and the colonized. The colonial city as the city of light that Fanon describes is an image that has been voraciously re-cited and has had long-standing resonance in postcolonial narratives, particularly when we recall Aye Kwei Armah's evocation of Accra in terms of a colonial gleam in *The Beautyful Ones Are Not Yet Born*, or Ngugi wa Thiong'o's Nairobi as the city of glittering metal in *Petals of Blood* (see Chapter 2).

Fanon's narrative of the emergence of postcolonial urban modernity represents the latter as fundamentally distorted by the colonial experience. The distortion is not just a physical or material one:

When the native is confronted with the colonial order of things, he finds he is in a permanent state of tension. The settler's world is a hostile world, which spurns the native, but at the same time it is a world of which he is envious . . . This hostile world . . . represents not merely a hell from which the swiftest flight possible is desirable, but also a paradise close at hand which is guarded by terrible watchdogs (52–53).

It is this double-edgedness of colonial urbanity—as both a hellish place and a longed-for paradise—that undergirds the postcolonial city as a "zone of occult instability" in which desire and power collide and provide a heady cocktail of repression and revolution. The figure of the "terrible watchdogs" adds to the poignancy and the valiance of the attempt by the native to aspire for that which is forbidden—a resolutely urban modernity. Fanon's writings seek to wrench open this forbidden zone to show that the articulation of western values (urbanity, civility, order) was possible only through dehumanizing the native; the native is what allowed for the West to urbanize itself.

The separation between the colonizer and the colonized in the space of the colonial city is underwritten by what Johannes Fabian has called the "denial of coevalness", in which cultural others are consigned to an altogether different temporal order.[27] The literal and perceived geographical separation between the two cities (the metropolitan and the colonial; the western *ville nouvelle* and the native *Casbah*) was meant to indicate two different historical moments in the history of civilization and progress, between the industrial European city and the pre-industrial Algerian city, and between western and non-western culture.[28] Colonial rule embedded culturalist notions of the city as the space of material achievement and autonomy free from the constraints of backwardness and tradition. Native presence in colonized cities came to stand in for all that obstructed the onward march of western cultural supremacy and economic progress. Thus different colonial regimes sought to preserve tradition for the natives while creating urbane spaces of modern citizenship and political participation for the colonizers and sometimes for the native elites within the space of the same city.

Race-consciousness as a constitutive principle of urban design was a specifically colonial manifestation. Whereas industrializing European cities such as London and Paris were, since the mid-nineteenth century, increasingly segregated along class lines, the colonial city gave rise to a new urban formation that Fanon calls "the Manichean city", in which racial, civilizational and national difference legitimated separate, hierarchized and distant spaces of work and habitation enforced by an authoritarian and rapacious colonial state.[29] The idea of the Manichean city denotes a splitting of both social space and consciousness and highlights the ethical possibilities and powerful potentialities that space bears in relation to social structures and political projects. It is this central concept of the divided city that becomes all-powerful in Fanon's analysis of the degrading effects of colonial oppression. It becomes the ultimate metaphor of the phenomenology of oppression itself, of how and in what geographical forms oppression is experienced.

This duality as a principle of the imperial project was institutionalized through metropolitan disciplines such as urban planning, ethno-medicine, tropical architecture, etc., producing a body of knowledge that made separation and spatial hierarchy seem natural. In effect, the Manichean city became constitutive of social relations between the colonizers and the colonized, involving regimes of surveillance, policing, hygiene and controlled social interaction on the one hand, and native feelings of despair and anger, envy and desire on the other. As a site that encoded power difference and racial and cultural hierarchy, the colonial city itself became "a cultural artifact", an "instrument of colonization" that involved the incorporation and re-designation of the indigenous city.[30]

As the major European metropoles concentrated the global and national administrative, financial and cultural networks within themselves, the colonized city emerged as the center of colonial administration and cultural hegemony.[31] It became a node in the circulation of capital and culture between the metropolis and the colony, constituting a semi-peripheral conduit. Through the development of private property, capital and the presence of new and consumerist household economies, ideas of modernization, westernization or civilization were introduced and a capitalist economy was grafted onto the colonies. As western manufactured commodities flooded the European parts of the colonized city and its homes, they became symbols of a new kind of class structure and class manifestation that were typically idealized and reproduced ideologically in the elite sections of the native city, even as raw materials that made the commodities themselves were evacuated from view, both literally and metaphorically. Thus, in the colonized city, metropolitan culture became "ossified", made ridiculous through being wrenched and transplanted out of context, even as the colonized city was instrumental in making the metropolitan ideal hegemonic.[32]

But with France's nineteenth-century history of social decline and urban unrest, following events such as the 1871 Paris Commune, the colony was considered the space from where the metropole could be re-imagined. It constituted itself as the metropole's self-representation in a colonial context. The colonized city would therefore be a reflection of the original metropole—Paris—only now in a more reactionary form. The experiments carried out in Algiers were consistent with the metropolitan notion that French colonies were laboratories in which the general rules of social organization were to be tested.[33] As such, Alastair Horne remarks that the *ville nouvelle* might well have been mistaken for Nice! The term "*ville nouvelle*" employed for the European section of Algiers, itself underscored the sense of newness and experimentation expressed by European planners and administrators. To use Paul Rabinow's concepts of "norms" shaping "forms", it could be argued that the norms of French society came to shape the forms of Algerian spaces.[34] The epistemic violence of the formulation of metropolitan "norms" shaping colonial "forms" inhered in the colonizers' material and social relations with the colonized. The physical layout of the French section of Algiers, with its imposing waterfront that comprised banks, mercantile companies, government offices, leading up to palatial clubs and hotels and an open forum, was in stark contrast to the densely packed lanes and bylanes of the Casbah. To these ends, segregation was rationalized sometimes as less a racial than a cultural affair. The colonial administrator in Africa *par excellence* Lugard opined: "what is aimed at is a segregation of social standards, and not a segregation of races".[35]

By destroying traditional economies and means of subsistence, and acquiring land through processes of dispossession, colonization spurred the movement of populations from the hinterlands to the city, turning peasants into an urban underclass for the most part (a history shared by English peasants, from the late-eighteenth-century enclosure movement in England).[36] Colonialism as a distinctive form of capitalist development (even as its racial and cultural logics were not always reducible to it) produced uneven economic and geographical development—almost all economic activity was now carried on for the benefit of the metropolis and its representative colonial government in the city. The indigenous city occupied the structural position of a periphery to the center of the colonizers' part of city.[37] Thus, underlying the particular colonialist divisions of space was a colonial political economy that propelled western capital accumulation. As Marx wrote in his analysis of what he called "primitive accumulation", capitalist development everywhere has been accompanied by violence and conflict. The colonized cities, prototypes of the late-twentieth-century third world city, thus became centers of economic, political and social disequilibrium with far-reaching implications for the postcolonial city yet to come.

For Fanon, the psychiatrist working with the natives' social and psychological fragmentation and alienation, the Manichean city made visible the role of lived space on the consciousness and sense of self of the colonized, producing an atrophied experience of modernity that was the very obverse of the "experience" of the *flaneur*, or the modern European secular man, who was celebrated in much of the literature of European modernity as its archetypal subject (see Chapter 1). Fanon explains the psychology of the colonized in the city as suffering from a double displacement—that produced by spatial segregation and that created by the simultaneous psychic fragmentation wrought by the Manichean colonial city and its discursive assignations of racial difference and hierarchy.

Critics like Homi Bhabha have foregrounded not only Fanon's apprehension of the ambivalence of colonial relationships but his emphasis on the spatial dimension of identity politics: "It is always in relation to *the place of the Other* that colonial desire is articulated: the phantasmic space of possession that no one subject can singly or fixedly occupy, and therefore permits the dream of the inversion of roles" (emphasis mine).[38] Fanon writes that the colonizer knows that the native wants to take his place, that "there is no native who does not dream at least once a day of setting himself up in the settler's place".[39] However, Bhabha suggests that the process of identification of the self-in-the-Other's place transcends its binary axes and splits up, caught as it is in the tension of demand and desire. It becomes "a space of splitting . . . 'Black skin, white . . . ' is not a neat division; it is a doubling, dissembling image of being in at least two places at once . . . ; the tethered shadow of deferral and displacement".[40] By extension, then, for Bhabha, colonial identity is at best liminal, the "being in at least two places at once" occasioned by the splitting of the subject in the Other. This presence/image of the Other is what surrounds the native body, de-certifies its existence and threatens its dismemberment.[41] Fanon's insistence that the black man does not have access to subjectivity because he is precisely denied a place in the self-Other dialectic exemplifies the process by which the black man experiences his self as an object. The blocked access to subjectivity then is what produces an awareness of place, of exile from one's proper place of belonging, indeed of the material displacement brought about by colonialism.

But one must go beyond, and indeed question, Bhabha's formulations, because the colonized subject is not fated to be permanently a liminal identity; rather, anti-colonialism, de-colonization and nationalist resistance seek to transform the terms of self and Other and of place itself. As discussed above, Fanon visualizes this through the spatial metaphor of the colonizer's city as "the forbidden quarter":

The violence which has ruled over the ordering of the colonial world . . . that same violence will be claimed and taken over by the native at the moment when, deciding to embody history in his own person, he surges into the forbidden quarters . . . The destruction of the colonial world is no more and no less than the abolition of one zone, its burial in the depths of the earth or its expulsion from the country.[42]

It is in light of this radical possibility of re-possession, of storming into the "forbidden quarter", that the urban space of the colonized city is wrenched from being an instrument of the colonialists into the very space of rebellion and self-making for the colonized. For it is precisely in the city that space is experienced in its most concentrated ideological form, encoding colonial relationships that need to be read, mapped, destroyed and ultimately re-drawn.

The foregrounding of space as the basis of identification, in which the Other is the one in one's place, has crucial repercussions for the analysis of urban space—its history of habitation, displacements and migration, and its centrality in the formation of modern political and gendered subjects. The spatialized material underpinnings of psychic oppression are unveiled in the anti-colonial struggle that highlights issues of territorialization and the politics of uneven development within the city and around it. Thus, the Manichean city as a purportedly stable marker of racial difference and economic inequality provides the very ground upon which, through political intervention, resistance and rebellion, a postcolonial city begins to be imagined and constructed.

The discursive parameters of urban space in both Fanon and Bhabha are limited to a masculine self and Other. What is so obviously elided is the issue of sexual politics that insists on the gendered constitution of selves and others. To live between identities is not available equally to whites and blacks as Fanon argued, in that the doubling of skin/mask as a reversal of subject positions does not have the same political connotations and social meaning for the two races. But the notion of the splitting up of identity has also very different meanings in modern culture for men and women. For if the black man experiences himself as an object, the black or native woman is twice removed from subjectivity, situated as she is within the overlapping structures of patriarchal native and colonial societies.

In particular, the gendered difference in the effects of split subjectivity is ultimately mediated through the Manichean city. Fanon's evocation of the Manichean city wrought by the colonial encounter and its enduring legacy of divisiveness is evident in representations of the figure of the nationalist woman who comes to embody a transcendence of private space/intimate self as encoded in the act of veiling in order that newer forms of public citizenship get articulated within the context of decolonization.[43] The ways in which the colonial city is transformed into a site of the politics of liberation of women in particular, and the colonized in general, are of course processes that are key to the main arguments of *The Postcolonial City* and will be elaborated upon later in this Introduction as well as throughout the book. The symbolic and material disjuncture that characterized the colonized city in Fanon's terms, in its divergent meanings and experiences for the natives and the colonizers, and for men and women, assumes new proportions of ambivalence in the postcolonial city.

Postcolonial Places

The postcolonial city, this book argues, is constituted by the tensions and contradictions between the global, national and the local concepts and practices of urban space; hence the idea of the postcolonial city as a conjunctural space. The use of the term "postcolonial city" as opposed to the more frequently used "Third World city", or the more recent formulation "city of the South" first needs to be explained here.[44] The Third World city evokes what Mike Davis refers to as the "canonical trajectory" that has dominated capitalist development. While it encapsulates the uneven economic development of global capitalism in the twentieth century, it nevertheless underscores the teleological view that has rendered the western metropolis as the paradigmatic urban space, increasingly encroached upon by the Third World city in the form of Third World immigrants in the First World city.[45] Moreover, the Third World city does not adequately denote the specificity of the legacy of colonialism's uneven development and its logics of rule that produced urban forms of colonial power and resistance within postcolonial cities.[46]

In an important sense, the term "postcolonial city" more provocatively keeps in productive play the contestations and articulations between national and global spaces, forms of neo-imperialism and the problem of (universal) citizenship. The postcolonial city is layered with multiple legacies. Its embeddedness in the histories and practices of colonial and postcolonial rule reflects both the unevenness of economic development under colonialism as well as colonialism's racialized modes of spatial organization. The postcolonial city confronts the contradictions of postcolonial state-making, late-capitalist development, and the polarizing effects of their discrepant diffusions and distribution. Consequently, the postcolonial city is where some of the most concentrated asymmetries of power exist; it is also the space where new political subjectivities are created through the very processes of marginalization and peripheralization on the one hand, and decolonization and nation-building on the other.[47]

Global city discourse focuses on the tendencies within late capitalism to erase older centralities, and in fact, on capital's propensity to eradicate the specificities of place. Because of its myriad contested legacies, the postcolonial city occupies only a tenuous position within this discourse.

Cities like Bombay (see Chapter 3) may possess some of the features of a global city, but are regarded only as "second tier" global cities in comparison to London, New York and Tokyo, only implicitly because of their very particular incubation within colonial history.[48] What is elided in the new theorizations of global urbanity is the way in which older centralities are re-instated or reproduced by capital's latest manifestation as a new imperialism (or neo-liberal globalization) that de-links the production of global cities from processes of industrialization, nation-building and economic development. As I show in subsequent chapters, complex processes of provincialization and nativization are unfolding in the same time and space as globalization. These trouble the neat distinctions of tradition and modernity, of capital's agency and citizens' claims, and of North/South, First World and Third World urban spaces. In the case of Bombay we can see how the global belonged to an earlier historical moment, when, for example, the model of westernization embodied in Bombay's elite classes signaled cosmopolitanism for the rest of India. The project of the Hindu Right since the 1980s has involved the articulation of Bombay as a regional or local city, home to the "sons of the soil" that is closed to outsiders, even as it paradoxically makes a belated entry into the elite club of global cities.[49] *The Postcolonial City* argues that the idea of the global city is better understood not only by noting its position in the global economy (North/South; First World/Third World), but also by analyzing its power in the places that surround it (even beyond the "global city-region"), places that are peripheralized by it, and places that aspire to hegemonic models of development and cosmopolitanism. The postcolonial city is thus precisely the site where the universality of global capitalist development comes up against the specificities of colonial history and postcolonial politics.

Postcolonial cities today are seen as experiencing deep incursions of western capitalist urbanity (as opposed to colonial urbanity represented in the idiom of cultural order, hierarchy and stability) via a representational avalanche of globalized images, signs and commodities. Postcolonial cosmopolitanism in the new global set-up is understood as no longer elsewhere, or as situated in geographic London or New York, but in the here and the now and in the everywhere that capitalism traverses.[50] The multimedia images purveyed through consumer shopping channels, the internet, popular cinema, malls, multiplexes and cable television networks, run through both urban and rural spaces, small towns and metropolises. In the process, they purportedly erase historical and local determinants, even as they produce the postcolonial city as "a place of new social disparities".[51] Social inequalities are no longer measurable solely through income and wealth indicators, or caste and religion; globalized commodity images provide sites for new desires and aspirations and encode a new calculus for success and happiness, for inclusion and exclusion. The global is now no longer the sole developmental fantasy of the urban elite imagination; it is always already in tension with nationalist and localized/regionalized moorings and class tensions.

The post-1990s retreat of manufacturing industry in many postcolonial cities across the world and the demands of first world capitalism paved the way to financial and service industries, such that the postcolonial city begins to function as a "node of an inter-metropolitan and global network carrying out information processing and control functions."[52] The concentration of the call-center and outsourcing business in former colonial cities is only one manifestation of the articulation of the postcolonial city in the new global financial economy. The whole apparatus of proficiency in metropolitan languages (erstwhile colonial languages), through "accent-neutralization programs" and English workshops that teach people how to speak in the colonial tongue are meant to erase traces of the postcolonial as a complex polyglot and resistant cultural and political formation.

In spite of these new expressions of a globalized urbanity, the new spatiality that the postcolonial city embodies is not so much virtual as material. After all it is the new economy postcolonial city in which slums and shantytowns are cleared for office blocks and shopping malls, where agricultural land is appropriated for ever-expanding urban conurbations and where a new managerial and technocratic elite overlaps with older elites seeking to maintain control of the processes of material and cultural accumulation in the city. Underneath these new projects of accumulation lie older logics of colonial rule even as the postcolonial state and social movements seek to foreground the postcoloniality of these cities—colonial buildings, spaces, trade networks, social rules and street names constitute the postcolonial city as a palimpsest of a messy colonial history.

It is therefore in the interactions and transactions between multiple spatialities and histories that the constitution of citizens and outsiders, locality and globalism, city and nation is effected in the postcolonial city.[53] To illustrate these complexities, *The Postcolonial City* places the global city in a relational dynamic with new articulations of provincialism, nationalism and neo-liberal globalization as articulated within the postcolonial city. It eschews the premature announcement of the demise of nation-based accounts of citizenship, belonging and solidarity. Implicit in its reading of the postcolonial city is a critique of the global city literature that re-marginalizes postcolonial urbanity through an occlusion of colonial history, even as nationalist discourses continue to incarcerate the city within the nation through an occlusion of critical processes of articulating feminist citizenship and social justice. This book is thus framed within the tense negotiations between postcolonial material spaces produced by colonial and neo-colonial capitalist development and representational practices emanating from historical constellations of urban power and challenges to it.

A key theoretical problematic that the question of the postcolonial city highlights is that of imagining and grasping the postcolonial as both inside and outside the west simultaneously, in a way that does not merely replicate and reproduce the centrality of western modernity, or simply negate it. This is one of the important challenges of postcolonial criticism. As a project it must attend to questions of how Europe's modernist ideas about urban space and its subjects translate into the spaces it colonized abroad.[54] For the discourse and project of postcolonial cities are imbued with both an enduring ambivalence towards modernity, and with a faith in recovering the "authentic" subject who can rightfully inhabit the postcolonial city.

Postcolonial critics have made more central the study of previously peripheral urban spaces, but have mostly replicated the model of canonical criticism by locating in the city the sites of fragmented and derivative modernity and hybridity on the one hand, and the chaos and degradation of postcolonialism on the other. For example, Sunil Khilnani's view of the modernity of India's cities is as "a split and discontented one, full of darker, mixed potential".[55] In his diagnosis, the colonial city that was the archetypal space of rule, where power resided, created a new geography of command such that the modern city as an idea and experience was never made available to the poor and the colonized. Khilnani writes of how

> the British Raj . . . created a masquerade of the modern city, designed to flaunt the superior rationality and power of the Raj, but deficient in productive capacities. The modernity of the colonial city had a sedate grandeur to it, but it remained external to the life of the society—few bothered about it.[56]

Khilnani's analysis reflects a deep pessimism about Indian cities that are for him above all embodiments of a failed idea, even as urbanization moved apace in postcolonial India. Partha Chatterjee expresses a similar view by arguing that Indian cities "had failed to make the transition to proper urban modernity". Citing the sociologist Nirmal Bose, who wrote of Indian cities as being "out of phase with history . . . having appeared in the setting of the traditional agricultural economy in advance of the industrial revolution that is supposed to beget the metropolis", Chatterjee endorses the sense of postcolonial cities as anomalies, as out of synch with the time of capitalist development and modernity.[57] In the case of Africa, Frederick Cooper furthers this point by arguing that, "the kind of society that emerged" in colonial Africa "was not a natural derivative of a social category known as urban".[58] Simon Gikandi extends the theme of colonial modernity (of which cities were seen as constitutive expressions) as an exclusionary and external project by posing the question: "why was the African theoretically excluded from modernity but politically forced into its institutional apparatus?"[59] On Gikandi's view, the colonial city was of course the perfect example of simultaneous exclusion and forced inclusion into the colonial project. But in the chapters that follow I suggest a far more complicated traffic between the *externality* of colonial urbanity (where it is a project of domination) and the *internality* of urban modernity (where it is a project of hegemony) as a condition of possibility for postcolonial citizenship.

An important preoccupation in postcolonial theory and subaltern histo-riography has indeed been the elaboration of "alternative modernities".[60] It emerges from what John Comaroff interprets as the apprehension of "moder-nity as a European cultural term" that formed an integral part of the civilizing mission.[61] Following on these terms, a culturalist critique of postcolonialism has entailed a rejection of modernity itself, seen as specifically western, and thus oppressive, in orientation.[62] Postcolonial critiques of ethnocentric mod-ernisms have pointed out the disjunctive nature of postcolonial sites where Europe's modernist ideas are made "uncanny by displacing them in a num-ber of culturally contradictory and discursively estranged locations".[63] The postcolonial city is precisely read as such an estranged site in these accounts. Bhabha asks:

> what happens to the sign of modernity in those repressive places like San Domingo where progress is only heard (of) and not "seen", is that it reveals the problem of the disjunctive moment of its utterance: the space which enables a postcolonial contra-modernity to emerge (244–245).

Whereas Bhabha's critique occludes questions of the materiality of moder-nity by foregrounding modernity as a sign, a more Left-oriented critique (as in the work of the Subaltern Studies historians) has focused on the post-colonial state and its continuity with the forms and substance of the colo-nial state—its privileging of bureaucratic institutions of governance and of abstract legal citizenship over material inequalities. In fact, it would be quite safe to assert that most critiques of the postcolonial state are predicated on a wholesale rejection of what is understood as the dominating project of colonial modernity.

I believe that critics from both Left and postmodernist orientations fail to take note of the ways in which the postcolonial state attempts significant breaks with the colonial state, through both popular politics and state-spon-sored planning encoded within socialist and emancipatory agendas. Further, the culturalist critique of modernity presents an ahistorical reading of pre-colonial culture as somehow pure and autonomous from modernity.

Whereas *The Postcolonial City* is embroiled in an attempt to shift the cultural location of modernity to the postcolonial city, the question it asks is a more fundamental one—whether it is a "contra-modernity", as Bhabha puts it, that needs to be theorized as a postcolonial project. Rejecting the primacy of an alternative modernity, the book argues that the urgent ques-tion today is not of decolonizing modernity from its western and urban orientation, but one of critically engaging with the multiple spatialities of postcolonial cities that cannot be disengaged from larger processes of capitalist development, colonialism and de-colonization. Instead of seeing modernity as a given, such that one either embraces modernity, or eschews it, or calls for de-hegemonizing it, the book foregrounds the question of how modernity is historically produced. In particular, the focus is on how that production of modernity continues to shape relations of power, especially in the context of the country-city dichotomy and the tradition-modernity opposition that have become modernity's foundational tropes.

The theorization of "a *singular* modernity" might help us reach out of the hole of such a dichotomous view, and enable us to articulate modernity with capitalism.[64] Of course this singular modernity is an uneven one even as it is irreducibly specific, shaped by the jagged itineraries of capitalist development and anti-colonial, socialist and revolutionary resistances to it.

This book then locates the postcolonial city within the twentieth- and twenty-first-century global arrangements of capital (its constantly shifting centers and peripheries, particularly its articulation as colonial and postcolonial rule), and a global cultural politics that renders urban spaces focal points for understanding both belonging and difference. It interrogates the centrality of the city within theorizations of modernity by examining the complicated genealogy of postcolonial cities and their representational histories. The book thus reads the postcolonial city as a theoretical and historical conjuncture through which contemporary contestations of identity and citizenship can be analyzed. Hence it suggests a far more troubled relationship of postcolonialism with modernism and postmodernism than the derivative analyses of much contemporary postcolonial cultural studies, in which postcolonial cities are read as either the past of western modernity (in the "progress" narrative, for example), or its apocalyptic future (as in the urban "crisis" literature).

The asymmetries unleashed by both the old colonialisms and the new imperialisms of globalization have not gone unchallenged. Historical reconfigurations of class and community in the postcolonial city around a range of issues such as housing, public services and the environment, generating what are known as the new social movements, have given rise to a proliferation of subjects and collectivities difficult to categorize within the individualistic terms deployed in modernist discourses.[65] These "new" subjects in the postcolonial city have emerged through a politics of contestation of space articulated with processes of decolonization and nation-building to which, as I illustrate in subsequent chapters, the idea and practice of a postcolonial city was central. Postcolonial cities have also, to an extent, remained not fully *inside* the grasp of neo-liberal globalization, eluding its logic through practices of claiming citizenship, just as colonial rule was never entirely *external* to forms of the postcolonial.

The new social movements and new contestations over urban space and public culture that have flourished in the wake of decolonization have renewed debates on citizenship as involving rights in the city and to the city, or whether citizenship as an idea needs to be jettisoned altogether in an era of increasingly mobile working people. At the same time, the formation of a de-colonized civil society that is the fundamental ground for hegemony has been one of the key challenges of the postcolonial state. Instead of reading the western liberal democratic notion of citizenship (which under colonial rule translated into a privilege of the civilized within the colonial order), as the precursor to postcolonial citizenship, this book locates citizenship within anti-colonial struggles (as also struggles against neo-liberal globalization such as those of landless workers, slum dwellers, refugees) that have left an indelible mark on, and indeed been constitutive of, the postcolonial city.

The Postcolonial City examines how postcolonial subjectivities in the city arise from contestations over political and economic formations, collectivities and practices that rewrite the binaristically entrenched traps of reading between tradition and modernity, city and country, and between colonial and postcolonial rule and resistance. In the process of this geo-political articulation of home, work and identity, a new understanding of postcolonial subjectivity can be forged in order to ground contemporary cultural concerns about identities and their relation to space in the realm of the possible postcolonial city as a socially just space for all.

Mike Davis writes of the

> cities of the future, rather than being made out of glass and steel as envisioned by earlier generations of urbanists, are instead largely constructed out of crude brick, straw, recycled plastic, cement blocks, and scrap wood. Instead of cities of light soaring toward heaven, much of the twenty-first-century urban world squats in squalor, surrounded by pollution, excrement, and decay.[66]

The majority of the inhabitants of the contemporary city are thus the "*new wretched of the earth*", an "outcast proletariat" that is "not a socialized collectivity of labor" (emphasis in the original).[67] At the same time, Davis concedes that this "outcast proletariat" does possess "yet unmeasured powers of subverting urban order."[68] The simultaneity of the assault on collectivity under neo-liberalism, most sharply on the collectivity named as class, and the eruption of radical creativity among the new social movements and contingent communities makes the task of analyzing contemporary postcolonial urbanity especially challenging. This book is written with a view to contribute to such an analysis. In doing so, the book tries to avoid the trap of romanticizing struggles for survival in the city as simply heroic and as autonomous of larger political and economic processes. After all, the self-help city of the urban poor is too often a product of the postcolonial state reneging on its contract with the destitute and the dispossessed in the service of global capital.

Patrick Chamoiseau's novel *Texaco* condenses many of the threads in the long argument that has been elaborated thus far.[69] Set in Fort-de-France, capital of Martinique (Fanon's native country), the novel focuses on the making of the city from the perspective of global capitalism's disposable populations, its "illegal" citizens. Ashley Dawson uses the phrase "squatter citizen" to describe Chamoiseau's central protagonist, a figure that he argues is "central to the urban imaginary of the twenty-first century's global cities".[70] In chronicling the story of Marie-Sophie Laborieux, a remarkable squatter citizen, Chamoiseau deploys a range of genres, languages, linguistic registers, textual fragments, indigenous and borrowed accents and literary traditions, making the text a highly hybrid entity. Such a textual entity then mirrors the form of the resistant city that the novel privileges, one that is able to challenge the hegemony of both colonial and neo-colonial urbanism, understood as intimately connected and dependant historical forces. The racialized and abjected others of Fanon's native city are transformed into neo-colonial capitalism's slum dwellers who remain unsightly in the city but whose labour enables the accumulation of capital globally.

Marie-Sophie arrives and exists in the city as one such disposable, unsightly citizen. Undaunted by the power of the state and of global capitalism, she decides to strike root in the city and build a home there. The ramshackle hut that she builds on a hillside, however, proves to be a threatening reminder of the symbolic power of the poor in the capitalist city. A local representative of the Texaco oil company reports her to the French police and invites them to evict Marie-Sophie and her comrades from their homes. The slum settlements are swiftly destroyed, but for Marie-Sophie that is an expected outcome that doesn't take away from her determination to build and build again. We see in this the novel's celebration of the power of a squatter woman/citizen to mobilize other squatter women/citizens to take on the might of global capital, and indeed, to defeat it.

(Un)veiling the Subject

The figure of "unhomely women" as postcolonial subjects negotiates between structure and agency and militates against abstractions that tend to dominate theorizations of citizenship. I want to return briefly to Fanon's elaboration of the figure of the nationalist woman. It is one that haunts my reading of gender in the postcolonial city through the ways in which it enables the conceptualization of postcolonial feminist citizenship as a process that entails historical consciousness of and material struggles over the city. It is in the tumult and clash of the historic forces pitted against French occupation that Fanon undertakes the project of exploring the role of the Algerian woman in the city in his landmark essay "Algeria Unveiled".[71] The essay is devoted to an examination of the conditions within which she entered the city in 1955. From the very outset, Fanon's project can be characterized as transformative and emancipatory in terms of both gender relations and nationalist identity. A transformation of gender relations that involves dismantling traditional divisions of public and private space becomes critical for the project of revolutionary anti-colonial nationalism. The essay is notable for the ways in which Fanon draws attention to the geographical specificity of the struggle for the transformation of Algerian identity that urban guerrilla warfare underscores in its particular negotiations with colonialism in the city. The Manichean city is what transforms Algerian identity such that it becomes a powerful agent of anti-colonialism.

So how does Fanon resolve the historically scripted incommensurability between the ideology of the gendered separate spheres and women as political subjects in the city at the time of revolution? Drawing critically on the traditional conceptual equation of femininity and space such that "both are charged with absence of politics" or "the inability to act politically", Fanon opens his description of the Arab city, soft, feminized, as surrounded and "immobilized" by the aggressive masculinized power of Europeans .[72] This dynamic of sexualized territorialization leaves the Algerian woman "exposed". In response to this siege, the Arab town weaves a "protective mantle" and "organic curtain of safety" around the woman in the city who is firmly located at home (51). It is precisely and specifically the revolutionary nationalist upsurge that changes these terms of engagement.

Uses of the Veil

For Fanon, the veil provides an apt metaphor and instrument for the analysis of women's agency in the city. The essay traces the checkered history of the veil in Algeria—its strategic adoption and repudiation, and a re-adoption in the final phase of the revolution—that, according to him, is entirely modern and evidence of the veil's "historical dynamism" (63), for the traditional sense of the veil had been exorcised through the medium of the revolution.

My discussion attempts to articulate the processes of the splitting of the female subject that the veil purportedly engenders with the geographical specificity of the Manichean city, with which the veil shares many effects on the body and the subjectivity of women. Like the Manichean city that splits the colonial subject, the veil is a specifically gendered instrument of such splitting in a culture that is simultaneously colonial and patriarchal. What is unveiled in Fanon's text is neither an essence (native woman) nor a passage into freedom (native woman who is emancipated), but a demonstration of the uses that Algerian women make of their assignation as subjects lacking agency, thereby enabling them to evade the logic of their discursive determination as such.

To begin with, the figure of the veiled woman walking down the streets of the city significantly revises western feminists' assumption of autonomy and what its physical manifestations look like in the city. Fanon's narrative follows this up by laying bare the preconditions for women abandoning the veil. They cannot throw away the veil without ostensibly becoming political subjects. It is only by constructing themselves as revolutionary subjects that they can overcome their essential feminine self and learn the idea of gender as masquerade. Alistair Horne's account of one real incident reveals the historical basis of some of these presumptions:

> They had been chosen for the job because, with their feminine allure and European looks, they could pass where a male terrorist could not. Noting the shock on their face, Yacef . . . told them that they were to avenge the Muslim children killed . . . Taking off their veils, the girls tinted their hair and put on the kind of bright, summery dresses and slacks that *pied noir* girls might wear for a day at the beach.[73]

After the call for revolution, Algerian women appeared with bare legs and free hips. The Algerian woman is now in an even greater conflict with her body than when she was veiled. As Fanon writes:

> to create for herself an attitude of an unveiled-woman-outside, she must overcome all timidity, all awkwardness (for she must pass for a European). The Algerian woman who walks "stark naked" (for that is the physical sensation she feels without the veil) into the European city re-learns her body, re-establishes it in a totally revolutionary fashion. This new dialectic of the body and of the world (59).

leads to a new understanding of political action and the space of women in the city. However, instead of recognizing how the revolution might construct women yet again as biologically essential, Fanon chooses to represent it as involving a kind of transcendence of a pre-political female essence.

After the beginning of the nationalist movement, the Algerian woman becomes a link across the city, a link in the revolutionary machine that attempts to break through the Manichean structure of the city. The hegemony of the revolution ensures that she now has family support and no shame or fear of dishonor among relatives. In effect, new relations between the sexes get articulated through the process of women entering the city. Not only does she move about in the native city freer than before, the Algerian woman now enters the European city. In this alien city, the Algerian man and woman have to assume they are strangers. Here the Algerian woman undergoes transformation into a European woman, unveiled, "completely at home in the environment", "like a fish in the Western waters", and the man "a stranger, tense, moving toward his destiny" (57–58). It is, thus, woman's ability to assume a different, more complex identity that enables her to infiltrate the enemy city. This assumption of a liminal identity (in terms of both gender and nationality) marks the first rupture between the woman and her male counterparts. After all, the need for revolutionary political action called for heroic efforts and a complex process of overcoming traditional habits. Fanon writes:

having been accustomed to confinement, her body did not have the normal mobility before a limitless horizon of avenues, of unfolded sidewalks, of houses, of people dodged or bumped into. This relatively cloistered life, with its known, categorized, regulated comings and goings, made any immediate revolution seem a dubious proposition. (49)

Having granted the Algerian woman her new role in the service of revolution, Fanon has no trouble considering the Algerian woman as a soldier; she is both "lighthouse and barometer", as she penetrates further into the enemy's city. Her participation in terrorist activity, through a skillful penetrating of cafés and places where police and colonialists hang out, becomes a primary tactic of the movement. The Algerian woman is no longer seen slinking around the city, but walking "with sure steps down the streets of the European city teeming with policemen, parachutists, militiamen" (58). Still, her newfound political role pushes the need for inner resistance against fears and emotions; it requires constant alertness against "the essentially hostile world of the occupier and the mobilized, vigilant, and efficient police forces" (52).

From 1957 onwards, Algerian women put the veil back on in response to the increasing French suspicion of unveiled Algerian women, and the long-standing French drive to "liberate" Algerian women from an oppressive, patriarchal native society. This time the veil was cut off from its traditional significance as gender separator, "stripped once and for all of its exclusively traditional dimension" (63). This phase of the nationalist movement in which the veil was adopted again led to new reconfigurations of the veil as a nationalist weapon: "manipulated, transformed into a technique of camouflage, into a means of struggle" (61).

The phase of re-veiling, according to Fanon, reveals "continuity between the woman and the revolutionary" (50). What the author does not make clear is precisely how the two supposedly separate identities—woman and revolutionary—are resolved and unified for a feminist project that may not be so easily subsumed within the national. The revolutionary's biggest challenge seems to be that she is a woman. Her political agency is contradictorily predicated on assuming a prior lack of agency traditionally associated with women (but this is more complicated when the disguise is that of the French Algerian woman—the further source of alienation for colonized women). Her disguise as French woman might represent autonomy from traditional patriarchy, but it also registers a far more complicated relationship between western feminism and its others.

After all, the project of un-veiling Algerian women had another, more destabilizing dimension—it was seen as part of the colonialist project of subverting and undermining Algerian society itself, in which women could be potential collaborators. Based on a process of simplification in which the wearing of the veil is attributed to the "religious, magical, fanatical behaviour" (41) of Algerians, Fanon draws attention to the sexualized discourse of the male colonizer who casts a lustful gaze on the native woman; a gaze that is equal to "baring her secret, breaking her resistance, making her available for adventure" (43). The European man imagines the native woman as a potential object of possession; in his dreams she appears never as an individual woman but in a harem of women. Thus, as Barbara Harlow suggests, women are de-politicized from their role as FLN (Front de Liberation National) partisans and are turned into "phantasmic representations of Western designs on the Orient".[74]

But there is a necessary connection, as Harlow suggests, between the phantasm and a political agenda. She argues that "more than analogy links the imperialist project of colonizing other lands and peoples with the phantasm of appropriation of the veiled, exotic female".[75] The political project of postcolonial feminist citizenship requires precisely the laying bare of this relation between colonialism and gendered exclusion from the processes and practices of citizenship. Fanon's essay demonstrates how it is in the city that sites of gendered citizenship exist and are struggled for. Like the notion of modern citizenship itself, the city, too, is both a symbol of westernization, and various affiliations with it, as also the product of anti-colonial struggle. Walking in the city as an attempt to challenge oppressive constructions of urban space takes on revolutionary proportions in Fanon's text. It is through the act of walking that women not only register their agency in a tumultuous Algerian society, but also use it to draw different maps of the colonial city.

Unhomely Women

In Fanon's account we see how the Manichean city is pressed into visibility in particular around questions of the native woman in the city. The colonized city was typically apprehended in the colonial imagination through discourses of sexual adventure and the danger posed by the native bodies in proximity to the colonizers in the city. The threat of miscegenation provided a key impetus to keep natives and colonizers in distant quarters. The physical separation between colonizer and colonized was thus sexually charged as much as it was racially motivated and gave rise to a number of new urban institutions, such as the club, the playground, and "civil lines" (demarcated colonial quarters) as spaces that would pre-empt, by isolating, the possibility of crossing racial and sexual borders. The colonial home was another such institution with its own apparatuses of designating inside and outside, culture and barbarism, domesticity and unhomeliness.

King asserts that a "distinctive demographic characteristic of the colonial city is the relative absence of females and, as far as the colonial community was concerned, of European women".[76] The belated entry of women into Europe's capitals and the long absence of native women from urban spaces in the colonies and the metropoles constitutes the theoretical and historical gap within which the "unhomely women" of postcolonial culture enter the city, a process, a phenomenon and a politics that this book engages centrally. The suppression of the gender question within the dominant narratives of modernity and the ideological embeddedness of urban discourse within imperialist practices historically articulated a public sphere based on white male ownership and male literacy. Colonial patriarchy's unsavory commingling with native patriarchies produced a generalized suspicion towards women seen in cities. When women, poor, foreigners and other figures began appearing surreptitiously on the city's margins, a series of "crises"—of representation and of the city's representational space—engulfed the modernist city. Their presence was experienced as an irruption of uncontainable difference, as recorded in the urban poetics of Baudelaire and of the generations of male writers, critics and social investigators who were to follow him (see Chapter 1). Thus even as the question of gender difference threatened to unsettle modernism's evocation of urban space as abstract, stable and cognizable, women played a constitutive role in modernist articulations of urban space and subjectivity, if only as modernity's Other, its occluded materiality as embodied in women's bodies, dwellings and labor. Women, relegated to the domain of the private and the domestic, could appear only as "unhomely" figures when sited/sighted in the city.

The figure of "unhomely women" performs an ironic gendered re-citation of the quintessential "unhomely" figure of modernist urbanism that was the *flaneur*. By examining the gender and colonial question suppressed or elided within the dominant narratives of modernity, we can begin to point to figures that disturb the notion of the "proper" urban subject. This book deploys the figure of "unhomely women" to enable a dislodging of the *flaneur* as modernity's subject *par excellence*, the prostitute as his perfect Other, and the fragmented racial and sexual identity of the colonized male as the subject to be recovered from the center of thinking about the postcolonial city. The book draws the figure of "unhomely women" as resolutely a collective one that provides a key to thinking about the possibilities and limits of figuring citizenship historically and politically.

Such a move requires a "refiguring" of modernity within a postcolonial framework. Gillian Rose has pointed out that many of the foundational assumptions of white feminism, such as the private and public sphere distinctions, have been "challenged by the elaboration of very different geographies of work, home and community from black feminisms", forcing the issue of the "diverse spatialities of different women".[77] Women writers who define their positions as belonging to the margins have expressed the need to forge new dwelling spaces that re-imagine the space of "home". Some of the new homes have been cast as borderlands, edges and peripheries.[78] Gloria Anzaldua writes: "If going home is denied me then I will have to stand and claim my space, making a new culture—*una cultura mestiza*—with my own lumber, my own bricks and mortar and my own feminist architecture".[79] Minnie Bruce Pratt, a white southern American lesbian feminist, finds that she was "homesick with nowhere to go".[80] Within a postcolonial feminist project, boundaries between the home and the world, the body and the city, the housewife and the prostitute, the metropolis and the colony, and the global and the postcolonial city emerge not as opposing entities, but as necessarily re-configured and inextricably articulated material and discursive categories.

Philosophically, the notion of the "unhomely" suggests existential issues of estrangement, alienation, exile and a metaphorical homelessness.[81] Departing from this dominant usage, "unhomely", this book suggests, destabilizes the inscribed meanings of home and homeliness and represents the state of lacking home in both a material and a representational sense. Through a simultaneous assertion of the political and the literary, the figure of "unhomely women" helps unravel the construction of the home as a refuge from the city, or as the site of an unproblematized and a priori community (see Conclusion). On the contrary, the figure of unhomely women brings to light the often hidden sources of modern terror, as the figure embodies domesticity's discontents, its perplexing and undomesticated Other that threatens to bring to a crisis the dominant regimes of urbanism and can be only represented as crisis.

One of the key organizing concepts that I wish to elucidate through the figure of "unhomely women" is the question of women's work. Karl Marx has written of how the worker in a capitalist society "is at home when he is not working, and when he is working he is not at home".[82] Marx is expressing a fundamental binary opposition that has been constitutive of theorizations of gender and labor—the disjunction between home and work. The structure and nature of production under capitalism has of course been directly linked to the production of space in Marxist urban theory. But Marx here is also elaborating the nature of work under capitalism. It is one of profound alienation, of not being at home in one's own place, body and consciousness. For women, the place of home is then paradoxically also a site of work and therefore of alienation. It is this doubled sense of home and work (particularly in late capitalism, when the two are intertwined in unprecedented ways) as simultaneously alienating and disabling, even as home and work are re-articulated in postcolonial feminism as sites of political struggle that provide the theoretical underpinning to the project of postcolonial feminist citizenship. The daily struggles of life in the home, the market, and the workplace might well elude the grand theoretical assumptions regarding capital and labor.

This book thus derives the figure of unhomely women from a materialist understanding of gendered subjectivity and political agency in the postcolonial city than from a primarily psychoanalytic one. The demand, negotiation, reconfiguration and subversion of women's proper home/place in the city, and of their proper "work", insists not on simply making home central to citizenship, even as it refuses to disassociate home and citizenship. By claiming the public and challenging the configuration of the domestic as out of place in "standard urban narratives", fictions of unhomely women suggest that home can be redefined as a place where to speak from, a place from where to challenge the debilitating anomie of late capitalist modernity, as well as a place of women's productive work and artistic and literary expressions. Even so, home must be pulled out of a false sense of security.

The articulation of the entrenched binary frameworks of home and city that have dominated gendered analyses of cities also entails a simultaneous project of disarticulation. It involves wrenching apart the city as the site of masculinist and colonial publics, reinforced by the asymmetrical and ahistorical privileging of Enlightenment-derived understandings of citizenship as a relation of state and (male, propertied) individuals. The challenge to extricate women from the realm of the particular, from their incarceration within an a priori community, has in political terms translated into struggles for access to universal subjecthood and to citizenship (see Conclusion). But a postcolonial feminist project must attempt to prise open the opposition between the particular (home) and the universal (city) that has plagued feminist strategies of claiming citizenship.

Postmodern and post-Marxist theorists like Chantal Mouffe reject feminist models of citizenship, arguing that

> the limitations of the modern conception of citizenship should be remedied not by making sexual difference politically relevant to its definition, but by constructing a new conception of citizenship where sexual difference should become effectively nonpertinent.[83]

Mouffe understands citizenship as "a form of political identity"; it is "an articulating principle" within which public/private distinctions are no longer distinct and discrete, but interlocking.[84] Whereas my readings would support the interlocking architecture of modern citizenship, the question of gender difference remains key to the very foundation of the question of rights and justice that citizenship is constituted by. The messiness of everyday life, of the operations of power and the materiality of bodies render the political goal of the nonpertinence of sexual difference not only untenable but politically questionable.

From a different position, the feminist theorist Iris Marion Young writes of "the unoppressive city" that is the paradigmatic space of "difference".[85] On this account, the racially marked woman's body in the city becomes an idealized site for the theorization of a radical democracy, such that the racialized woman's body becomes the reified carrier of liberal and postmodern conceptualizations of difference as a privileged political and ethical category. But the fetishization of urban space in modernist thought—as the space of consuming difference—hides the workings of patriarchal, capitalist and imperialist systems of dominance that structure urbanism (see Conclusion for a fuller discussion).[86]

These disjunctions between competing feminist versions of a radical democracy made possible in the city, one making a case for the non-pertinence of gender difference and the other privileging the woman of color's body as the marker of absolute difference, need to be pulled into a project of feminist citizenship whereby citizenship as a form of politics and political identity is negotiated and struggled for, instead of allotted by the modern state or produced by the market. For this, too, feminist theories of citizenship need to take into account, and account for, the processes of de-colonization and neo-imperialism.

Women's increasing access to the city throughout the twentieth century has, however, been jeopardized by the simultaneous erosion and privatization of public spaces within contemporary urbanity. On a material and political level, women are not only among today's homeless, but the home itself has become the site of concentrated and new forms of violence and alienation, even as women abandon it for the worlds outside. The diminishing of social service programs, the expansion of the informal sector and the exponential increase of inequalities in the city under neo-liberal globalization have all exacerbated the pathologization of women's bodies as carriers of global epidemics like AIDS, as progenitors of a population explosion in cities and as sites of new insecurities about identity and sociality. Fundamentalist political and religious ideologies continue to seek to stabilize gendered public/private divisions, and resort to violent tactics to maintain them. Thus violence against women now emanates from an ever-widening range of sources—patriarchal ideologies, neo-liberal globalization processes, security apparatuses and varieties of religious fundamentalisms seeking to simultaneously liberate and rescue women from "unhomeliness". So an important question that *The Postcolonial City* asks is: how can sexually and culturally different bodies become signified and politicized as citizens without being privatized by patriarchal, capitalist and colonial discourses, or consumed by reactionary nostalgia politics?

Postcolonial feminist citizenship as a project and politics recognizes that the city has been at the crux of modernist thinking about home, that citizenship lies in the constantly traversed paths between homes and other places, and that citizenship is constituted in the struggle to obtain the right to inhabit the city as a political subject, and to be represented as such. Postcolonial feminist subjects are elaborated through this process of critical citizenship, enabled by women's simultaneous alienation from and imbrication in the postcolonial city.

By posing the question of women's relationship to urban space and by interrogating the theories that describe those relations, this book furthers the debate on the value of re-instating women as subjects in their own right. Pierre Bourdieu has argued that the subject possesses connotations of unlimited capacity of the will to rise above social constraint; he prefers the concept of "agents" who strategize to maximize their interests within the rules of the game.[87] But unhomely women as subject are neither a static nor a limitless category. The overall argument of *The Postcolonial City* consistently moves between making a larger theoretical claim for urban women

in the re-figuration of modernity and the formation of a postcolonial feminist subject as an agent of political change.

Accounts of women in postcolonial cities, as they are consistently displaced (and often disfigured) by enduring, rejuvenated or frustrated patriarchies, and as they are impoverished and eviscerated by new alliances of
global and national capital, pose a serious challenge to the project of postcolonial feminist citizenship. Priscilla Connolly presents this image of women
in Mexico City: "as much as 60 percent of the city's growth is the result of
people, especially women, heroically building their own dwellings on unser-
viced peripheral land."[88] The "heroic" women in Connolly's account are the
very women who are rendered as disposable, surplus population; yet in this
account, they are not only integral to the growth of the city but are actively
involved in "building their own dwellings", in making home in the cauldron
of a gigantic and in-hospitable city.

The challenge for postcolonial feminist theory and politics is to turn
these displaced subjects' predicament, the globe's surplus humanity, into a
demand for justice that is also a demand for a right to space in the city and to
citizenship itself. These subjects mediate and reconstitute spatial narratives
and arrangements in ways that contribute to a reassessment of postcolonial
literary and feminist theories. I try to show how fictional texts work by both
creating autonomous literary spaces *vis-à-vis* a masculinist urban modernity,
as well as by reconfiguring literary spaces, to claim agency for the unhomely
women who are central to my formulation of postcolonial feminism and its
claims to citizenship.

Fictional Spaces

For Marx, urbanization was both an outcome of the development of the
productive forces of capitalism and contained the potential for a new cosmopolitanism and cultural exchange. In this, cities are important nodes or
sites for the formation of a world literature, or a literature that would travel
across national and cultural borders and boundaries. In fact, on Marx's
reading, Andy Merrifield points out how "arguably, one of the authors of
this world literature is, of course, urbanization itself".[89] But whereas cities
have been read as important sites or nodes in the formation of a critical
cosmopolitanism and in the circulation of ideas and texts, this book hopes
to show that the idea of the city as this locus of cultural interchange was a
highly contested one.

In its more substantive and groundbreaking articulation, critics are suggesting a re-conceptualization of "world literature" in terms of a "world
literary space", defined by Pascale Casanova as "a set of interconnected
positions, which must be thought and described in relational terms". She
writes that "at stake are not the modalities of analyzing literature on a
world scale, but the conceptual means for thinking literature *as* a world".

Such a re-conceptualization would enable a restoration of "the coherence of the global structure within which texts appear".[90] In an influential formulation in his essay "Conjectures on World Literature", Franco Moretti has suggested that this world literary system can not only be mapped on to the world capitalist system, but that the two imbricated systems are structured not so much on difference but on inequality. He writes:

> I will borrow . . . [my] initial hypothesis from the world-system school of economic history, for which international capitalism is a system that is simultaneously *one*, and *unequal*; with a core, and a periphery (and a semi-periphery) that are bound together in a relationship of growing inequality. One, and unequal: *one* literature (*Weltliteratur*, singular, as in Goethe and Marx), or, perhaps better, one world literary system (of inter-related literatures); but a system which is different from what Goethe and Marx had hoped for, because it's profoundly *unequal*.[91]

If this book is written against the grain of dominant urban theory that displaces and disperses the postcolonial city into the imperial and the global city, it is also fashioned against the premature announcement of the demise of postcolonial literary studies as having been rendered irrelevant by world literary studies. Following on from these new conceptualizations of reading world/ly texts, postcolonial literature can be read not as simply appropriating or borrowing the norms and forms of modernity, but as engaging "an art of distance" that is in itself a struggle against varieties of cultural imperialism. By extension I would like to argue that fictions of postcolonial urbanism could be read as expressing distinct modes of asserting a complicated aesthetic and political articulation of resistance to the dominant world system that is simultaneously "one and unequal". Postcolonial urban fictions as "world literary space" are the very sites of struggle in which the world and the text come together and collide and make visible the unevenness of both urban form and text.[92]

The context of a renewed interest in the politics of global readings, now apparent in the resurgent theorization of "world literature" and the search for a Third World aesthetic is relevant for the ways in which this book might possibly be read. The precipitous rise and multiplication of global cultural flows and of new modes of trans-nationalism has in effect produced "globalism" as a dominant strategy of reading in the analysis of contemporary cultural conjunctures and forms. The novel, in particular, has been hailed as "planetary" in its form, history and scope, even as the global city becomes the template for twenty-first-century urbanization.[93] The elaborations in subsequent chapters of this book concerning the debates about the postcolonial city and citizenship have been situated in the novel and in different forms of fiction. They draw upon Fredric Jameson's analysis of the general "spatialization of form", the forging of "a new spatial language" that "becomes the marker and the substitute . . . of the unrepresentable totality" of modernity.[94]

On Jameson's account, the very self-consciousness about space in modernist writings paradoxically points to the larger sense of an un-representable world that cannot be fully grasped. Postcolonial fictions, I argue, operate in significant tension with the modernist aesthetic of the spatialization of form, as well as with the modernist assertion of an un-representable totality. The task of the works discussed is precisely to map out and to foreground the spaces rendered un-representable (because buried, subsumed, commodified, erased or destroyed) by colonial and neo-colonial rule. The book engages postcolonial fictions as opening up literary space where some of the most telling contestations of identities and subject formations have taken place in reference to the material locations of postcoloniality.

In effect, my readings elaborate how postcolonial fictions not only transform the cultural representation of cities by engaging the "others" that modernity produces, but historicize the imperial (and neo-imperial) history of the production of space that is both national and global. In doing so, postcolonial fictions provide a literary realm that does not simply duplicate Eurocentric presuppositions of culturally specific forms of literacy as universal or normative for democratic engagement. In this vein, Nicholas Brown suggests a "reconstellat(ion)" of Euro-modernism and African literature "in such a way as to make them both comprehensible within a single framework within which neither will look the same. This framework will hinge neither on 'literary history' nor abstract 'universal history' but on each text's relation to history itself".[95] The constant traffic between English, the language of the Anglophone fictions, and the profusion of street languages, popular culture, oral narratives, local and regional languages such as *sheng* and *bambaiya* and languages of the underground, result in multiple, broken, regional, vernacular, sub-national and trans-national public spheres that co-exist in the worldly and literary spaces of postcolonial fictions.

The novel, with its purportedly bourgeois origins in Europe, was based on the assumption that the world was knowable through human experience—in Lukacsian terms, the novel internalized the external world. But the politically charged assumptions of what it meant to be human in an unequal world, to have a worldly consciousness and to possess the capacity to experience the world, remained repressed within colonial abstractions in languages of universal freedom and citizenship. When the novel appeared elsewhere, in Africa or Asia, it was subjected, in its production and reception, to the bourgeois colonial logics of its origins in Europe. The Kenyan novelist Ngugi wa Thiong'o writes of how the novel in Africa, controlled by missionaries and colonial printing presses, was authorized to narrate "stories of characters who move from the darkness of the pre-colonial past to the light of the Christian present, yes. But any discussion of or any sign of dissatisfaction with colonialism. No!"[96] This is perhaps what Jameson meant as the "crisis of representation" in non-metropolitan cultures that were and are "locked in a life-and-death struggle with first-world cultural imperialism . . . a cultural struggle that is itself a reflection of the economic situation of such areas in their penetration by various stages of capitalism."[97]

This painful repression is unlocked in the literary struggles over urban form and politics undertaken in postcolonial fictions. *The Postcolonial City* suggests that postcolonial fictions have had to confront in a concentrated form issues of geographical and cultural location as tied to the very genre they inhabit. The disjuncture between an inherited narrative form, the novel, and an authentic experience of colonization mirrors the disjuncture expressed by Fanon in the struggles over space between the colonizer and the colonized. These broken, mottled histories of contestation over urban space and form are expressed most vividly in fictions of the postcolonial city as a conjuncture.

Mapping/Reading/Walking

The discourses of urbanism that postcolonial theory inherited from colonial rule and modernist aesthetics, such as the country-city dichotomy and the idea of the city as the quintessential space of bourgeois masculine citizenship, are shattered and reconfigured in postcolonial cities. Specifically in this book, I identify London, Nairobi and Bombay as three key sites of postcolonial re-articulations of colonial capital and citizenship in three different historical moments that have been "critical" to the formation of gendered modern citizens. The first chapter of the book is a study of London around World War I, the second is focused on Nairobi during Kenya's anti-colonial struggle in the mid-twentieth century, and the third examines Bombay in the context of the 1992 riots orchestrated by the Hindu Right and the city's subsequent turn to a neo-liberal economic agenda. The texts I read are written in or around a particular historical convergence of urban discourse as crisis, (post)-imperial power and the gender question. I interpret these moments of crises as productive of dissident subjects within the representational histories and accounts of the postcolonial cities I have chosen to examine.

All three cities considered here come out of British colonialism's constitution of a logic of rule that concentrated the city as the site of citizenship and civic rights. In particular, both Nairobi and Bombay were creations of British rule—one was purportedly part of bush-country and the other existed as a fishing village—before they were integrated into the colonial geography of the regions. Taking the arguments elaborated in previous sections—i.e., the suppression of the gender question within dominant narratives of modernity on urban space, and the embeddedness of urban discourse within widespread notions and practices of imperialism, postcolonialism and globalization—each chapter in the book is a reading of the urban and the postcolonial feminist subject together and against the grain of what I call "standard urban narratives" (see especially Chapter 1).

As method, I invite the reader to a series of walks in these three very different cities. The walks are occasions to conduct an argument or a debate, as the epigraph to this book suggests, with the hegemonic narratives of postcolonial modernity. "Eccentric Routes" analyses Jean Rhys's novel *Voyage in the Dark*. In the imperialist London of World War I, working-class women, "foreigners" and Caribbean immigrants move about the city as eccentric figures. I explore how Rhys uses the figure of the woman walking in the city to subvert and appropriate masculinist and imperialist claims to the city. Anna Morgan, a chorus girl recently arrived in London from Dominica, occupies a tenuous but suggestive relationship with the colony itself, recording the anxiety of London at the very heart of empire. I read the text, along with C. L. R. James's novel *Minty Alley*, to explore how the idea of London as the unshakeable imperial metropolis was never such a stable one, and that questions of race, class, gender and imperialism were always just around the corner. The novel is read in the context of the emergence of the "new woman" asserting her rights as citizen and questioning her scripted role as white woman in the metropolis, and within other dissident moments and movements unsettling the fabric of the imperial city. Rhys's novel not only provides insights into women anxiously weaving their way into the city, but also implicitly invites us to consider what was it like to be a woman writer or a woman at the margins of imperial narratives recording this instability.

In "Different Belongings", the book travels to Nairobi. Historically established for connecting the east African "interior" to the world economy, Nairobi has gone through different phases of development—from a railway depot and an administrative site to the "white man's city" at the center of a settler colony, to postcolonial capital, and a city now plagued by crime and chaos. Ngugi wa Thiong'o's *Petals of Blood* and Marjorie Macgoye's *Coming to Birth* fictionalize the transformation of the Kenyan peasantry into urban proletariat during and after the period of colonial rule. Ngugi's novel stages an epic journey to the capital city, where the disenfranchised although newly independent citizens of Kenya hope to find justice. The journey's narrative parodies and satirizes the novel of bourgeois capitalist development. Macgoye, too, chronicles the coming into Nairobi of a village girl that parallels the "coming to birth" of the nation. But her novel reveals in pointed ways how the process of becoming a "national" citizen (moving away from tribal/ethnic identity) is a highly gendered one. The persistence of the countryside as the locale of tradition and authenticity in postcolonial discourse is debated from starkly different positions by Macgoye and Ngugi in their fictional accounts—for Ngugi, Nairobi is the ultimate space of degradation and neo-colonialism; for Macgoye, women find new ways of being a citizen in postcolonial Kenya by living in the city. "Different Belongings" reads both novels as narrativizing the complex modernities of its urban subjects in the postcolonial city.

Moving to Bombay in "Uncivil Lines", the book illustrates a highly contradictory staging of postcoloniality where women intrude into the city and disrupt masculinist claims to political agency. The 1993 communal riots, in which women of the majority Hindu community played a key role in violating the rights and personhood of the minority Muslim community, provide the historical framing for the chapter. The discussion in this chapter intervenes in the contemporary debates in postcolonial feminist theory over women's participation in right-wing movements and questions some of the feminist constructions of women's identities in terms of false consciousness. Instead the chapter makes a case for the necessity of reading women's agency as complex and contradictory, as articulated in their multiple positions within an increasingly communal and neo-liberal postcolonial city. The chapter reads Shashi Deshpande's novel *That Long Silence*, a section from Vikram Chandra's *Love and Longing in Bombay* and Thrity Umrigar's *The Space between Us* to analyze how these fictions narrate postcolonial and feminist literary and political traditions, and open up space to forge new possibilities of feminist solidarity in a deeply divided and increasingly neo-liberal city.

In the Conclusion, entitled "Situated Solidarities", I return to the city of London in the twenty-first century and examine its interpellation within a range of contradictory and convergent discourses on multiculturalism, neo-liberalism, the "war on terror", religious fundamentalism and the question of gender. Reading new writing by women writers and by activists of Southall Black Sisters, the book concludes by enumerating contemporary challenges of postcolonial feminism in a variety of different sites in the city—places of work, worship, community and activism. The chapter revisits the theoretical and political necessity of renewing the political project of postcolonial feminist citizenship while also making a case for reading the postcolonial within the global city and the complicated traffic between them. In other words, the Conclusion provides a re-iteration of imperial and colonial history and narrative as an inextricable part of the postcolonial city as conjuncture.

The chapters stage a thematic progression that corresponds to historical reconfigurations of postcolonial modernity and urban space. The book presents the historic junctures of each chapter to highlight some important moments within hegemonic urban discourses that were challenged in unusual places within the postcolonial city, enabling a reading of urban culture as a whole, in which writers, political activists and workers form part of a dense urban text. In particular, the chapters cohere around the figure of unhomely women. Clarissa Dalloway and Anna Morgan and her cohort of chorus girls, the veiled and unveiled women of Algiers, mistresses and servants in Bombay, the citizen of the un-oppressive city, and the Southall Black Sisters are all united by their positioning *vis-à-vis* hegemonic notions of the city and citizenship. These unhomely women are simultaneously fictional and real. Above all, they force an opening up of space for re-theorizing the postcolonial city, its dominant representations, and for questioning the inequitable arrangements of a late-capitalist order in the global city.

1 Eccentric Routes

London: Take One

> Women in modernist literature by men appear via . . . illegitimate or
> eccentric routes.
>
> —Janet Wolff, "Invisible Flaneuse"

> After all, London was the capital of India.
>
> —London Calling

I begin my study on postcolonial cities with a discussion of early-twentieth-century representations of London. The question that is likely to arise for most readers at the very outset would be: why should a feminist reading of postcolonial urbanism begin its itinerary in imperial London? This chapter will attempt to answer this question via different, if somewhat eccentric, routes.

I start by taking you to the opening scene of Virginia Woolf's 1925 novel *Mrs. Dalloway* that provides one possible pathway into this question. In it, the novel's protagonist, Clarissa Dalloway, a middle-aged, upper-class woman married to an important politician, prepares to take a walk in London. As she sets out to soak in the wonder and the glory of imperial London (albeit in the aftermath of World War I), she is *haunted* by the specter of a time when London would be "a grass-grown path and all those hurrying along the pavement this Wednesday morning (would be) but bones."[1] I underscore the word *haunted* to suggest another way of looking at modernism's understanding of its "present", proposing a spectral view of the postcolonial futures yet to come. From this perspective, we see that the idea of the death of imperial London, as figured by Woolf in the image of bones, preceded the historical demise of the imperial city. Clarissa Dalloway's ruminations underscore the fact that even at the heart of the British Empire, intimations of its mortality, destruction and fragmentation were already present, later to be interminably re-iterated in the discursive thread that binds London as a city constantly engaged in processes of regeneration and re-invention.

In this opening scene, the time-space limit of the imperial city is refracted through Clarissa's stream of consciousness that is both individual and part of a collective unconscious of modernity in the traumatic time of war. The imperial city is already the site of what is to be later theorized as its postcolonial melancholia, characterized by a pervasive sense of the irrecoverability of the lost object of Empire.[2] The still-to-come postcolonial city marks the imperial metropole's internal limit, and becomes its phantasmatic, shadowy double. It contains what remains (bones) of the colonial city even as it is the site of the scattering of imperial significations assembled at home, such that the coming postcolonial city can be imagined worldwide.[3] This projection into an unknown future of the city, I propose, offers us another way of not just looking at Woolf and her aesthetic unfolding of the modernist "present" but of London's precarious modernity in the context of Britain's imperial project. It is this ability of Woolf's art to imagine, as Jacques Derrida wrote of the texts of Marx and Engels, its "own possible 'ageing' and (their) intrinsically irreducible historicity" that becomes the defining feature of its modernism.[4] The mode of spectral presence evoked by the image of an emptied out city populated with bones apprehends the very destabilization of temporal and spatial co-ordinates that allows the Other to enter modernity as an apparition.[5] In this scene from *Mrs Dalloway* Woolf projects the image of bones that might typically signify archaic time, the designated time of the Other, into the future, as a time that is yet to come, that is "not yet there".[6] The image of the evacuated imperial city is thus a dialectical one, in Benjaminian terms, as it allows for a theorization of the relationship between the archaic and the modern, between the local and the global. Thus I use the moment from Woolf's text that I refer above to make visible the trace of the idea of the postcolonial city within the high imperial metropole.

Of course metaphors of death and regeneration have been integral to progressivist urban sociology and other related social sciences that envisioned the evolutionary cycle of urban growth as movement from the countryside to city, and from urban conurbation to megalopolis, culminating in the proverbial necropolis of a shadowy and ultimately destructive modernity. Lewis Mumford wrote of this "cycle" as descriptive of "the course of all the historic metropolises, including those that arose again out of their own ruins and graveyards."[7] This chapter attempts to trouble the progressivist narratives of urbanism that secured London's place at the center of global imaginations of modernity by offering other readings of imperial London that are nevertheless coeval with representations of a hegemonic imperial metropolitanism. At the core of the British imperial project, London was translated, even in the literal sense of being borne across, in the Empire's margins, only to create new and sometimes unexpected narratives and logics of centralities and peripheries.

Narratives of imperial subjectivity, as in Woolf, are inseparably linked to the material vagaries of colonial capitalism and the uneven forms of metropolitan rule that it generated. The re-iterative discourse of London's enduring vitality has been constantly mediated by the presence of new bodies and subjects that came to inhabit, albeit surreptitiously, what were the hegemonic representations of the city. If modernist urbanism tended to abstract urban space such that, as David L. Pike puts it, the human itself constituted a "spectre of irrationality", attention to these bodies and subjects helps us re-frame some of the central assumptions of political agency and citizenship, especially in gendered terms, within the modernist city.[8]

While placing the modernist city in the context of a world (imperial, capitalist) system, the arguments in this chapter are constructed around embodiment and trans-nationality (both products of the historical processes unleashed by colonial capitalism but occluded within world system theories), or around what postmodern thinking in a less materialist way has called "difference". Such a reading challenges the uneven universality of global citizenship that purports to transcend local, national and regional spheres of belonging and to supersede abstract and embodied differences. Rather, the chapter re-articulates the possibilities of a universal feminist project of citizenship with a materialist critique of capitalist modernity and the aesthetic forms it generates. The citizen (when male, white, propertied), whose body is largely immaterial, is placed alongside different subjects of politics such as this book's "unhomely women". Whereas modernism's aestheticized abstraction of urban space that rendered it coherent, homogeneous and exchangeable glossed over the messy terrain of everyday life in the city and its embedded inequalities, the figure of unhomely women in all its unruliness and ir-rationality disrupts the process of abstraction, loss of coherence, and the easy assumption of groundless universalism.

The Whole Empire in Little

Whereas the scene from Woolf's novel opens up the pathway between an interiorized subjectivity and a worldly consciousness, the British Empire exhibition of 1924 provided Londoners in general with a powerful sense of the world that was encased in their city. The cognitive leap of faith in apprehending the contradictory scale of the world contained in the city is dramatized very effectively in Andrea Levy's novel *A Small Island* (2004). In the Prologue, the young Queenie (daughter of a provincial butcher), one of the four protagonists in the novel, describes the experience of going to the Exhibition:

> The year we went to the Empire Exhibition, the Great War was not long over but nearly forgotten. Even Father agreed that the Empire Exhibition sounded like it was worth a look. The King had described it as "the whole Empire in little". Mother thought that meant it was a miniature, like a toy railway or model village. Until someone told her that they'd seen the real lifesize Stephenson's Rocket on display. "It must be as big as the whole world," I said, which made everybody laugh.[9]

What stands out in this passage is the idea of the overlapping and contending scales of the imperial city and of the world it had colonized. Can the city contain the world in miniature, or is the city a miniature version of the world? The process of miniaturization involves producing an exact replica, but scaled down. It thus allows the world to be contained in the city, even as the city, in miniature form, represents the world. Within the space of the exhibition miniaturization as a mode of representation is directly linked to the social relations produced by capitalism, in which the commodity (coffee, tea, chocolate, machines, crafts) stands in for and indeed congeals whole networks of historical and cultural difference and economic relations.

The over-wrought pre-eminence of London as the "metropolis" that stood against all the negative (backward, non-modern) associations of the "colony" was indicative of how the capital city encapsulated in the early decades of the twentieth century both the glory and the changing status of the British Empire. Malcolm Bradbury notes that by the end of the nineteenth century, rapid industrialization, technological growth and urbanization had made London the world's biggest city and Europe's commercial center.[10] Although London's significance as a major center of modernist artistic output and *avant-garde* cultural practice remained uncertain and was consistently out-flanked by Europe's other capitals like Paris and Berlin, there is little doubt that on the eve of World War I London had succeeded in establishing an artistic reputation as well, albeit a more politically conservative one than that of continental Europe.[11] The idea of London as the acme of modern culture and international commerce in general, combined with a distinct national identity predicated on its global reach through Empire, was a powerful one especially in the colonies, translated and transmitted in the cultural work done by English administrators, planners, missionaries, social workers, writers and educators.[12] London thus played a central role in creating empire in its image, even as its institutions—commercial, political and cultural—carried on the *realpolitik* of governing almost a quarter of the earth's surface, a task increasingly difficult and often unwieldy by the time of World War II.[13]

In the account that I offer below I take as implicit broad continuities between late-Victorian and early-twentieth-century renditions of urban space in literature, culture, policy and politics, even as I seek to highlight the ways in which the twentieth-century city represented some radical discontinuities of experience and representation from the preceding century.[14] The multiplicity of European modernisms emanating from different cultural contexts and geographical locations, and articulating varied political agendas and aesthetic forms, also needs to be meticulously taken into account. But these differences do not obviate the *singular* effect of metropolitan power on the global scale.[15] Therefore, while focusing on the modernist city of London, the discussion draws upon the often very similar assumptions shared by different geographical contexts of modernisms.[16]

The material conditions of colonialism and industrial capitalism that shaped London's contours as well as of those other European metropoles in the early decades of the twentieth century found shape in what I call the "standard urban narratives" of modernism. These narratives describe not only the features of the modern city; they also *prescribe* the city's role as central within various national cultures. A generalization such as "standard urban narratives" is not meant to erase the presence of other competing narratives on and of the city (as found in popular culture, and in the writings by women, working-class, gay, lesbian and black artists), nor of varied modernist practices and philosophies. Rather, it is deployed to enable the disclosure of where and how these oppositional narratives pressed against the imaginative and political limits of the "standard urban narratives" of modernism. In this my analysis is aligned with recent readings of "postcolonial London" that represent the city's imperial history as always complex and conflicted, pitting those multiple histories against the "totalizing and abstract concept of the 'colonial centre'".[17]

As we read the city's contours and fault-lines in these standard urban narratives, London expresses not just the prevailing imperial, class and gender arrangements during and in the aftermath of World War I, but evokes modernity's rationalization of space, in its configuration of public and private realms, of legal and affective spaces of citizenship and belonging, and of the demarcation of the spaces and temporalities of production and consumption. The imperial city came to signify what Daniel Bell calls "the 'rational cosmology' that underlay the bourgeois world view of an ordered relation between space and time".[18] This 'rational cosmology' found further vigorous expression in ideas of civic order and political regulation. The need to manage territorial possessions from a center, to control the growing domestic population in the city, and the resultant unruliness of London's urban sprawl legitimated the rise of new forms of knowledge such as social reform, cartography and urban planning; created novel regimes of policing and surveillance; and produced persuasive discourses on hygiene, sanitation, civic self-fashioning and improvement, and the ideology of a proper ordering of the home and the world.

But of course London's "internal order" was inextricably linked to its "imperial fortunes", even as Richard Sennett suggests, "this unimaginably wealthy place had placated . . . its poor with the spoils of conquest".[19] Studies of London's spatial arrangements in the early part of the twentieth century reveal that although the colonial spoils were not distributed equally across class divisions, the illusory possibility of their acquisition by any Briton was inscribed in spatial divisions of "class-homogeneous, disconnected spaces" that served to both contain desires of upward mobility and to inscribe those desires into the very fabric of the city.[20] These new arrangements of capital and property in London were meant to indicate social stability, making the separation and insulation of "the relentless continuity of (London's) ceremonial fabric" from "equally vast scenes elsewhere in London of poverty and social distress" seem natural or at least the inevitable end result of capitalist development.[21]

In particular, the East End of London (an area that was "discovered" by social investigators and named as such in the 1880s) provided observers with simultaneously intriguing and repellent scenes of poverty and chaos that needed to be kept at a distance from the core of the imperial city.[22] As London's population grew, so did the number of social observers who deployed methods borrowed from scientific empiricism and colonial ethnography in order to both rationalize London's class-divided spaces and to provide a unifying narrative for the growing city.[23] The presence of the poor signaled the risks of contagion and death, a slide into the abyss of disease and poverty, and a loss of imperial metropolitan power. The working classes and the poor immigrants who inhabited the marginal spaces of the city were widely pathologized as evil and degenerate in the middle-class imagination. To admit these "outcast" city dwellers as proper residents of the city would have amounted to recognizing the rot of civilization within the imperial metropolis.[24]

Interestingly, descriptions of the London poor in the East End borrowed key notions of social difference from the ever-expanding repertoire of colonial discourse. Ian Baucom writes of how the London poor came to function as "local allegories of the empire's distant 'savages'".[25] Slum quarters were perceived as "a zone of cultural primitivism and racial alterity".[26] From parliamentary reports to censuses, surveys and urban plans, colonial discourse drew an analogy between the untamed savages on the frontiers of the British Empire with those within it, eating away at the metropolitan center's civilizational fabric.[27] An impending fear of nihilism was displaced on to "darkest" East End pitted against the "blaze of light" that was the imperial capital.[28] Recall the discussion in the Introduction to Frantz Fanon's evocation of colonial cartography as made visible through a contrasting economy of light and darkness. In London, race terms displaced and reinforced class categories and enabled the fortification and policing of social and economic boundaries within a new discourse of difference. Typically elided in these narratives of the London poor were blacks and racial others that were also physically present in the imperial city.[29]

But the fact that even the centers of ceremony and power were constantly under threat by, to use McClintock's evocative phrase, "the impossible edges of modernity" that were the slums, the ghettos and the brothels of the city, was an ever-present reality in London.[30] Baucom writes of the "uncannily persistent return of this scabrous city into the spaces of the nation's cultural imaginary".[31] As images of a London swollen with disease aroused feelings of dread and distaste, the new social-scientific regimes of city planning and social services attempted to manage the unruliness of the growing metropolis while new imaginative constructions of the modernist city in literature and art also played their part in imposing order over what was in reality a terribly messy city.

It is possible to speculate on the historical context in which the fear of the loss of racial, economic and civilizational boundaries was situated. After all it was the city that had been the site of working-class struggle historically. Friedrich Engels had written of how "without great cities and their forcing influence upon the popular intelligence, the working class would be far less advanced than it is".[32] By the end of the nineteenth century, the East End had begun to hum with socialist desires and with what Engels called the "new unionism" in which the masses of unskilled workers were to forge a new identity within the urban industrial economy. A series of strikes in the 1880s and the 1890s by women workers in match factories; the growing suffrage movement in which at the start of the new century, in 1903, Emmeline Pankhurst formed the Women's Social and Political Union; the rise of anarchism and trade unionism more generally were all events that sparked resistance to the dominant forms of metropolitan rule mediated by the exclusionary and exploitative demands made by capital and empire.

A series of political upheavals in the colonial realms throughout the nineteenth century lent credence to the fact that the imperial project was relentlessly subject to insurrectionary pressures. The year 1807 had marked the end of the British slave trade; slavery itself ended in 1833. Further challenges to colonial rule were signaled by the 1837 Morant Bay rebellion in Jamaica and the 1857 Mutiny in India. By the turn into the twentieth century, nationalist movements were gaining ground in several colonial territories, most notably in India. A crucial part of the story of imperial London that is beginning to be told now is that of London as a center of anti-colonial dissidence, as intellectuals and radical political activists from the colonized world—members of the first Pan-African Congress that met in London in 1900; the early delegates of the Indian National Congress followed by Gandhi, Nehru and the Communist M. N. Roy from India, C. L. R. James and George Padmore from the Caribbean, Kwame Nkrumah and Jomo Kenyatta from Africa; and numerous other revolutionary figures—met, debated and created visions of freedom and rebellion in the crucible of the imperial metropolis.

The socialist and feminist struggles that gained ground on the one hand, while swelling poverty, deepening economic depression, spiraling scarcity of housing and jobs that proliferated on the other, produced a sense of precariousness as part of the experience of living in the city. All varieties of popular resistance paradoxically reinforced class boundaries for the time and escalated bourgeois anxieties about maintaining them. The social upheaval wrought by such mass movements (exacerbated by the influx of masses displaced from the countryside) thus gave rise to a deepening suspicion of masses in general, perceived increasingly as essentially disruptive of social stability, national culture and bourgeois order.

London was thus both a contested place of self-making (in subjective and material terms) for the bourgeois individual and by that same logic a place of exclusion of all others.[33] London in this analysis then is not just a bounded container or an incidental site for exploring the web of gender, race and class relations. The city can be read in fact as both produced by historically delineated relations between genders, races and classes and by the logics of colonial capitalism, even as it is producer of those relations and logics in turn.

Modernity's Divided Subject

Within canonical modernism, the "essentially" chaotic and unruly elements associated with the masses in the city were aligned with feminine subjectivity that threatened not just bourgeois society but specifically male order within it. Andreas Huyssen notes how "the fear of the masses in this age of declining liberalism is always a fear of woman, a fear of nature out of control, a fear of the unconscious, of sexuality, of the loss of identity and stable ego boundaries in the mass".[34] What the masses needed to be ferociously shielded from was their articulation as class antagonists. Walter Benjamin points out that one key feature of the French poet Charles Baudelaire's representation of the modern city is that the masses in it do not stand for any kind of collective, nor do they represent any classes.[35] Rather, they are shadows of the male artist's sense of emasculation and distance from a collective politics. Feminist critics have rightly turned attention to Benjamin's reading itself and pointed out that in remaining silent on the sexual politics of Baudelaire's writings on the masses in the city, Benjamin reveals his own masculinist appropriation of modernist urbanism.[36] Benjamin's reading of "A Une Passante" in which Baudelaire's unknown woman in a widow's veil is "mysteriously and mutely borne along by the crowd . . . bring(ing) to the city dweller the figure that fascinates" illustrates the modernist theorist's fascination with the anonymous transient encounter with women in the city.[37] Rey Chow argues that the "anonymity", the facelessness of the masses in modernist representations of urban space, is analogous to the facelessness of woman in modernist culture. Both the undifferentiated masses and the woman in the city seem to defy "figural representation".[38] Mass cultural production, which was an arena that was shunned by high modernism, had nevertheless emerged as a site in which new social relations were produced, and through which new versions of masculinity and femininity were expressed. Novel technologies such as the automobile, modern weapons, security regimes, advertising, household gadgets and cinema began to pervade the cities. They not only extended the reach of the market into domestic spaces and the intimate sphere but also began reconstituting the very idea of the public as a sphere always already saturated with commodities, images and social relations produced by capitalist development. Through these new technologies of production and consumption, mass consciousness was simultaneously commodified and homogenized. In particular, women came to be seen as mass culture's primary consumers and instigators. Thus by the early-twentieth century, shopping as an activity attained gender specificity and emerged as a key activity that allowed bourgeois women access to the city.

But this activity was disconnected from agency. Drawing an analogy between women consumers and spectators of cinema, Kracauer pointed out how capitalist modernity produced women as passive objects such that the experience of modernity produced radically different consciousness and subjectivity in men and women. Whereas bourgeois men experienced an increasingly rarefied self-consciousness through separation and distancing from the masses in the city, women were unable to emerge as proper subjects of modernity.

Theorizations of such a distorted and eventually aborted attempt towards female subjectivity do not, however, account for the ways in which women were pouring out into the streets of the modern city as agents of social change and as subjects re-making the gendered self—as suffragettes and citizens, as workers and consumers of a new capitalist economy and as reproducers of imperial capitalism.

Modernist literature's vexed relationship with this confluence of mass culture and the threat of feminization can be traced in the work of nineteenth-century male writers such as Charles Baudelaire, Emile Zola, Charles Dickens and Gustave Flaubert. The naturalists' observant and scientific explorations in the nineteenth-century city are transmuted into *fin de siècle* aestheticism and decadence and eventually into the modernists' more experimental, and as among the Surrealists, sometimes revolutionary and shocking metropolitan forms. Whereas Baudelaire, Edouard Dujardin and Louis Aragon became famous for their perambulations in the various Paris *arrondisements* and shopping arcades, their art itself sought to represent and reflect urban form—its labyrinths and passages in particular were read as representations of the complex, layered experience of urban modernity. They paved the way for a number of literary experiments in European modernism that took the city's artifice as a natural habitat.[39] These later experiments of high literary modernism were typically distilled through the consciousness of the aesthete as artist who kept both an objective distance from his subject matter, the city, as well as experienced it first-hand by appropriating its vast alienated spaces as sites of self-fashioning.[40]

What is also activated in this modernist discourse is the notion that while the male modernist revels in "the almost unequalled fascination of publicly accosting a whore in the street" and flirts dangerously with her image of subversion, it is the woman as historical agent and embodied subject who is banished from view. She is seen both as an *instrument* of bohemian masculine self-fashioning and a *threat* to the stable, bourgeois mentality the *flaneur* purportedly shuns but ultimately safely returns to.[41] After all, underlying the discourse of sexual adventure with an anonymous female figure are the "pleasures of 'crossing' class boundaries and 'hovering' on the brink" of society without entailing any material or subjective risk.[42]

The *flaneur* at one level even appears to feminize masculinist subjectivity through his expression of love for pleasure, ease, hedonism and bohemianism. But his reliance on a radical autonomy and his psychic alienation from the family and from women (even as they become the objects of sexual adventures), and on processes of repression and commodification of the feminine, leave little doubt that it is a variation and not a subversion of the preferred masculine qualities of reason and productivity as expressed in the more blatant modernist projects of colonial domination and urban planning. The self-definition of the artist as a distanced and objective innovator, which paradoxically reified the notion of a unified self, was thus a constitutive aspect of the dominant male bourgeois modernist aesthetic. The modernist aesthetic of the loss of self and of impersonality in the artistic product, espoused especially by its Anglo-American practitioners such as T. S. Eliot, E. M. Forster and others,[43] could be seen as emanating from the larger pervasive aesthetic of urban individualism—characterized by estrangement and detachment, and what Sennett calls "civic solitude"—found in such different discursive sites as architectural practice, urban planning and literary theory. Such a prevailing anxiety about personal space could only fortify the distinctions between male and female experiences of modernity, emerging as they did out of the previous century's stabilizing assignations of gendered space (public/male; private/female).[44]

But the paradoxes inherent within the modernist celebration of the *flaneur* perhaps point us towards something else as well—a veritable "epistemological crisis" that was eroding male writers' sense of "being at home in the city".[45] Anxieties about intimacy and public power, desire and restraint, leisure and work, especially intellectual labor in the context of increasing work specialization and professionalization, technological growth and mass production, were creating new experiences of precarity and opportunity.[46] These anxieties prevailed even as the city was offering bourgeois men the space to fashion themselves as proper subjects of modernity, and to imagine life across and beyond the comfort of class and gender privileges. The opportunities to step outside the bounds, always available to upper-class men, were nevertheless kept in check for the majority of middle-class men, through fears of economic destabilization and the possible dissolution of the familiar, although routinized, comforts of work and family. Within middle-class domestic ideologies home was figured both as the space of the feminine that could be potentially emasculating, and as the antidote to the city's alienation and chaos, providing material comfort and an emotional retreat from the heady messiness of the city.[47] It is in this contradictory milieu of gendered spaces that the ideological contestations of the standard urban narratives can be located, and from where new subjects of modernity emerged.

Modernity's Other Subject

Literary modernism, I argue, disappeared women from the city. This was the major transformation in women's representation in the city from the nineteenth to the twentieth century. If representations in the nineteenth century had been marked both by a consolidation of separate spheres and contestations over women's right to the city, the early-twentieth-century representations dealt with women's actual appearance in the city with an artistic sleight of hand that rendered them as apparitions and specters, fleeting images that defied figural representation. From Breton to Eliot to Benjamin, women in the city were unrepresentable.

But there was a singular female presence that provided continuity between older and newer apprehensions of women in the city. As bourgeois men trafficked in working-class women in both public and private domains, the prostitute represented the most visible female body in the city, one that both fascinated and perturbed male writers. The *flaneur* who went about eroticizing city life and expanding his repertoire of novel sexual experiences in the city also "enabled a mapping of the dangerous influences of sexuality exclusively onto women and the spaces they inhabited".[48] Sophie Watson and Katherine Gibson argue that the figure of the prostitute in fact "colonized the public role for women in the city, rendering "respectable" women's movements in urban space a subject for strict regulation".[49]

The prostitute became, in modernist writings, an allegorical figure representing the city's corruption and its dangers. She embodied the putrefying waste (as in the city's deadly sewers) and the pervasive disease of modern industrial urbanism, an idea materialized in such legislation as the Contagious Diseases Act.[50] The representation of the prostitute was also accompanied by a corresponding discourse of commerce that attempted to create equivalence between commodities and sexually exchangeable women. Benjamin reads the figure of the prostitute as allegorically personifying "the decline of the aura" in the high capitalist world—"where the commodity attempts to look itself in the face" and where "it celebrates its becoming human in the whore".[51] The abstraction and fragmentation of the female body in prostitution must thus be read in the context of urban capitalist expansion at the turn of the twentieth century. In the new public spaces that were emerging in the modern city, women were being looked at as "commodities" while also doing the looking as "consumers", or from the point of view of consumers, internalizing their gaze.[52]

The gendering of shopping as a particularly urban feminine activity reinforced the cult of domesticity within capitalist urbanism even as it reinforced passivity as a feminine attribute. Whereas the labor of working-class women was rendered invisible, the labor of reproduction within the home was naturalized and both symbolically and materially embedded within the logic of capitalist urbanism. The relationship of women to both capital and labor was blurred in the dominant optics of modernity that divided the city into the private sphere of reproduction while relations of production, work and consumption were firmly embedded in the male public realms. Thus, whereas middle-class women could now buy commodities to make their homes both more comfortable and enticing, prostitutes were deemed to be threats to this growing complex of bourgeois economic and sexual politics. Prostitutes, after all, were willing to provide sex (and more threateningly, affective relations in some cases) to men for monetary remuneration, rendering certain forms of female sexuality to be in excess of the reproductive economy of the public-private divide.

There was a significant racial dimension to the discourse on prostitutes, crime, and the commodification of sex, such that prostitutes, poor and working-class women were seen as being proximate to the savage races.[53] McClintock asserts that prostitutes were typically considered the "metropolitan analogue of African promiscuity".[54] The presence of primitivism within modernist artistic and spatial practices and discourses reflected the increasing space for perverse sexual fantasies of slavery and bondage and of the dangers of miscegenation within the metropolitan imaginary. But, as the cult of domesticity became central to imperial class fantasies, the space of the middle-class home was re-inscribed in terms that emphasized whiteness and stable gender divisions in which women stayed at home and men worked outside it. The domestic ineptitude of the poor and the non-whites, whose unkempt homes symbolized that their women were not home, reinforced racialized class superiority.[55] Thus whereas Englishness was constructed as a certain kind of domestic space for women (being "at home"), it had to also negotiate an increasingly heterogeneous and contaminated public sphere in terms of the presence of race and class others. Above all, this was a public sphere in which women were making serious inroads in terms of industrial work for the war machinery and domestic work for imperial masculinity.

In general then there are two main questions key to this issue of the purported incommensurability of women and the public sphere in modernity—the question of (in)visible gendered labor and the question of the prostitute as the spectacular female figure allowed into the representational space of modernist cities. Women's invisibility in the modernist literature on cities supposedly stemmed from women's general invisibility in the bourgeois public sphere until the early decades of the twentieth century. The severe restrictions placed on the mobility of women as political subjects attempted to (unsuccessfully) exclude them from public discourses on citizenship, political participation and modernity (coded as public) in general. At the same time of this supposed invisibility was gathering evidence of women's participation in labor struggles, social struggles against societal and state restrictions, and in the movement for gaining the vote, producing the figure of what came to be known as the "new woman". The working classes remained problematically hidden from view in influential literary narratives of modernism; especially invisible were working-class women and colonized subjects who historically had to negotiate and engage with public spaces in the city as its "others".[56] The standard urban narratives thus only ostensibly concerned themselves with bourgeois masculine activities and subjectivities in the city that were considered foundational to the emergence of the modern public sphere.

This invisibility had historical antecedents in the ways in which gender difference was consolidated, mediated by the demands of colonialism and industrial capitalism that restructured notions of work, domesticity and sexuality.[57] Elided in the preoccupation with individualized modernity that privileged dislocation and fragmentation as essential conditions of modernity, as exemplified in the figure of the *flaneur* or the urban dandy, was the question of how imperial spoils were being channeled as capital accumulation, urban wealth and grandeur in the metropolis, and how the city in the colonies from whom value was constantly extracted was constructed to hold up a mirror to the western metropolis. It was to be but a mirror that would distort as much as reflect reality.

Unfortunately, even feminist criticism has tended to appropriate many of the tropes of the standard urban narratives. It has often merely reversed the gender "bias", expressed through appropriating the figure of the prostitute as modernity's exemplary other and through gendering the practice of *flaneurie*. Liz Heron, for instance, asserts that the modernist city for women writers was "a place where family constraints can be cast off and new freedoms explored".[58] Such a view persists in seeing the city as primarily a male public sphere that progressively opens up for women, but remains divested of familial and domestic issues. The attempt to feminize the role of the *flaneur* also does not grapple with the dominant conceptions of the city, including the material conditions in which gendered spaces are allocated and produced through labors of production and reproduction, mediated via an imperial economy. A related counter-move within feminist criticism has been to focus on the history and the insurgency of the private as opposed to the public, and to disengage the scholarship on modernism from a purely formal and political preoccupation. But such re-readings still tend to gloss over the much too resilient separation of the public and private spheres, and consequently of capital and labor, of production and reproduction, as processes that underwrite the logic of imperial capitalism.

The tying in of the regulation of women in the city and their economic and sexual labor to prevailing ideas of imperial power and order that shaped understandings of sexuality and gender difference in the western metropolis has thus emerged as an important challenge for postcolonial feminist scholars.[59] Postcolonial historians have shown how Britain superimposed Victorian notions of sexuality and morality onto a colonized population.[60] But the reverse could also be argued—that Britain's preoccupation with controlling colonized bodies and subjects affected notions of sexuality and the public in the metropolis itself. We can thus trace genealogies of citizenship as it pertains to rights and responsibilities, to labor and (re)production, to civic spaces and public spheres, in these standard urban narratives in order to refigure it within a new conception of feminist postcolonial urbanism that might also be committed to an anti-colonial and justice-oriented critical project.

(De)Mobilizing Public Space

To walk is to lack a place. It is the indefinite process of being absent and in search of a proper.

Michel de Certeau, "Walking in the City"

Standard urban narratives privileged the mobile body in search of novel experiences. Indeed, notions of both velocity and constant dislocation became central to the modernist idea of the impossibility of holding on to the present, graspable only as fleeting and transient flickers of experience. Although some of the nineteenth-century prohibitions against women entering the city alone were eroding at the beginning of the twentieth, women were still circumscribed by the spatial limits imposed upon the female body in the early decades of the twentieth century. Ironically, it was within the hyper-masculine public world of politics and business that loitering about in the city's formal labyrinth gained a high degree of subversive signification for the male aesthete. It was here that the *flaneur* framed his self as anti-establishment, and represented bohemian fantasies of inhabiting the other, even while maintaining his class privilege as a man of letters about town. Drawing attention to gender differences in terms of access to the city, Susan Buck-Morss argues pointedly how "sexual difference complicates the politics of loitering".[61]

The *flaneur* walking about in the city's streets, resolutely not at home, embodied what was to be a fundamental feature of modernity's self-representation: a complex mode of unhomeliness. The image of the *flaneur* walking alone was a departure from more romanticist notions of-walking together as an important expression of friendship that also evoked older modes of community. The figure of the *flaneur* helped privilege the act of walking in the city as the most intense way of experiencing it, drawing upon a long tradition in western narrative in which the act of leaving home to go out into the public world is imbued with heroism. In the end in that story, of course, the hero returns to his home and to a stable identity. These self-constituting narratives of departures were thus also narratives of arrivals and returns to home.

Whereas walking in the city was marked as male privilege, it was nevertheless an everyday activity undertaken by most city dwellers. Michel de Certeau's excavation of the meaning of such routine activities, what he calls "everyday practice", necessitated by the very form of the city, invests the act of walking with significance of immense existential proportion, constituting a "trace" that is a reminder of absence itself, of difference, of otherness.[62] De Certeau writes: "The moving about that the city multiplies and concentrates makes the city itself an immense social experience of lacking a place".[63] Following his analysis, one could read the city as instrumental in producing in modern subjects a universal and profound sense of homelessness. But one must ask the question: are modern subjects destined to repudiate or be expelled from the home in search of the unhomely streets of modernity? The disturbing presence of colonized, working and female bodies in the city, not to mention the historical limits imposed upon women's mobility within urban spaces, certainly raises questions not dealt with in the universalizing narratives of urban modernity. The terms "home" and "street" after all are inextricably linked to a complex history and materiality of the politics of gender, class and race, an engaged consideration of which could surely offer a less fatalistic view of modernity.

One must then historicize the act of walking as a specular (observing) practice articulated with the very production of the modern self, of urban space as spectacle, and with particular forms of consumerism, imperial trade, commerce and advertising. Romantic tropes of walking in nature and communing with it were transformed in the modern city into window-shopping and strolling by middle-class consumers, prostitutes and working-class women looking for and going to work and *flaneurs* seeking escape from boredom, thus rendering the modern city as an essentially artificial and un-natural space, refracted through the fragmentation of value, increasing alienation from production, loss of community and the fracturing of organic space.[64]

Plans of nineteenth-century European cities had aimed to create a crowd of freely moving individuals, without letting them obtain the character of organized groups or a social collectivity. Sennett states that "individual bodies moving through urban space gradually became detached from the space in which they moved, and from the people the space contained."[65] As space became devalued and open to exchange through motion, individuals gradually lost "a sense of sharing a fate with others".[66] Sennett's descriptions of the outdoor cafés in Europe's capitals that contained people as spectators with the right to be left alone provide us with an intensely urban symbol at the threshold of modernity—that of "a public realm filled with moving and spectating individuals" who "no longer represented a political domain".[67] A proliferation of public spaces in the city was thus paradoxically contained by transformations in the very idea of the "public" itself as consisting of atomized individuals joined by the accident of sharing urban space. In fact, the paradox of western modernity for the story of feminism has been just that—as women were to gain space in the public sphere as citizens and workers, the notion of the public itself was weakening, becoming increasingly instrumentalized, privatized and commodified, and subject to both subtle and obvious forms of surveillance and control.

Shifting the focus back to London, one notes how the political economy of London produced and privileged what Baucom calls "a cultural aesthetics of movement and speed" that was simultaneously "the cultural aesthetic of modernity".[68] Baucom goes on to suggest that London, as early as the middle of the nineteenth century, had become the center of a great national and imperial economy of circulation that had written the social cartography of Victorian England as a chart for the distributive and redistributive flow of the nation's and the empire's commodities, texts and human bodies.[69]

But by the turn into the twentieth century, discourses on citizenship and national belonging struggled to reconcile the loss of unified geography in the city with the urgent need of the English nation to assert cultural and spatial unity in the face of the crisis of World War I, the colonialist projects abroad, and the women's and workers' movements at home.[70]

Analyzing the tension between the freedom associated with movement in the city and the limits imposed upon raced and sexed bodies and collectivities thus forces open productive spaces within the new public domains that were relentlessly under contestation. The cartography of modernist London, even as it privileged the moving body—propelled by the necessity of negotiating shops, the traffic on the streets and the crowds in parks, as well as by encounters with racial and sexual differences—also facilitated new relationships and social and political affinities.

De Certeau argues that "the long poem of walking manipulates spatial organizations, no matter how panoptic they are".[71] In Foucauldian terms, circulation in the modern "site" overturns previous, more fixed notions of "place", revealing a grid or network of structural relations within a defined space.[72] It is precisely the instability of circulation (Foucault characterizes it more problematically as "random") and the diverse readings offered by the grid that might be highly productive for the insertion of gender into the matrix of the modern urban site, within the barred/closed-off circuits of male power distributed across capital's production of local, national and world systems.

Gendered routes in the city might thus provide us with critical strategies to circumvent "the geometrical' or 'geographical' space of visual, panoptic, or theoretical constructions".[73] The use of walking as an illustration of a gendered activity further avoids the pitfalls of attempting to invoke a romanticized tradition of pure spaces for women, while at the same time opens up ground for rethinking the politics of citizenship.[74] According to Benjamin, salient to the experience of urban space itself was a key mechanism central to the apparatus of capitalism—a "tearing things out of the context of their usual inter-relations".[75] Walking might thus be construed as a social and political practice that makes possible not only the thinking of alternative, indeed eccentric routes, but also of reading and placing things in context, of reading against the grain of capital.

Inside Modernity

Feminist critics have already challenged the ways in which modernism came to be understood primarily as "a body of experimental writing produced by a group of expatriate men" from 1900 to 1945.[76] Virginia Woolf, whose novel *Mrs Dalloway* provides this chapter with its opening scene, has assumed a place as an exception in elite and masculinist configurations and accounts of literary modernism.[77] In taking up Martin Fuchs's suggestion that we open up modernity from its inside—"to its own countercurrents and to significant others"—this chapter turns to themes that are both central to modernist literary criticism in many ways and appear in a marginal relation to it—those of imperialism, racialized urbanism, and the gendered political economies of representation under capitalism.[78]

Patrick Williams reviews the salient ways in which modernity's relationship to imperialism has been largely theorized. On the one hand, modernism has been read as "incorporating" the cultural effects of imperialism; on the other hand, postcolonial critics have seen imperialism as a disturbing presence, and as radically disruptive of modernism, signaling a double crisis of both European colonialism and modernism.[79] The double crisis, of modernism and colonial capitalism, as I argue throughout this chapter, has been most forcefully figured in the modalities of urban rule and its gendered representations.

In the following sections, I explore the complex relationship of modernist urbanism and imperialism via a consideration of Jean Rhys's novel *Voyage in the Dark*.[80] A writer like Rhys has occupied a more or less peripheral position *vis-à-vis* the modernist "tradition". Her own writings evoke a perpetual sense of the problem of placing her within any canon, locating her uncertain place partly in the gender politics of the modernist literary tradition, but partly also in her mixed national heritage as a white creole from Dominica, itself a hybrid, multi-layered place with its own history of multiple colonizations and diasporic movements.[81] The daughter of a Welsh father (whose own mother was Irish), Rhys referred to her cultural origins as "pseudo-English" in her memoir *Smile Please*.[82]

Perhaps as an extension of this, Rhys also occupied an ambiguous place within the racial and sexual demarcations of the imperial metropolis. Views of the Caribbean in the metropole associated it with degeneracy, vulgarity, sexual immorality, illegitimacy, as a resolutely "unEnglish kind of place".[83] In particular, white creole women, the West Indian heiresses, were likened to the figure of the Hottentot Venus, a nineteenth-century racialized vernacular image for pathologically sexualized women. The most celebrated literary example of a white creole woman who meets a tragic fate is of course the crazed Bertha of Charlotte Brontë's *Jane Eyre*—violent, bestial, degenerate and transgressive of Victorian codes of femininity and domesticity.

In 1907, at the age of sixteen, Rhys left her family in the Caribbean and arrived in England. She spent the years leading up to World War I and the subsequent wartime years in London, returning to the city again after spending the decade of the 1920s in Paris.[84] Her remarkable biography weaves together dispersed geographies even as it displaces metropolitan modernity onto the black trans-Atlantic routes of migrating and circulating bodies, cultures, texts and commodities that she was herself a part of. It also questions the predominantly Anglocentric framing of Rhys's output as a modernist writer, a reading that this chapter implicitly questions by placing her work within trans-national European/Continental and Afro-Caribbean literary traditions, political concerns and theoretical innovations. Such a reading allows for modernism to be read as a trans-national movement and project located within the imperial world system. At the same time, it can be viewed as a dissident project aimed at interrupting the dominant routes of the global trade in people, commodities, texts and cultures through the insertion of the peripheries as important centers of artistic activity, creative sensibilities and revolutionary energies.

If in her memoir, *Smile Please*, Rhys represents herself as an alienated and reviled stranger in the imperial heartland, other fellow writers and critics have echoed those views. In the Introduction to her collection of short stories, Ford Madox Ford identified Rhys's national origin as the source of her peripheral vision of the imperial metropolis: "Coming from the Antilles, with a terrifying insight, and a terrific—an almost lurid!—passion for stating the case of the underdog, she has let her pen loose on the Left Banks of the Old World—on its gaols, its studios, its salons, its cafes, its criminals, its midinettes."[85] Taking their cue from Rhys's own ambivalent pronouncements about her origins, critics like Helen Carr point out that "as a white creole from Dominica she was 'West Indian' in a different way."[86] Kenneth Ramchand goes further and writes of the historical predicament of the white creole as consisting of a "terrified consciousness" emanating from a sense of belonging to nowhere.[87] Judith Kegan Gardiner notes that "on both sides of the Atlantic (Rhys) felt in the position of a member of a racial minority living among a resentful majority", a fact that led Rhys to continually contest boundaries of identity, nation and culture.[88]

Critics have picked up on this pervasive mood of estrangement from the colonial metropole and have increasingly read Rhys as a black writer, although it is unclear how satisfied she would have been with such a classification.[89] Such a critical move is complicated by the fact that as a white descendant of slave-owners, she could never make the West Indies home, in either a moral or an existential sense.[90] Nevertheless, Rhys's readability as a black writer only underscores her troubled relationship to metropolitan modernity. Rhys has thus emerged in Anglophone modernist literary

history as the quintessential outsider figure.[91] In particular, her female protagonists embody this sense of being outside class, race and nationality
assignations. Thus the unhomely woman on the edge of modernist urbanism was to become a defining figure of resistance in Rhys's fiction.

Situated Intersections

Voyage in the Dark is situated at the intersection of colonial and postcolonial worlds, the latter haunting the former, the former displaced onto
future dreams of difference erupting in the metropolis. The discussion
below illustrates how Jean Rhys appropriated, complicated and sometimes liberated the colonialist and masculinist claims of modernity and its
rationalized organization of urban space. Within a geometric imagination,
colonial and postcolonial urban relations could be figured as a series of
concentric circles. In the inner circle, the masculine sphere constitutes the
center of power in the city, with the women at the periphery. In the global
sphere, the European city constitutes the core of the empire, its colonies
the periphery. These very geometrics of modernist urbanism and imperialism, ultimately uncontainable even in the spatially articulated sym-
metries of urban planning and colonial knowledge systems, are mapped
and then unraveled in Rhys's novel, the site where the ideological and
emotional hold of such totalizing representational systems can at least
rhetorically be undone.

The concentric circles break off into the eccentric routes that Rhys's figures
embark upon. Walking these wayward pathways in the imperial city, the bodies of women, and those of black and working-class people, both resist and
desire (in)visibility and (in)direction. These figures trouble the assumed intel-
ligibility of possible insurgencies that seek to challenge the hegemonic constitution of London within the discourse of imperial urbanism. My thematization
of the ways in which the novel represents reading, walking and mapping as
interlinked urban social practices framed within a global imperial system foregrounds a historical dynamic for grasping the challenges facing the figuration
of citizenship within postcolonial feminism.

In particular, Rhys's representation of female labor in the city, or wom-
en's work more generally, provides a critical counterpoint to the capitalist
arrangements that underpinned the modernist city. Whereas the *flaneur*,
the man about town, embodied modernist anxieties about intellectual labor
(elaborated through a veritable elision of domestic and sexual labor), this
chapter suggests that the labor of fashioning oneself as a modern subject
in the city is not entirely a male prerogative, nor is it a narrowly representational one. Rhys's focus on women's (sexual) work opens up the issue of
women's political agency, as it enables a re-reading of the work of making
self in the home and the world as a work-in-progress within the larger
project of gendered citizenship in the capitalist city. It is also the labor of

a critical feminist reading that re-inscribes work (creative, affective, material) as central to modernist urban representations.

Set in London on the eve of World War I, *Voyage in the Dark* seeps into the interstices of literary modernism's hegemonic representations of the city that signify masculine and feminine modernities as disjunctive and differentially available to literary representation. The novel makes implicit use of the radicalizing moment of the years preceding World War I (without naming it) and its attendant rupturing of a plethora of social, especially gendered meanings of public and private, capital and labor, colonial power and class struggles. Rhys's modernism consists of elaborating these various discrepant realities (in modernist fashion, the discrepancy is sometimes apprehended as an opposition between the inner world of the protagonist and an uncomprehending, seemingly messy objective reality) while registering the impossibility of maintaining these distinctions. This allows her to curtail and question the monumentalizing drives of the capitalist colonial modernity both produced by, and producing, the standard urban narratives discussed earlier in the chapter. Rhys provides narrative space for the problematic of modernist subjectivity, especially that of working-class women involved in increasingly alienated sexual labor in the service of the capitalist urban machine. Oiling this machine are men with new money, engaged in City-based trans-national transactions that operate alongside, if not entirely depend on, the traffic in the underclass of women.

Typically, Rhys's women characters have been read as paradigmatic expressions of feminine psychology. Critics have pointed to Rhys's women in the city as the "walking wounded", or as "dispossessed urban spinster(s)".[92] Her fictional women, from Anna Morgan in *Voyage in the Dark* to Julia Martin in *After Leaving Mr Mackenzie*, are interpreted as passive, narcissistic and masochistic victims in a world dominated by men and capital. In Elaine Showalter's more positive reading of Rhys, the Victorian aesthetic that celebrated the polarized psychologies of men and women is to blame for the predicament of Rhys's female characters.[93] Another feminist critic, Judith Kegan Gardiner, reinterprets the critical reception of Rhys's fictional women as psychologically alienated. She argues that their alienation is based on the fact that Rhys's characters are often "female, poor, and sexually active" in a historically alienated world.[94]

Against these generalized critical responses that represent Rhys's fiction as either reflecting the fixed gender ideologies of late Victorianism or as celebrating authentic, albeit embattled femininity in a masculine world, the discussion below reads Rhys's fiction as a project of rethinking citizenship in a high imperial city through the figuration of alternative, dissident bodies that challenge hegemonic narratives of modernist urbanism. Rhys interpolates her protagonist Anna's sexual, economic and ultimately political body within the spaces of London in order to insert, quite materially, the question of women's materiality within the framework of colonial capitalism. Such a reading also opens up a re-theorization of the city and its subjects as it challenges the boundaries of literary, cultural, domestic and public spaces and foregrounds the ideological and material work that goes into producing and maintaining them.

Ultimately, Rhys's novel does much more than just disturb the standard urban narratives. In spite of the critical consensus that reads the novel as melancholic, closed and limited in its political aspirations, my reading shows how the novel itself points to other ways to enter the text and engage with that sense of the exhaustion of politics as signaled in its melancholic mood. In other words, I read the novel as in fact self-consciously respond-ing to a critical moment within capitalist and colonial urbanism, and in doing so, as offering possibilities for critique as a form of feminist politics.

The Textual City

Rhys created *Voyage in the Dark*, published in 1934, out of a series of journal entries written in the aftermath of a failed love affair in London in 1910.[95] The novel reads as a series of episodes that refuse the status of meta-narrative or social commentary; rather the novel strings together fragmented interior monologues that traverse diverse geographies and temporalities and are ren-dered in a first-person narrative voice. This particular choice of narration underscores the tension between the protagonist's inner and outer worlds. It narrates the problems of a troubled gendered subject moving about in a rapidly changing modernist city, enabling Rhys to re-evaluate, indeed to re-write, existing narratives of political agency and gendered citizenship. In doing so, Rhys mounts a literary challenge to what had been a largely masculine preserve—the analysis of urbanity as emblematic of the modern human condition. She thus disturbs prevailing notions of both gender and genre. The novel narrativizes not only the seemingly contradictory while also complicit relations between modernism and imperialism, but also draws attention to the questions of the uneven development of textual production and circulation within trans-national modernism and its gendered routes, prompting critical questions of who and what travels where and why.

The figure most prominently straddling the disconnected and heteroge-neous spaces of the imperial capital of London in *Voyage in the Dark* is the novel's protagonist Anna Morgan, a white West Indian girl newly arrived in the metropolis. In order to "get by" (economically, but also in other senses) in the city, Anna is precariously dependant on the vagaries of her job as a chorus girl, on infrequent monetary support from her stepmother, Hester, and on the beneficence of the men she gets involved with, who promise to "provide" for her for unpredictable durations of time. Like Rhys herself, Anna exists in the interstices of the English class system. She is a product of the Dominican plantocracy who is caught in the double bind of increasingly limited economic opportunities in the colony and uncertain status in the mother country.

The simultaneously listless and hysterical tone of Anna's interior monologues evokes her vexed relationship to the monotone of the standard urban narratives of literary modernism. Anna's accent, her sing-song voice, become the most palpable signs of her difference and her disempowerment in the imperial city. Hester talks of how "exactly like a nigger" Anna talked (56).[96] We see in these references Rhys's insertion of her narrative into a longer literary history of the representation of the white Creole woman who is racially suspect.[97]

The difference of tonality and accent profoundly sharpens Anna's experience of the city as that of a foreigner who is also an exile or a refugee, as well as her experience of relentless degradation and ever-increasing dependence on an exploitative system that condemns her to moving about in the city, both unhomely and homeless, and between London, the grand imperial metropolis, and England's dour, peripheral small towns. But even as Anna descends economically into poverty, culturally she remains unplaceable, both in terms of class and race and in terms of her national origin. Even without money, Anna still has access to a vanishing colonial cultural capital that shows up starkly and poignantly against her seemingly bleak future in capitalist London.

As a chorus girl Anna occupies a particularly tenuous position in the social hierarchy of London. The imperative to be constantly on the move, as employment seems scarce and housing remains unpredictable, is propelled by her sense that she must look for her "chances", however infinitesimal they might be within the palpably weighty apparatuses of imperial capitalism. After all, unlike prostitutes, chorus girls had some possibilities of upward mobility, an issue, Anna notices, that is often highlighted by the popular press in headlines such as: "'Chorus-Girl Marries Peer's Son.'" (46). These narratives of upward mobility, of trying to "settle down" or "get on" with life, made chorus girls and other working women in the public eye to be looked upon with a great deal of ambivalence and anxiety by bourgeois society. In many senses, the uncertain predicament of a chorus girl (or a masseuse or manicurist), often from the working class, was worse than that of a prostitute who could offer sex and charge money for it on a regular basis, thus ensuring a degree of financial independence. In contrast, chorus girls existed in the intermediary realms of the city, not quite policed as the prostitutes, but not quite treated as decent, proper women. Moreover, whereas the woman on stage within modernist culture could be the center of male romantic fantasies, attitudes of the upper classes towards mass entertainment in general continued to be riven with ambivalence[98] While mass theatrical performances were perceived as providing a widening arena for cultural expression and autonomy, they still represented un-reconciled contradictions with the economic and social repercussions of the massification of culture. Women workers in the theatre, such as actresses and chorus girls, were thus positioned somewhere between subjects of economic independence and objects of social disdain.

The modernist ambivalence towards mass entertainment is echoed in the debates on literary genres that sought to draw sharp distinctions between the popular pulp fiction that indulged in sensationalism, the naturalist/realist fiction that explored the lives of everyday people in the city, and the experimental, formal high-modernist novels. Within these demarcations, pulp fiction's dominant themes came to be associated with fallen or loose women walking about in the modern city. The Goncourt brothers referred to such popular fiction as "those spicy little works, memoirs of street walkers . . . scandals that hitch up their skirts in pictures in bookshop windows".[99] The melodrama in which such stories found a generic home emerged as a despised form of popular culture. But the increasing popularity of literature based on the lives of working-class women and their sexual escapades revealed the paradox of the middle-class fascination with sexually provocative details of working-class women's lives. Such narratives provided vicarious access to the pleasures of crossing class boundaries through sexual fantasy and fantasy alone, and palliated the feelings of boredom and anomie brought about by modern life in the alienating city.[100] The different class dimensions of the overly commercialized and at the same time moralizing depictions of poor and sexually active women reinforced generic distinctions and instigated new questions of culture and taste.[101]

The debates on gender, genre and the space of the city form crucial subtexts of Rhys's reworking of the possibilities and the limits of gendered political agency in the city.[102] On the surface, Anna's life proceeds along the familiar scripts of the "slice of life" narratives about sexually available women in cities who were typically represented as victims of unnatural and unrealistic desires for social mobility within a class-bound and narrow-minded society. Thus, if "Anna" anagramatically echoes "Nana", the heroine of Emile Zola's celebrated novel *Nana* about a society prostitute whose life ends in tragedy, it is perhaps Rhys's attempt to take on one of the standard bearers of sexuality and morality in the modern city. Zola's Nana spreads degeneration and disease within the body politic through the medium of her own simultaneously aestheticized and debased body. Rhys's novel re-cites the moral of the story through Anna's more worldly wise friend Maudie's words: "Everybody says the man's bound to get tired and you read it in all books. But I never read now" (46). In repudiating those books and reading (of canonical narratives) itself as an alienating activity, Maudie hopes to be able to circumvent her fate, to follow a different script. After all: "a man writing a book about a tart tells a lot of lies . . . books are like that" (5).

In raising the issue of the gender of the author, his authority on the subject itself is questioned here, underscoring issues of the truth of representation and its relationship to experience. Recognizing the inscription of her life in the standard urban narratives, Anna deploys textual mimicry, an ironic re-citation, in refusing one man's advances: "'Some other night,' I said. '*Ca sera pour un autre soir.*' (A girl in a book said that. Some girl in some book.)" (79). The city itself then becomes an allegory of the drama of false representations. In his writings, Baudelaire had referred to that "vast picture gallery which is life in London or Paris" providing the city dweller an encounter "with all the various types of fallen womanhood".[103] The question elicited by Rhys is the question of the gender of the generic "city dweller". It is through such textualized negotiations of the simultaneous familiarity and estrangement with the dominant texts of modernist urbanity that the novel begins to write itself as an alternative text to the standard urban narratives of modernist London.

The City of Images

The circulating bodies of women in the city are articulated with the movement of cash and images in London's economy. Cash appears in the novel almost exclusively from rich businessmen who use it to flaunt wealth and lifestyle, even as it transmutes into a surreptitious, almost magical thing in the handbags and purses of women sleeping with such men. Advertisements that take on a reality of their own underscore the pervasive presence of commodities in the space of the city. The modernist city's commodified spaces (and spaces that are themselves commodities) tear things out of context, blurring the gap between image, the materiality of bodies, and the in-vestment of the subject with rights and personhood.[104] Karl Marx had noted how "the *devaluation* of the human world grows in direct proportion to the increase in value of the world of things".[105] The capitalist city afforded an ever-increasing disjuncture between things and their value, predicated now on the image being sold (in place of the thing). It was transforming all human relations as a relationship between things. This is the very condition in which Anna experiences her body as a fetish, such that London becomes a city where "a girl's clothes cost more than the girls inside them" (28).

In a critical scene, the novel focuses on revealing the process by which Anna dresses herself up as a commodity and experiences it as such. She ponders: "There was a black velvet dress in a shop-window (on Oxford Street), with the skirt slit up so that you could see the light stocking. A girl could look lovely in that, like a doll or a flower" (81). The imbrication of the commodity in discourses of the female body imaginable as a "doll" or "flower" evokes a Surrealistic image of modernist alienation as it fractures the smooth images of over-determined representations of femininity. Placing these images in the context of a capitalist city, the phrase "like a doll or a flower" not only points to the construction of femininity as fragile, commodified, passive and submissive, it also underscores the way in which the female body enters the discourse of modernist capitalism as a set of floating, fleeting, reproducible part-object images to be consumed, becoming part of what Benjamin calls "the phantasmagoria of commodities" in the city. Commodity fetishism, so integral to the logic of capitalism, defines the very condition of being human under capitalism; its critique particularly exposes the ways in which the human is also a profoundly gendered category.

Here I am suggesting that Rhys's text can be read in the context of the Surrealists and their work with mannequins and automatons through which they sought to artistically respond to the politics of the capitalist rationalization of the body and the city.[106] Like the Surrealists, Rhys seeks to highlight the unrepresentable in capitalism—i.e., the making of the female body as commodity. Read through the metaphor of clothing that Rhys deploys throughout her novel, the fetishization of women's bodies under capitalism is presented with a sharp eye towards the pedagogical—the lesson to be learnt for women in the city is regarding the value/lessness of women. But there are also more practical lessons about the importance of being "dressed up to the nines" (18–19). After all, Anna's "hideous underclothes" signify very powerfully to her the "beastly lives" of women like her (15). In another scene that illustrates the imbrication of women in the commodified spaces of the city, Anna finds that her new clothes make "the streets look(ed) different that day". But she learns as well that the difference between her self and the city is as "a reflection in the looking glass is different from the real thing" (17). After all:

> the clothes of most of the women who passed were like caricatures of clothes in the shop-windows, but when they stopped to look you saw that their eyes were fixed on the future. "If I could buy this, then of course I'd be quite different". (81)

The melding of commodities, social value, personal worth and sexual image here signals the ultimate limit of the rationalized languages of capitalist modernity to apprehend the full scope of the gendered experience of modernity. The city itself is nothing but a labyrinth of signs and images that need to be constantly decoded but whose meanings are ever shifting and subject to the vagaries of capital. In this, urban space is entirely transformed into a site of commodity spectacle, but it also where the fault-lines of capitalist culture become visible.[107]

The spectacle of commodities that advertising engendered, involving the production of images that were meant to be both looked at and that in turn looked back, led to individuals experiencing the city through constant self-observation. Throughout the novel, Anna looks at mirrors for assurance of her worth that she can only evaluate by turning herself into another object—"as if I were looking at somebody else" (13).[108] Such an objectification extends the domain of the image (such that the past is "like looking at an old photograph of myself" [26]), even as it expands the hegemonic filter of the male gaze. Looking at her own body Anna realizes how: "I hated the looking-glass in his room—it *made* me look so thin and pale" (24;

emphasis added), granting a curious agency to the mirror as the source of self-reflection. This anxiety about "wondering if I looked all right" is one that holds "three-quarters of (me) . . . in a prison" (47). The image is thus also a space of incarceration. The phrase "made me look" suggests that the mirror is in fact not a blank space, but one that conceals the dominant gaze and makes it invisible in order to make it all-seeing; it performs a disciplinary operation. Capitalism itself here is figured as a mirror that reflects and simultaneously regulates the continuous traffic between use value and exchange value, between nature and culture, between the city and its subjects. Capitalist modernity emerges as an ideology effect in crisis.

In another variation of this idea, the street becomes a mirror, providing a mobile vantage point that destroys distinctions between public and private spaces, self and other. This mirror reaches into Anna's consciousness even as it moves relentlessly outwards to the interiors of hotels and houses to that of the shop windows and streets. Streetlights merely illuminate, make visible, what is otherwise experienced as the all-knowing masculinized, capitalized public gaze. For Anna, the intensely physical experience of being looked at in the street—"I felt cold and as if I were dreaming" (22)—is also the paradoxically disembodied experience of looking at herself, "as if I had gone out of myself . . . in a dream" (14). Such a complex representation of Anna's body as always already disembodied and alienated does not erase her experience of it as oppressed, pressed upon; rather it complicates the way in which sexual and economic oppressions are reflected in the city of images and how they structure her subjectivity.

Anna Morgan stands out as a modernist protagonist whose admittedly experiential understanding of the mechanisms of capitalism's commodity fetishism opens up the question of subjectivity within modernism. Her ability to make faces in the mirror illustrates how the narrative's evocation of mirroring as simultaneously external and internal regulation is pitted against the possibility of self-fashioning, of making face. Paradoxically, the novel provides virtually no physical descriptions of Anna's looks. It is Rhys's microscopic portrayal of gestures, of Anna's acts of changing and putting on clothes, of her walking and creeping within both architectural and bodily confines as she struggles to engage in self-fabrication and in finding a home, that Rhys's depiction of Anna's physicality can be read as inextricable from her interiority.

The novel presents a very complicated portrait of Anna's ineffable, seemingly innocent sexuality that evokes both sympathy and mystery. It becomes another site of making self, of exposing the mechanisms of sexualized commodification in gendered terms. Anna's anomalous sexuality is expressed through her bouts of moodiness, in moments when she pretends to be a virgin, or affects weakness and sickness. Her demeanor remains a puzzle throughout, as she plays the role of a betrayed lover, a sick woman and a virgin alternately. Anna's main talent, which draws upon her complex, interstitial class background, is that she can simulate being a "lady" who has hit upon bad times. Her ability in part to pretend to bourgeois ladylikeness prompts a colleague to express optimism about Anna's potential for upward social mobility: "I always knew you'd get off with somebody with money" (27). Even so, Anna's emotional and economic calculations intersect precariously, offering her a mode to just about get by in the city. Anna uses her sexuality to gain access to agency in her very limited situations. Paradoxically, this tenuous control of her sexuality is predicated on a streak of impracticality and un-worldly, idealistic recklessness. Her friends advise her not to "get soppy" about men because "that's fatal" (27). Instead, the more worldly women advise her "the thing with men is to get everything you can out of them . . . You ask any girl in London . . . You ought to make him get you a nice flat up West somewhere" (27).

The novel makes productive use of the un-decipherability of Anna's precise situation—she is not a prostitute, but neither does she belong in any family situation—in order to draw attention to questions of gendered sexual work. It doesn't focus so much on the working conditions of women (although material questions of housing, clothing, food and law and order remain key) as much as on the effects of sexual work on gendered subjectivity. In being sickly and in refusing to have sex under duress, Anna shows both a romantic delusion as well as a refusal, however temporary, to relinquish agency even as she has to suffer from poverty and homelessness. The novel provides an instantiation of how intricately and intimately capitalist enterprises are woven into the very fabric of London and in the bodies, gestures, affects and emotions that populate it. The interchange of women and commodities provides a critical lens through which we are to read this imbrication. The materiality of the city—represented in advertising billboards, working conditions, property relations, real estate values, rent, etc.—crucially shapes gender relations and gendered subjectivities in the novelistic city.

Bedrooms on Tour

Twentieth-century London's cartography as laid out by Rhys is heavily commercialized, dotted profusely with hotels and restaurants, shops and arcades that represent key aspects of capitalist development as urbanization. Anna comments on how "All the houses seemed to be hotels. The Bellevue, the Welcome, the Cornwall, the Sandringham, the Berkeley, the Waverley" (80). Not all hotels of course represent the purported exuberance of high capitalism—the insides of many of these hotels with their musty, gloomy, "lugubrious" (76) rooms full of "funereal smells" (60–61), the boarding houses (where Hester, Anna's step-mother. who is an independent woman, lives), the innumerable rented spaces in the city simulating domesticity, reveal the precarity of a construct of the home and the city that has nevertheless an incalculable stranglehold on bourgeois sensibilities. The critic

Helen Carr has picked up on this and characterized Rhys's description of the inside of these spaces as evoking "an in-between world, where identities are indecipherable, uncertain, confused . . . her characters live in transitory, anonymous boarding houses and hotels, strangers to those who surround them."[109] Anna herself moves among more than fifteen towns on her first winter tour in England, living in a series of makeshift homes—in hotels and in bed-sits presided over by unpleasant landladies, or the "ghastly" hostels for chorus girls where they "make you come down to prayers every morning" (10, 12). She recalls "all the bedrooms . . . and how exactly alike they were, bedrooms on tour". One is described as "a small, dark box", "getting smaller and smaller", and cold as the street (14, 18). The detailed descriptions of smell (stale breakfast trays) and color (dirty red carpets), leaking into the structure of a claustrophobic urban geography, of "streets like smooth, shut-in ravines" (9), of "spiked railings" (80) everywhere, re-inforce unhomeliness, that simultaneously material and affective experience of lacking home in the modernist city.

The "hotel" has typically been read as an allegorical space within theoretical evocations of modernism and postmodernism. The anonymous, transient, interchangeable and transnational flows of money, people (businessmen, tourists, travelers) and encounters (business deals, sexual services) locate the hotel firmly within urban space (such that the hotel can be read as an allegorical space) while seemingly affirming rootless modernist cosmopolitanism as a condition of modernity itself. Kracauer's essay "The Hotel Lobby" emphasizes the sense of stasis and repetition pervading the space of the hotel. His hotel lobby is peopled with guests wearing a plethora of social masks that transform them into "mannequins", "ghosts" or "marionettes". The hotel provides the space of anonymous, temporary encounters allegorically signifying the evisceration of sociality within the modernist city.[110] And yet, the hotel is an intensely gendered space. Rhys shows that although women can be seen at upscale restaurants and hotels, they can do so only when accompanied by well-to-do men: "With the hotel half-empty they'd still say that they hadn't got a room" (90). Thus the sexual politics of the hotel as the allegorical space of modernist urbanity is evoked most starkly in Anna's material situation—she is a woman without material belongings, a male escort or social status. The question of sexual difference thus complicates the notion of the seemingly anonymous nature of capitalist transactions within the transient space of the hotel.

Walking about in the city, "thinking about (my) room in Camden Town" that she "didn't want to go back to" (81), Anna reflects attitudes of both profound alienation from and embracement of the city, as the rhetoric of sexual propriety reveals itself as being also that of urban space inasmuch as the latter is embedded in social codes. Although her perambulations along London streets appear to bourgeois society as "just bumming around" (70), they point sharply to the gender difference underlying the discourse of movement in the modern city. The cosmopolitanism associated with London's businessmen and global travelers who come to the city is not available to the women whose work consists of escorting rich foreign men and "showing (them) round" London (71). Cosmopolitanism and metropolitan culture are thus deeply imbued with gender difference; the spaces of commerce and public culture in the city are as stratified by race, class and national origin, as are spaces of intimacy and privacy. From this perspective, women like Anna can gain access to only a kind of subaltern cosmopolitanism.

In this high imperialist city, some of the more upwardly mobile men keep mistresses in alternate, second homes, paying for transgressing the sanctity of bourgeois marriage through transacting in real estate. Some of the makeshift spaces of sexual encounters mimic proper homes—when "spruced-up" and made "dainty" they can conjure "a nice flat to bring anybody to", as an astute landlady advises Anna. After all, the landlady has rightly calculated: "people don't give you what you're worth . . . They give you what they think you're used to. That's where a nice flat comes in" (96). The novel shows how in a way any place can be made to look like home, and it is what *looks* like home that matters—after all, there is nothing intrinsic about home in the modernist space of the city. As Rhys illustrates it, the space of the home is not only not immune from the visual and moral chaos of the city and its rampant commercialism, it is produced by that very contradiction between order and chaos, between the public and the private, between the affective and the calculable.

Anna is acutely conscious of the unhomeliness of her particular dwellings when she does have a place to live—rooms appear to possess "a secret feeling" (13). Even furniture and art objects such as Voltaire's bust in her lover Walter's home are felt as "sneering" at her (54). Constantly rebuked by landladies for "showing (y'self) at (my) sitting room window 'alf-naked" (4), Anna has to often go "crawling up the stairs at three o'clock in the morning" (17–18). The scene of her "crawling up the stairs" becomes a recurrent image of illegitimacy in the context of the pervasive policing of poor and single women in the city as figures of unrepressed sexuality and even criminality. The complex network of policing operates both inside and outside, institutionally and intimately. In the streets of London and at "home" in the city, Anna hears voices rebuking her: "They watch you, their faces like masks, set in the eternal grimace of disapproval. I always knew that girl was no good" (101). While the presence of detectives and policemen, not to mention landlords and hotel owners in the city, circumscribes possibilities for finding and sustaining work, the image of masked faces evokes Surrealism's critical evocation of the facelessness of capitalist domination and modern power. Anna internalizes the gaze and redirects it upon herself: "I got out into the street. A man passed. I thought he looked at me funnily and I wanted to run" (63).

In an essay on the French photographer Atget, "who, around 1900, took photographs of deserted Paris streets" as if they were "scenes of crime",

Benjamin reflects on a new perception of urban space as one of subversion, crime and danger.[111] Borrowing from the modernist aesthetic of the city as empty, abstract space, Rhys's London is also a city of deserted streets that evoke a sense of moral and physical danger. Baudelaire's coupling of kept women and criminals rendered through the perspective of the privileged poet strolling the urban streets is here reversed and presented from the perspective of a "kept" woman.[112]

Inhabiting these unhomely spaces in the city, the novel's task is to precisely re-situate the search for home from an over-determined context of hegemonic domesticity (marked as the space of the feminine) into the matrix of an imperial city. In "the bed small and narrow" where he (Walter, the man who has abandoned her) "never comes" (27), Anna experiences first-hand, in the aftermath of her failed love affair, the absence of intimacy and emptiness of life in the imperial metropole. The lack of communication between her and the world is concretized as walls between people. The only possibility of personal interaction, of community and social relations, depends on the chance encounter on the street enacted within the framework of the everyday act of walking in the city. The encounter carries within it the potential of a personally transformative experience but also represents its limits with regard to sociality, especially when it pertains to gender difference.[113] A pervasive sense of modernist alienation—melancholia, homelessness, anomie—seeps into the uncanny spaces of Rhys's novelistic city. The city of images, crowded with restless figures, modern buildings and flashy street signs, is drained of meaning. All activity relating to work and leisure, community and self-making, seems repetitive and empty. In this context, "the everyday" becomes "impenetrable", even as "the impenetrable" is experienced as "everyday", according to Benjamin's characterization of Surrealism's mode of apprehending daily life in the metropolis.[114] Domesticity is then lifted from its incarceration in the everyday and becomes something impenetrable. It is this transaction or negotiation between the everyday and the impenetrable that provides an important way of defining the unhomely in Rhys's novel.

But as before, the task of my reading is to articulate the experience of unhomeliness to its materiality. Moving about in poor, working-class districts of London, Rhys's representation of the grimness of the city has an element of social realism to it.[115] She counters the standard urban narratives of literary modernism through shocking juxtapositions of urban and bodily spaces. Anna's body, "cold as ice" (7), fuses with the coldness of the city—its life and its surfaces. In utter contrast to the *flaneur*'s experience of endless variety in the city, Anna finds that London as a city is doomed by alikeness with "the rows of houses outside, gimrack, rotten-looking, and all exactly alike" (18).[116] The image of "loathsome London, vile and stinking hole" finds artistic utterance in the poem she finds left behind in a drawer in her hotel room (29). It is the trace of the transient traveler to the city, an intimate expression left in the ambiguously public space of a hotel room.

The novel picks up on the enduring motif of the city as the space of death, or as dead space, as much more than physical reality. Even the air of London is "used-up and dead, dirty-warm" (47), "the dead smell of London" (48). The city's air of death and emptiness is thickened by the ghostly fog that envelops the city and seeps into its every nook and cranny. It evokes images of death and stagnancy, of a heavy emptiness, but also of opacity. The fog constructs mobile screens (the opposite of mirrors) that blur the lines between spaces, objects and subjects. But above all, "parts of London are as empty as if they were dead. There was no sun . . . looking out the street was like looking at stagnant water" (25, 28). This image of stagnant water is presented with a variation when Anna notices men watering the streets after a night of alcohol. London is the space of excretions and bodily remainders. D'Adhemar, the Frenchman visiting the city, too, notices "the dead streets, and the blank faces of the houses. 'It's terrible, . . . The sadness, the hopelessness. The frustration—you breathe it in'" (105).

Within the contradictory mixture of a socially conservative city where Anna and her friends face insults "just because we haven't got a man with us" (29) and an imperializing urban form, Rhys also narrates the emergence of new public spaces in the city where women could walk around, and where they could reside with varying degrees of autonomy. The singular image of Anna walking in London dominates the novel. She walks alone and with other women—Maudie and Anna go into the city to eat, they take a bus to go home, they shop, and go to the cinema in Camden Town. The space of the cinema not only projects images of the city on the screen, it itself becomes a screen of and from the city. Within the cinema hall, urban dwellers become anonymous. Its dark interiors mimic the fog that pervades the city outside. The cinema is both in and of the city.

Such an evocation of urban space in its simultaneous everydayness (routine, anomie, the fixed geography of the city) and magic (cinema, shopping, transportation) points to the ways in which Rhys attempts to imagine new publics in which women could be effectively figured as (historical) women, and as subjects in modernist literature, even as the novel is the starkest rendering of an imperial metropolis in which women, poor and migrants can only traverse eccentric routes.

Placing Race: Rhys and Her Others

Among the key theorists whose work I harness to understand the conjunctural space of the modernist postcolonial city is Fredric Jameson. For Jameson, the modern imperial system circumscribes literature and art's ability to apprehend the global within representational systems, such that the project of "mapping the totality" is an impossible one. He argues that colonialism has meant that a significant structural segment of the economic system as a whole is now located elsewhere, beyond the metropolis, outside of the daily life and existential experience of the home country . . . Such spatial disjunction has as its immediate consequence the inability to grasp the way the system functions as a whole . . . Pieces of the puzzle are missing; it can never be fully reconstructed.[117]

It is against the theorization of such an impossible project at the heart of literary modernism that Jean Rhys delivers a distinctive geo-political understanding of modernity's evocation of space—its binary hierarchization of center and periphery, metropolis and colony, as well as its abstraction of space as instrumental, containable, mappable, made amenable to the dominant tendencies of modernist aesthetic representation. My analysis of Rhys's fictional re-presentation of the representational dimension of the world system in the codes recognizable to, and as, aesthetic modernism, links the previous sections of this chapter—on Rhys's evocation of an imperial capitalist city and everyday life in it—with the following discussion on the ways in which racial difference and colonial rule structure the economy of the city of images.

To begin with, as a modernist, Rhys deploys memory against official history in order to make sense of the world system from its peripheries. Memories of slavery and of the long history of "miscegenation", of the black Atlantic as an imaginary double of metropolitan modernity, enable the political imagining of the destruction of the colonial center. Such a dissident imagination would no doubt problematize the subjectivity of a woman inhabiting these intersecting worlds. As the novel "cuts", to use a cinematic metaphor, between the Caribbean and London, Rhys frames her narrative in geo-spatial terms, situating Anna Morgan's movements within a global traffic in goods, cultural artifacts, performances, texts and migrants. While the plantation on which Anna grew up had been at the center of an international capitalist system in a previous century, in which slavery was linked with finance, industry and domestic consumption in the metropolis, in the imperial world of modern twentieth-century London the Caribbean plantation comes to be seen as remaindered from an earlier, now outmoded form of colonial culture and economy. Yet, as Gautam Premnath points out, in terms of the new circuits of imperial power and global capitalism, the old plantation has been continuously re-invented as a "transnational hinterland".[118] *Voyage in the Dark* turns on the gaze from the hinterland in the direction of the metropolis itself, the center of a new imperium made possible through what Kumkum Sangari calls the "internalization of jeopardized geography".[119] Such a narrative evocation is also an instance of what Patrick Williams refers to as "modernism from the empire" that displaces the western imperial metropolis as the key to modernity.[120]

Alongside Rhys's literary output whose task was to de-center the metropolis, one might place the work of the generations of writers to come from and of the Caribbean to make London their "home", including those whose time in the city might have overlapped with Rhys's. Consider a figure like the Trinidadian writer C. L. R James, whose *The Black Jacobins* was published in London in 1938, when Rhys herself was living the life of a writer there. In it James chronicles the history of the revolution in San Domingue, Haiti, in the implied context of twentieth-century anti-imperialism. James's work was, remarkably, pointing to an earlier modernity of the Caribbean, before the arrival of official colonialism. Equally significantly, James's writing on Toussaint L'Oueverture, the hero of the Haitian Revolution, suggested the revolutionary possibilities in twentieth-century Africa, of the possibilities of postcolonial autonomy and nationalism being born in the crucible of colonial exploitation, in what David Scott has called "the paradox of Enlightenment".[121]

Placing Rhys's work alongside James's provides a parallel that might enable one to approach another answer to why a book on postcolonial feminist urbanism must begin its itinerary in imperial London. For it is in the heart of the metropolis that political imaginings and real insurrections seem to challenge the purported order of the world system. James recognized his own coming of age as a product of this system, having "come to maturity within a system that was the result of centuries of development in another land . . . transplanted as a hothouse flower is transplanted and bore some strange fruit".[122] Thus it is also Rhys's peripheral, exilic, strange Anna Morgan, whose memories of the Caribbean world evoke the sense of the imperial metropolis as one haunted by death and destruction.

But there is another dimension to this relation, in the sense in which Rhys's vision of the metropolis stands in a complex relationship with the representations of slum life in the Caribbean world as found in James's only novel, *Minty Alley*, set in 1920s' Port of Spain and published in 1936, two years after the publication of *Voyage in the Dark*. Stark in realism, comic in spirit, *Minty Alley*, along with James's other short stories set in Port of Spain's backyards, could be read as *avant-garde* in the ways in which it delineates characters, relationships and situations from the world's periphery. The lives of the slum people are depicted not as representative, but as replete with the complexities of love, desire, hate, joy and sorrow. More pointedly, like Anna Morgan in London, Mrs. Rouse, the landlady (therefore not unhomely like Anna) from whom the protagonist Haynes rents a room, seems to be immersed in a life-struggle in an economy devastated by the First World War I around the question of money and property that is nevertheless also interlinked with issues of love and emotional stability. The young, sexually active female residents of her boarding house on Minty Alley become foils for her middle-aged frustrations and failures to establish a family or a romantic relationship.

But unlike Rhys's novel in which Caribbean figures walk about the city as alienated, displaced subjects, James records, as Paul Buhle suggests, both "the life of the masses, their joys tainted by sorrow and their collectivity tainted by conflict", as well as "the rise of the Black middle class" and "the passing of the old ways."[123] For James, the golden age of the masses, of collective existence, comes to an end with the rise of the middle classes in Trinidad. This is exemplified in the very last paragraph of the novel as Haynes walks past his former home in Minty Alley, now a "respectable" home housing a nuclear family:

> The front door and windows were open, and from the street he could see into the drawing-room. Husband and wife and three children lived there and one of the children was sitting at the piano playing a familiar tune from Hemy's music-book. Over and over she played it, while he stood outside, looking in at the window and thinking of old times.[124]

But unlike the inescapable biographical seepage in Rhys's depiction of life in seedy homes in London, James knew the life in the slums of Port of Spain from a distance, as a *flaneur* strolling through the backyards of the city, albeit as an attentive intellectual with responsibility. Critics like Kenneth Ramchand see this fictionalized in the novel in the figure of Haynes. Ramchand argues: "By making Haynes a plausible character and the centre of consciousness through whose limited point of view the novel unfolds, James achieves the distance necessary to explore his own alienation from the West Indian proletariat."[125] Like James, Haynes is a middle-class man who temporarily moves into the yard, "to make a break with all his monotonous past life" (23), and slowly but inexorably, albeit always at a remove (often "through the crack in the wall", 40) gets sucked into the lives of its inhabitants. Miss Atwell, a fellow resident, says of his situation there: "We has all liked you from the day you come here. You sits in your room, you doesn't go out, you reads your book, you plays your gramophone, you troubles nobody" (149–150). Haynes might be an unmoving spectator, with the backyard serving as the book of life, yet everyone including himself knows that his situation is at best temporary, until he resumes his path towards middle-class upward mobility.

In London, James would acquire a similar kind of mobility, that of the acculturated man of letters, that allowed him to attend lectures in Bloomsbury, visit art museums, remain unimpressed by the city traffic and tourist sites, orate on Trotskyism in Hampstead, heckle Marcus Garvey in Hyde Park for his racialism, perform the roles of Toussaint and Dessalines with Paul Robeson at Westminster Theatre, work with figures like George Padmore towards a new pan-Africanism and publish *The Black Jacobins*.[126] James the reporter who can "sit in a corner and watch" seems as active a figure as James the political and cultural activist.[127]

London, then, "indisputably the West Indian literary capital", is a profoundly different city for James than for Rhys, who both in real life and in her literary works is unable to conjure the kind of collectivity and political possibility ("of life's triumphs over narrow surroundings") that someone like James does with seeming ease.[128] In his Introduction to a collection of essays written by James about his life in London in the 1930s, Ramchand wonders if James had read Rhys (Ramchand sees "no sign" of that) but suggests that James would have definitely empathized with Rhys's depiction of young women floating about in the city.[129] James's own ambivalence towards the city is reflected in his valorization of Bloomsbury as a district that inspires him with intellectual ambition, while the jail-like dour lodgings in which he lives his daily life seem ever-present reminders of the sheer hardness of material life in London. He writes of his dwelling: "Whatever you do the loneliness of the room is dreadful."[130] Although in his reportage of women in London, James describes them in terms of "phenomena" and "types", he nevertheless devotes an extended passage to how, "even in these dreadful lodging houses you will find many girls with woman's natural instinct, and the opportunities which London gives, making a fine room out of this unpleasant material".[131] For James, women in London are strong, visible, "at home" in the city. Although he is aware of differences of class, what he admires most about an English woman in London, especially "the Bloomsbury girl" but also the Bohemian student "type", is "her independence, her ease, her total lack of constraint. They have a lot of freedom, these girls. They go where they like, when they like".[132] These are of course not the "normal type". But even the "average girl working in a bookshop, draper's shop, bureau of some sort, the million and one occupations which London offers", can be seen in "the streets or in the cafés, shoes and stockings always very fine, and clean."[133] James of course adds the cautionary note: "Please remember that these are not girls of the street".[134] Yet James himself is aware of the slippage between the two, a slippage that may mean a certain kind of moral ambiguity, especially from the perspective of a Trinidadian. Faced with the dizzying array of the types of women in London, James throws up his hands, arguing that it is too "difficult" a subject, one that he must leave alone for his "data is highly insufficient".[135] Thus, Rhys's and James's own particular depictions of high colonial London (the one deeply sensual, the other drily sociological) could not be further apart: "Hers was a voyage in the dark. His was a pilgrimage to a place of light and learning" in which women possessed the talent to give beauty and meaning to life in a very harsh metropolis, even for a coloured man from the Caribbean.[136]

In Rhys's fiction, the catastrophic consequences of Europe's wars and colonial adventures haunted the imperial space of London in the form of mobile, shadowy, stateless persons, unhomely women whose presence nevertheless shaped the political economy of urbanism. Feelings of insecurity and precarity co-existed with new assertions of cosmopolitanism *and* xenophobia, a structure ironically replicated at the beginning of the twenty-first century as well (see the Conclusion, "Situated Solidarities"). Rhys reads the figure of the white creole in the metropolis as that of the racialized stranger whose cultural origins seem un-mappable. She is a veritable reminder of the disconcerting presence of the other in the metropolis.

She represents both the impossibility of dissident interpellations within an imperial national identity and the possible anxieties and melancholia that structure imperial subjectivities.[137] Her presence in the city pushes against something "unknown and threatening", signifying the imperial repression of other time zones and latitudes (148).

Two articulated processes come to view in the ways in which the presence of the other is reconciled within the logic of urbanism in the time of imperialism—commodification and exoticism. The history of "exhibitions" which made a spectacle of black women such as Sara Baartman, the so-called Hottentot Venus, in London and Paris in the nineteenth century had both provoked an abjection of the black female body as irreducibly other in its sexual pathology and had rendered it as the site of racialized fantasies. These spectacles are embedded as cultural memory within Rhys's text.[138] Rhys's text remembers, sometimes through mimicry and sometimes through memory, the conventions of popular ethnographic script. During her affair with Walter Jeffries, Anna's subconscious registers the subsumed presence of a mulatto slave named on a slave list at her grandfather's ruined estate at Constance. In other places, the textual referencing of Caribbean carnival, its foods, colors and heat that circulate as memory in the alternative geographies suppressed within metropolitan space, veers between nostalgia for the past and a presaging of a different future, for a city yet to come.

Kenneth Ramchand has famously argued that *Voyage in the Dark* represents the Caribbean's "first Negritude novel".[139] Negritude's inversion of European racism's abjected black bodies into a celebration of blackness finds an echo in the modernist trope of the loss of an organic, more vital past (but also place) in the confrontation with a mechanized, spiritually barren modern world. Modernism's, and especially Surrealism's romance with ethnography and the exotic facilitated a globalizing, transnational project of modernity, as evidenced in the widespread cult of *art negre* and of primitivism in general.[140.] In Surrealist works, ethnographic artifacts were typically juxtaposed against machines and modern gadgets in various art exhibitions and publications, drawing attention to the elaborately technological, sophisticated barbarism of modernity that displaces its own advanced capitalist pathologies on to another savage purported to be elsewhere.

Rhys's narrative project can be understood as an attempt to turn the imperial gaze in upon itself through the perspective of the stranger. Such a narrative move makes visible a profound ambivalence about what Bill Schwarz calls "the unanticipated strangeness of the imperial center" that forever creates "new and unpredictable meanings" for the colonized other who finds herself transported or trafficked within it. If imperial adventures involved battles abroad and economic transactions on a world scale, they also sought to harness zones of safety and comfort, places where the imperial subject could return to for national sustenance (experienced in a familial setting), where Englishness could be constantly recycled as a cultural dominant. After all, it was in the center itself that the ideologies of domesticity played a crucial role in securing the place of the British imperium in the global imagination. London was not merely a global city in economic and geo-political terms, but also a domestic parlor where citizens showed off the best their civilization had to offer to a world looking enviously in.

On this view, Rhys places London firmly as an English city, even as she maps it on to a global system. Maudie's incomprehension of Anna's dislike of London—Anna "must be potty" for "whoever heard of anybody who didn't like London?" (28)—only underscores London's hegemonic status as the quintessential global metropolis. It is Anna's belated and uninvited arrival into this city—imperial capital and imperial city—that Rhys stages in her novel. The horrors of London experienced by the stranger in the house become indicative of the cracks within the walls of the imperial parlor even as it could be spruced-up and made to look inviting. In Anna's view the experience can be summed up thus: "this is England, and I'm in a nice, clean English room with all the dirt swept under the bed" (18).

It is precisely the complex ideological working out of the hegemonic status of London as simultaneously a global city and an imperial national parlor that the novel attempts to make visible. Rhys rewrites the interior architecture of the clean and dainty imperial parlor as a space where its dust and rubble are barely containable, deliberately kept out of the frame and out of sight. "Voyage" in the dark spaces of London thus evokes something deeper—a kind of Conradian moment in which a whole culture as concentrated in the imperial city is exposed as unsightly, hollow and brittle.

The ideology of metropolitan English domesticity exported to the periphery or the colony was a crucial aspect of colonial hegemony. Anna's abodes in the West Indies, such as Morgan's Rest and Constance Estate in New Town, were replicas of the imperial home in London's more middle-class districts, evoking an uncanny displacement inherent to the colonial setting that is "shut-in there, between two hills, like the end of the world" (42). Hester's view of Morgan's Rest as "nothing but rocks and stones and heat" is compounded by her "never seeing a white face from one week's end to the other". It is here that Anna grows up, disturbingly, "more like a nigger each day" (38).

Inside these prototypes of metropolitan homes are bookshelves full of "Walter Scott and a lot of old Longmans' Magazines, so old that the pages were yellow" (43), illustrating both a temporal lag and a spatial displacement characteristic of the colonial modernity of elsewhere. The verandah that provided a space for looking out from the vantage point of a secure home outwards at the colony, at the town full of natives, becomes the veritable symbol of colonial exile for Anna. Life in the Caribbean for such shadowy colonials in their shut-out locales consists of unrelieved monotony, absence of opportunity; it constitutes an ironic reversal of the shadowy status of Caribbean and other black migrants in the imperial city.

But if Anna's Caribbean home was one kind of exile—from a sense of self and opportunity, as well as from metropolitan culture—the voyage "in the dark" to the metropolis of London constitutes another kind of exile, to an eternal rootlessness and loss of class status and racial privilege. It is in London that paradoxically Anna mourns the loss of her Caribbean home that was never hers in the first place—she both idealizes and reviles it in its rural setting, seeing how it barely contains the brutal legacy of racial hatred and colonial violence.

This being not at home in both locales complicates the notion of home itself. As Premnath points out, *Voyage in the Dark* sets out to "disrupt(s) the discourse of 'home'" so important to the metropolis-colony relationship within high imperial discourse.[141] He points out how Rhys re-arranges imperial geography to present an interpenetrating landscape that is "virtually postimperial", where the distinctions between metropolis and colony unravel. The destabilizing juxtaposition in which London in fact is experienced "as a dreamscape", a dream of home that is "a figment of the colonial subject's imagination", "constructed out of scraps and fragments", enables Rhys to open up, as Premnath puts it, "interfaces to the Caribbean within the very landscape of the imperial metrology".[142]

The Caribbean emerges as a ubiquitously hidden alley in the topography of London in the novel. In contrast to the cold disgust and grey fear London evokes in Anna, home (the Caribbean) is "white-paved and hot", a "firecolour" (26). The unstable contrast between the metropolis and the colony is explored in images of "the narrow street" in the West Indies which "smelt of niggers" (3) to that of an almost cataclysmic image of "hundreds of thousands of white people . . . rushing along", engulfing London (9). The antinomy is also built up by developing narrative analogies between food and space, such as the sensuous image of Francine, the black servant, eating a mango, in contrast to images of the cold, stale breakfast trays in London's hotels. Francine's stories, jokes and laughter echo harshly and hauntingly against an English culture that is repressed and machine-like. Sue Thomas writes of how the black Caribbean figures as "a site of nurturant corporeal memory activated by a mnemonics of pain and loss" in Rhys's fiction.[143] Yet, the West Indian streets' "forlorn sound of voices" with the "heat pressing down" is not an idealized contrast, for "the sun at home" is "hot and terrible" (45); it only emphasizes Anna's ambiguous longings: "I hated being white. Being white and getting like Hester" (44). While "being black is warm and gay, being white is cold and sad" (19). The existential dissonance recorded here animates Rhys's narrative of ambivalent imperial unbelonging throughout.

The memory of the West Indian colonial home, however ambivalent, provides Anna with an outsider's perspective on London and English culture at large. The novel, in fact, consistently uses the displaced experiences of other expatriates, who like Anna find England "claustrophobic" and Englishmen full of "scorn and loathing of the female". One woman caustically comments: "I wouldn't be an Englishwoman . . . for any money you could give me or anything else . . . The women here are awful. That beaten, cringing look—or else as cruel and dried-up as they're made! . . . most Englishmen don't care a damn about women" (50–51). The misogyny of imperial English patriarchy also meant that the task of maintaining a sacrosanct private sphere fell upon British women in the colonies, including women such as Anna's teacher, Miss Jackson, and her stepmother, Hester. The experience of privatized, domestic ideology takes place in the context of the Caribbean's occupation, crucially built upon a repudiation of the "other" race, even as Englishwomen are themselves reviled by Englishmen.

Rhys presents the colonial context not as mere background, but as *constitutive* of the very condition of possibility of metropolitanism as a dominant ideology. *Voyage in the Dark* contrasts metropolitan bleakness with Caribbean warmth, but without nostalgia. The West Indies is also the site of terror, and of guilt for Creole women who are widely pathologized in a culture of misogyny. Throughout the novel Rhys reveals how the construction of "authentic" English womanhood is based on notions of decency that are inextricably tied to an understanding of public space as simultaneously masculine, colonial and English. The novel then records the familiar strangeness of the colonial world such that the (post)colonial subject's arrival into the imperial metropolis is always belated but always also indicative of a future yet to come. The narrative opens up the moment of imagining what the metropolis would look like once decolonized, from the perspective of what it means to become West Indian in the English city. Anna's strategies of living dislocated lives simultaneously were to be re-iterated in subsequent literary texts that seek to come to terms with "postcolonial London".

In this chapter I have read *Voyage in the Dark* as inaugurating a particular kind of critical postcolonial feminist urbanism that pierces the standard urban narratives of its time, and paves the way for reading imperial metropolitanism through the figure of the stranger, the unhomely woman, who unsettles colonial understandings of citizenship and belonging. Long attributed to male writers such as James Joyce, Joseph Conrad, Sam Selvon, Salman Rushdie and Hanif Kureishi, the exilic aesthetic that has come to dominate discussions of postcolonial London is subjected by Rhys to questions of gender, and in ways that are much ahead of her times, so to speak.[144]

Voyaging Out

Rhys's counter-narrative on the spaces of imperialist and modernist London proceeds from Anna's consciousness of her out-of-place, unhinged existence on the margins of society in London. Anna's complex subjectivity deriving from her origin in the Caribbean, and therefore as an outsider to London, enables her to negotiate the many ways in which she is marked as "different". Resistance against the dominant ideology that represented bourgeois women as primarily consumers and facilitators of an expanding capitalist economy, and of working-class women as simultaneously instruments of perverse sexual desire as well as recipients of social uplift, is registered through the evocation of the eccentric routes and the insurgent bodies that populate the city in the novel.

Rhys appropriates the mobile position of a narrator in the city, thus gendering and elaborating a plethora of possible relationships between the everyday, gendered subjectivity, citizenship and the city. Instead of a *trajet* that traces an urban male sensibility that simultaneously desires autonomy from and imbrication with the private domains, Rhys presents juxtaposed spaces in which the private and the public are no longer separate realms but integral to one another and to the city. The novel's complicated class-based readings of the city critique analyses that make certain kinds of "work" central to social analysis, and hence marginalize women's position in the city, relegating them to the periphery of urban space. The text injects the modernist project of urbanism with an insurgent angle by shifting focus from the city as the signifier of high modernity to its position in an intricate network of quotidian use-value, of spaces and places of exchange, of everyday practices of consumption and habitation and of an imperial world system.

In Rhys's fiction, the social imaginary is unthinkable without women's presence, however shadowy, in the circuits of power in the city. The nexus of the invisibility of women in the public sphere, of the repudiation of mass culture as feminine, of masses having female characteristics, of the city being precisely the space where such femininity could potentially be unleashed and where women's bodies needed to be controlled, as found in the "standard urban narratives", is effectively unfolded in the novel.

But the novel also challenges the limits of imagining citizenship from the spaces of marginality, of embodying the urban experience in alternative figurations, even as the modernist city is hegemonically the quintessential space of abstraction, commodification and imperial rule. Does this incommensurability, if it is such, between a postcolonial feminist reading and the imperial city that it must read against necessarily give rise to a defining melancholic urban sensibility and by extension, politics? Must we work with the simultaneously disabling and liberating modernity of our times in which metropolis and colony, center and periphery, selves and others are forever and inextricably linked? I will return to these questions in the Conclusion entitled "Situated Solidarities".

2 Different Belongings

> Men heard that women who went there (Nairobi) to sell potatoes and
> beans remained to sell themselves to strangers in cars.
> —John Lonsdale, "Jomo Kenyatta, God and the Modern World"

In his introduction to the "Five Year Plan of Research", the anthropologist
Bronislaw Malinowski invites his reader as "a passenger flying over the inland
route of the Imperial Airways" to a view of Africa. From such a vantage
point, the houses and the natives over many parts of the continent appear
to be no different from those in Birmingham and Manchester, he notes! But
on reaching Nairobi, "we enter a world where natives and things African
seem to play but the role of mutes and properties respectively". The place
is "dominated by large European administrative buildings, banks, churches
and stores. The white inhabitants go about their European business and live
in a world almost untouched, on its surface, by Africa".[1]

This view from above condenses a long history of colonial urbanization
in which cities like Nairobi were established as centers of colonial power. In
this chapter, the book moves from a discussion of the idea and the materiality of high imperial London to its scattering in the so-called peripheries (so-
called because the process always involved the creation of new centers and
margins). Nairobi's origins can be traced to 1896 when it became a depot on
the railway line from the port city of Mombasa on the east coast of Africa
to the East African interior in Uganda.[2] In 1907, when railway headquarters
were moved to Nairobi, it became the capital city of British East Africa. In
the following decades it grew to become a typical colonial city "with clusters
of African neighborhoods and shantytowns scattered around a white official
and residential core".[3]

Over the years, the image of Nairobi in the popular imagination has
undergone significant twists and turns—from the colonial ideal of the par-
adisal "green city in the sun",[4] an oasis of European culture in the midst of
bush country, to a city that became independent Kenya's symbol of modernity and progress (visible through landmark colonial buildings such as
Nairobi House and monumentalized postcolonial spaces such as the Jomo
Kenyatta Conference Center), to one that is in the contemporary moment
on the verge of collapse, torn apart by civil war, crime, corruption, decaying infrastructure and proliferating international terror links. Nairobi's
modernity is equally evidenced in the stark delineation of space according
to ethnic, class and race differences, concentrated within the parameters

of the postcolonial city. The general sense of Nairobi's present is summed up well by the oft-repeated formulation—"Nairobi is in a state of crisis".[5] The 1990 Saba Saba pro-democracy riots, the 1997 general strike, the 1998 bomb explosions at the US embassy that rocked the city and killed hundreds of Kenyans, the recent explosion of urban corruption scandals and the ongoing political crises, have all contributed significantly to the perception of Nairobi's permanent state of confusion and of its ultimately profound unruliness, with a reputation for high crime and low tricks.

The ever-increasing chaos of Nairobi has seemed to parallel Kenya's postcolonial politics. In 1978, the death of Kenya's first President, Jomo Kenyatta, signaled the end of the era of nation-building that had been formulated in the 1960s, that heady decade of decolonization hopes in Africa. The setting in of postcolonial disillusionment picked up pace under the regime of Daniel Arap Moi, whose rule became best known for its unabashed authoritarianism and corruption. The end of the Arap Moi era came about in the elections of December 2002. One of the first tasks taken up by the new government was a clean-up operation targeting corrupt city politics. The new President, Mwai Kibaki, also announced his commitment to neo-liberal economic reforms, with hopes of better integrating Kenya into the global economy. Now even that purported political arrangement is being torn apart with controversy and violence raging around the issue of political legitimacy.

Whatever the current state of its crisis might be, Nairobi is still the most important urban center in postcolonial East Africa, a region that continues to sit relatively peripherally to the contemporary centers of the global economy.[6] The city's transformation from a railway depot to an administrative node and the quintessential "white man's city" at the center of a settler colony,[7] to a postcolonial city connecting the hinterlands with national capital and East Africa with the global economy (as a tourist hub, Nairobi connects the African "wilds" with metropolitan centers in the West), could well be read as indicative of the ways in which the city has functioned as an important locus of historical change, and of East Africa's transition into a capitalist modernity that was crucially incubated within colonial rule.[8] Integral to the representational economy of Nairobi are thus the overlapping and contending frames of postcolonial identity that are simultaneously local, national, Third World and trans-national.

The view of the unruliness of Nairobi is of course not unique, nor is it exclusively rooted in the specific political and material conditions of the city per se. Simon Gikandi draws attention to the centrality of the "notion of crisis" in "theoretical reflections on postcolonial Africa" in general.[9] Mahmood Mamdani reads such analysis as an instance of what he calls "Afropessimism". In a related vein, AbdouMaliq Simone writes:

> Most African cities don't work, or at least their characterizations are conventionally replete with depictions ranging from the valiant, if mostly

misguided, struggles of the poor to eke out some minimal livelihood to the more insidious descriptions of bodies engaged in near-constant liminality, decadence, or religious and ethnic conflicts.[10]

On his view, images of incessant movement—of throbbing, migrating bodies, of lives lived on the edge—jostle with and reinforce the idea of the African city as a "stage too clogged with waste, history and disparate energy."[11] This chapter seeks to trace how the idea of Nairobi within postcolonial representations of the nation's modernity, especially in its literature, has a highly contested history—understood predominantly as a contest between the inherited forms of the colonial modern and the postcolonial imperative of decolonizing those forms. It is a history whose analysis is central to the understanding of the postcolonial city as a conjunctural space of global capitalism and culture. In this discussion, as throughout this book, narrative and urban form are seen as interlocking postcolonial formations. Even when the African novel has been ostensibly set in the countryside, and is read through the lens of folk and oral traditions, it is possible to read for the ways in which the relation between African-ness, African culture and urbanity are pushed outside the frame, and how both the rural and the urban face the dangerous possibility of becoming artifact instead of being considered products of historical processes and material forms. Reading outside that frame, the chapter explores how literary contestations over the space of Nairobi have structured the discourse of citizenship in Kenya, particularly in its gendered articulation.

Urbanizing Rule

The story of Nairobi as the space of political ferment and as object of rule begins with British colonialism when the city was organized as comprising the core of modern, western values. It was a place to be protected from the contamination of uncivilized natives in the countryside. This understanding of the colonial city as an oasis of western civilization in what the British perceived as alien and hostile country both reflected and constituted the fundamental underpinning of colonialism's logic of rule in Africa, articulated most sharply in a thoroughly racialized urban form. In fact, Mamdani goes as far as to suggest that the very construction of the opposition between the rural and the urban is a product of colonial legacy, emanating out of what he calls the "bifurcated" form of the colonial state in Africa.[12] Such a form was embodied in the British colonial state's mode of indirect rule in the countryside where tribal elites were put in charge of the administration of law and order, while cities came to be ruled through a more direct form of "urban civil power". The discourse of rule was consequently bifurcated as well, employing "the language of civil society and civil rights" in the city which was "first and foremost the society of *colons*", and the language of "community and culture" in the countryside.[13] Thus, a "racially defined citizenry" that was bound by the rule of law in the city was integrated into an "associated regime of rights" that included rights of free movement and association, leading up to political representation.[14] On the other hand, the local state was embodied as ethnic power enforcing custom on tribespersons who were distinguished from citizens.

To extend Mamdani's terms to a city like Nairobi which was primarily a construct of the colonial state, between the "rights-bearing colons" and "the subject peasantry" one has to pay attention to the question of the natives in the city who "languished in a juridical limbo"—free from the authoritarianism of the customary law of the countryside but not from what Mamdani calls "modern, racially discriminatory civil legislation".[15] Colonial policy thus created two kinds of Africans—the native urban dweller of the racialized state with no status in the city, and the "containerized" African in the countryside, seen "not as a native, but as a tribesperson".[16] The bifurcated state thereby shaped the unequal constitution of African urban society and the accompanying legal apparatus that was empowered to determine citizenship. A further and related effect of this unevenness of rule was that the city became the symbol and instrument of civility and by extension of modernity, while the countryside was rendered as the repository of tribal authority, tradition and custom.

The bifurcated logic of rule is made manifest in such disciplinary sites as urban planning, law and anthropology. For Malinowski and other cultural functionalists, the stark differences of social order in the colonized city would eventually lead to a new urban culture arising out of the very same historical and spatial juxtapositions. David Simon, on a more pessimistic note, writes of the colonial legacy of African cities that is "a legacy of physically and socially structured inequalities" that derived from European forms of urbanism speaking in the name of modernity and progress.[17] Simon writes of the city plans forged under the influence of modernist urbanism: "Eurocentric, supremacist, discriminatory and exploitative they frequently were, but they provided a comprehensive justification for suppressing, deprecating and/or ignoring the alien, the different, the 'other' in the name of this presumed 'greater good'".[18] Frantz Fanon, reading a similar racialized cartography under French rule in Algiers, had referred to such a colonized city as the "Manichean city".[19] On Fanon's analysis, the divided parts of the city are ideologically and spatially organized to signify a whole universe of representations and practices of domination through geographical difference. The difference thus articulated at its core is not only about a racialized administration of urban space but is anchored in sedimented notions of civilizational superiority and ultimately of the incommensurability of cultures. The notion of incommensurability exposes a fundamental contradiction in the project of European urbanism as a civilizing mission. It reveals how the discriminatory apparatus of rights and rule was to provide the linchpin of European hegemony operating under the sign of urban modernity.

As an experiment in urban planning, Nairobi was both the model of the Garden City (an idea that had great currency in British urban planning since the late-nineteenth century) and of an essentially European city in an African setting, following the Algerian and South African models. Urban planning mapped the bifurcated logic of rule into racially distinct areas of town that were built into the design of Nairobi.[20] Thus were created spacious open areas for whites in the north and west while densely populated African sections were located in the south and east of the city. Even though Europeans never formed more than 10 percent of Nairobi's population, colonial administration kept a tight control of the city through pass laws and residential zoning restrictions that would maintain the white core of the city. The Nairobi City Council followed clear policies of the containment of Africans in these spaces. In 1901, a law allowed for the forcible removal of "unauthorized" people from the city. As workers were not allowed to bring families into the city, Africans were considered only "temporary" residents of Nairobi. After a 1919 law enabled the establishment of "native" areas, Africans were allowed to live in "satellite villages" outside of the city center, which were typically seen and represented as wild areas and as zones of political and psychic insecurity. After all, the Municipality of Nairobi in 1920 had declared that anyone "lodging in any verandah, outhouse or shed, or unoccupied building, or in a cart, vehicle or other receptacle", without an ostensible occupation, would be considered a vagrant.[21] Frequent demolition of African settlements was carried out to prevent more Africans from entering the city, more than would be necessary for the labor needs of the colonialists.[22] These "settlements" subsequently became some of Nairobi's largest slums. It was only in the aftermath of World War II that Africans in Nairobi experienced a brief moment of government support, typically directed towards returning black soldiers demobilized from the army. In 1939, the first housing estates in Nairobi were set up for Africans. These became increasingly cramped and decrepit as rising commodity prices and rents in the post-war period forced a new type of communal living in the city in which married workers were often forced to share homes with friends and kin from the countryside. But as resistance to British rule grew and dissent spread from the countryside to Kenya's cities, Nairobi's geography was written over by barbed wire, dividing not just whites from blacks, but one tribe from another.

Right of Entry

The selective and uneven deployment of rights in the city along racial lines was propelled not least by the labor demands of the colonial state. But the bifurcated logic of rule also both uniquely produced and exacerbated already existing gender inequalities in terms of women's work, their right to belong in the city and to contest the domain of rights associated with living and working in the city. Historically, colonial rule first kept Africans out of bounds of Nairobi, and then when they were selectively let in, native men were preferred over native women. Thus, Nairobi as a colonial city was first and foremost a white man's city, with selective entry granted to native men. Women came into Nairobi from the countryside as prostitutes or domestic workers in search of livelihood, as victims escaping violence and abuse, or as transient wives visiting their migrant city husbands. Colonialism thus produced newly precarious gendered subjectivities that were products not of the breakdown of families and communities as typically understood, but of new relations forged by colonial rule between gender, work and urban space.

As discussed in the previous chapter, the most visible *and* theorized women's work in the city is sex-work or prostitution. It is the most visible because historically prostitutes had access to cities before other women did (so that they could sexually service urban men). Theoretically prostitution provided the strongest evidence of women in public spaces; it complicated the analysis of work and sex and of public and private spheres by straddling the divides between seemingly antithetical concepts. Luise White writes: "in colonial cities built by male migrants, prostitution was a specific relationship between men and women, their families, and private employers."[23] White attempts to radically re-interpret the role of prostitution within Nairobi's history by focusing attention on questions of political economy. Through a study of the city's gendered and material history, White shows how prostitution is re-inscribed within the economic framework of "family labor" in which the "daughter's revenues" as a prostitute helped to "restore(d) the shattered fortunes" of increasingly impoverished, mostly male peasants. In White's reading, "women's work" provides "a way to study the workings of a colonial society from its most intimate moments—the interaction of the work of daughters, the makeshift arrangements of male migrants, and the long-term strategies of rural lineages and urban employers".[24] The work of prostitutes is thus firmly placed within familial and colonial frames, rather than as outside them. Crucially as well, it is sex-work that renders any easy opposition between the urban and rural as separate spheres of economy and culture untenable.

In the city, White argues, prostitution provided a way for some poor women to enter the ranks of the urban petit-bourgeois. Prostitutes invested in real estate and acted as heads of households, epitomizing and "caricaturing the values of a commoditized, accumulating society". They also supported the communities of male migrants and transients by forging complex affective, economic and sexual relationships. Rural relationships were thus extended into the city's back alleys and lodging houses, producing "a vast number of the relationships we tend to think of as anonymous, furtive, and sordid".[25] The figure of the prostitute or of the woman brewing beer or working as a barmaid was hence one that consistently evaded control, "a dangerously autonomous person, with too many ties to other people, with too few official eyes on her".[26]

Such a historically informed reading of the complex position occupied by prostitutes in the economic, social and affective realms of the city cannot occlude the ways in which prostitutes were subjected to both colonial and native surveillance. Viewed as runaway women, their mobility was policed not only through colonial state technologies, but also through a native civil society comprising a plethora of welfare associations and communal organizations. In a stark pointer of how both the colonial and the native forms of urban rule viewed women in Nairobi as interlopers, the Kikuyu General Union in the pre-independence period identified the four groups of women who should be allowed to remain in towns: legally married women living with husbands; householders; registered domestic servants and old prostitutes (women no longer capable of engaging in sex-work). This classification of women's roles exemplifies various orders and hierarchies of labor—from domestic to reproductive. What remains unnamed and inadmissible is the labor of sexual work in the urban economy.

By the time of independence, then, Nairobi was an overwhelmingly male domain.[27] The traditional labor model of men at work in the city and women and children left behind in the countryside had been endorsed and encouraged by the colonialists. Within both colonialist and nationalist discourse, women were associated with tradition and hence with the countryside, a notion that put them at two removes from any claim to citizenship in the city where previously native men had been denied rights as individuals. When Nairobi became a postcolonial city, native men continued to be the rightful inhabitants of the city and trustees of the modernity it emblematized, while native women were re-deployed as symbols of tradition and of the populist roots of Kenyan nationalism. This version of nationalism structured its discourse by way of a rhetorical reversal of the colonial state's logic of rule, while maintaining continuity in practice. Substantially shifting and undermining the focus from critiques of the colonial state and its domination in the private domains of African life, White argues: "the colonial state . . . when it did have impact on women's private lives, it did not have it for very long".[28] Because traditional culture (variously figured as tribal or African) was represented as patriarchal by the colonizers, and subsequently defended by anti-imperialists and nationalists as an authentic and indigenous sphere that needed to be protected from colonial modernity, gender relations within Kenyan society were deliberately and often cynically shielded from the influences of modernity, ironically perceived as embodied in the colonial state or the Christian Church. Thus, the very nature of the struggle over *uhuru* (freedom) and its discourse reinforced affiliation of women with traditional country life. Tradition became the rallying point, and practices including circumcision and polygamy were often defended in the name of freedom and a resistant indigenous culture.[29] Lonsdale writes of how

Kikuyu men saw modernity as a twin subversion of gender discipline. Alien rule emasculated self-mastery, urbanization inflamed female sexuality . . . Conquest deprived youths of the warriorhood in which they once proved their mettle. Land loss denied many the virtues of domestic production and ancestral guidance.[30]

Drawing attention to the simultaneous anxiety about urbanization precipitated by the loss of an agrarian order and the moral panic of the loss of a stable gendered social order, Lonsdale writes: "Towns alienated not only male production but female reproduction. Nairobi, the nearest, was Kenya's capital and a Kikuyu market."[31]

Anti-colonial struggles were thus paradoxically predicated on "traditional" values, even as colonial rule itself harnessed some of the most authoritarian features of custom in order to secure its own rule in the countryside and in the city. This politically opportunistic and strategic respect for culturally sanctioned authoritarianism on the part of the colonizers was often disingenuously framed as a liberal recognition of native culture.

Belonging in the city thus continued to be subject to gendered prohibitions in the postcolonial period. The question of belonging and citizenship remained glued to the contested terrain of tradition that had to be defended against colonial modernity that was followed by a more blatantly rapacious neo-colonial culture, even as the colonial modern sought to leave tradition as the sacrosanct sphere of the colonized. In postcolonial nationalist discourse, race and class discrimination quickly gained precedence over issues of gender inequalities as challenges for the new nation, a displacement that has been a classic feature of masculinist nationalism. Without recognition, then, the question of gender became key to postcolonial contestations of citizenship as properly belonging to the nation and to the city, with its associated norms of rights and civic privileges.

Refashioning the City

As African states prepared the ground for decolonization, albeit in very different ways, the object of reform and change, and the subject of tensions came to include civil society, whose most visible and material manifestations was the city itself.[32] I am interested in this chapter to further the inquiry into the city by focusing on new urban subjects created in the colonial encounter who are engaged in transition and translation, as much as in negotiations and contestations over the meaning of citizenship, often against the dominant logics of rule as articulated in the state-civil society debates. These debates tended to create polarities between legality and illegality, between hard work, respectability and social order in the service of capital versus the lazy drunken behavior of native Africans antithetical to economic efficiency and growth. As Frederick Cooper writes: "What the (colonial) planners had to face was not merely the mobilization of labor power, but the control of human beings, of people living in societies and immersed in cultures."[33]

Given that the city had been rendered out of bounds for Kenyans during the colonial period (even as the rural could only be signified as a lack), it was very much an act of resistance and defiance to learn to inhabit it, control it, and to re-signify it as *Kenyan* space in the postcolonial period. As Cooper writes, the project of colonial urban rule had had to contend with "people living in societies and immersed in cultures". Reclaiming the city was thus as much an act of repossession as it was of self-making, based in the material realities of their own "irregular" neighborhoods, anarchic streets and traditional communities.

The loosening of control on movement in the city after independence paved the way for a dramatic spurt in Nairobi's population. Though city living was typically depicted in the colonial period as a form natural to western modernity, with its concomitant associations of civility and citizenship and its historical rootedness in the processes of capitalist industrialization, it proved to be a highly contentious mode of being for Kenyans. The project of reshaping Nairobi as a postcolonial city became integral to redefining citizenship in Kenya, and to determining the nation's development. Nairobi became the postcolonial project *par excellence*—it was where the visible, material symbols of colonial rule were to be reinvested with African meaning, and where people of different ethnicities and tribal affiliations would become national citizens. Postcolonial civil society in Kenya, shot through by the contradictions of a brutal colonial legacy figured as a contest between rights (such that every citizen of independent Kenya would have rights previously denied under colonial rule) versus justice (such that the state would take into account the history of colonial rule's unequal treatment of various tribes, sexes, etc), took on the Africanization of cities and urban culture as its rallying cry. A key independence goal was the establishment of an indigenous de-racialized and democratic urban civil society.[34]

As it turned out, the postcolonial project of re-fashioning Nairobi as a national city was an extremely fraught one. On the ground, de-racialization translated into a strategy of replacing white rule by black rule while civil society remained deeply embedded in tribal and racial hierarchies and inequities. Postcolonial rule maintained the logic of the colonial state, keeping intact older hierarchies of power between different tribes, sexes and classes. Further, as the rural sphere was not de-tribalized to the same extent as the urban sphere was purportedly de-racialized, tribal affinities (translated as inter-ethnic rivalry in the city) continued to play a major role in African politics.[35] Ethnic or tribal identities, which had provided a strategic instrument of control over natives by the colonial state, were used to express revolt against colonial rule during the anti-colonial period and to lobby the postcolonial state for advantages.

Colonial forms of rule and processes of governance shaped the sorts of resistance to colonial rule that were formulated in the nationalist postcolonial period. Thus the salient experience of most African peoples (both rural and urban) in the postcolonial period has been that "nothing much changed".[36] In fact, the post-independence stress on indigenization or nationalization did not uproot or reorient urban-centered reform. In the city, those who had been the beneficiaries of the colonial order—upper-class native elites—defended and reinforced their privileges even as they articulated their demands for a new order in the language of nationalism and anti-imperialism.

The forging of postcolonial civil society came to be understood via a rethinking about cities as places where people could come together in a sociality that was based not on ethnic or kinship affinities but on solidarities arising from shared space and a common historical experience. In the city individuals and communities could live simultaneously as strangers and neighbors as well as form the imagined community of the nation. In reality, Nairobi and other African postcolonial cities became the very sites of concentrated ethnic violence and struggles over resources, processes held to be inimical to national unity and to the consolidation of a decolonized, deracialized civil society.

Kenyan nationalism (like other varieties of nationalism throughout Africa) thus inherited both the colonial logic of the opposition between the urban and the rural and the idea that the formation of the decolonized city was key to postcolonial civil society. These ideas were of course contested as well as absorbed by nationalists as the urban bias of development planning coexisted tensely alongside rural populism. Leaders like Jomo Kenyatta, for instance, emphasized the traditional tribal culture of the countryside as the repository of Kenyan values even as development projects in independent Kenya concentrated power and resources in the capital city. Kenyatta, Kenya's first President was born in 1894 in a family of Gikuyu farmers and received his early formal education at the Presbyterian Church of Scotland Mission. As a young man he arrived in Nairobi and secured work on a clerical position in the government. By 1920 Kenya had become an official colony, and the colonial state was now engaged in openly paving the way for increasingly exploitative policies towards African labor. It was in this political context in the city that Kenyatta came into contact with anti-colonial politics—through the East Africa Association (EAA), and a new organization consisting primarily of Gikuyus called the Kikuyu Central Association (KCA). In 1929 the KCA sent Kenyatta to England with the task of representing the Gikuyus, who were being dispossessed of their lands and turned into squatters on European farms. Kenyatta stayed in Europe until 1946 (with one brief return to Kenya in 1930), traveling through the Soviet Union, Sweden and Norway, among other places. In London, Kenyatta famously attended the seminars of the Polish functional anthropologist Bronislaw Malinowski at the London School of Economics in 1936. This encounter with western anthropology led to the writing of *Facing Mount Kenya* (published in 1938), one of the first anthropological accounts on Gikuyus written by a Gikuyu. Simon Gikandi has referred to it as a foundational text of the tradition of "national romance", later to be re-cited and critiqued in the work of other Kenyan writers like Ngugi wa Thiong'o.[37]

Kenyatta's biography is striking for the unique way in which it reconciles "his stylish representation of Africa in London's imperial political theatre" against a "conversion" to his people's cause in Kikuyuland upon his return to Kenya.[38] Kenyatta's cosmopolitanism is typically narrated in accounts of his social fluidity at negotiating the various layers of London society and his eloquence in English. Descriptions take note of how he enjoyed London's "splendours and temporary delights", leading what was a profligate lifestyle by most standards. Still, Lonsdale points out, doubts persisted about Kenyatta's real predilections as he was more often than not found to be "disappointingly tribal in focus", even by other African friends in the western metropolis.[39] On this view, Kenyatta was always an authentic Kenyan, nativist, tradition-bound and doggedly refusing to be contaminated by his exile in the cosmopolitan West.

Gikandi argues that "the turn to African traditions" in the works of African nationalist intellectuals as diverse as Kenyatta and the Ghanaian leader Kwame Nkrumah:

> was part of an elaborate search for a decolonized vista on modernity. If the African crisis now seems to be mapped out as the failure of modern categories, ideas and institutions in the history of Africa, it is precisely because modernity and modernization were the cornerstones on which the promise of nationalism was built.[40]

Other writers have noted how attitudes towards the idea of modernity in the postcolonial period shifted from being regarded as contagion to one of necessity, or contingency. Modernity came to be looked upon both as "a historical necessity and an object of social quest".[41]

The figure of Kenyatta has loomed large over modern Kenya as a shaper of its relations of past and present as elaborated in a project of postcolonial modernity and nationhood. On December 12, 1963, Kenya's day of independence, Kenyatta voiced the national policy towards the past: "Today, the tragedies and misunderstandings of the past are behind us. Today, we start on the great adventure of building the Kenya nation".[42] The ironic rhetorical distancing in Kenyatta's pronouncements from the colonial legacy of modernization while committing to it in policy has led critics like Simon to blame the modernist project embraced by African nationalists for many of the problems facing African cities today. He critiques the various strands of radical nationalists and socialists who shared the modernist ideology which often consisted of a single path to a desired outcome of development.

He argues that these ideas were alien and inappropriate to Africa and had immense internal contradictions that have remained irresolvable.[43] In the writer Ngugi wa Thiong'o's words:

> The rural areas of Africa were to the big cities what African countries were to the metropolis and countries of the West . . . The turning of the peasantry into semi or full-fledged proletarians by alienating them from the land is one of the most crucial social upheavals of twentieth century Africa.[44]

Ngugi here draws a direct and forceful analogy between the country-city dichotomy and the colonizer-colonized antinomy in distinctly materialist terms, exposing the ideological underpinning of postcolonial development and civil society committed to modernization in terms laid out by the West.

Certainly by 1963, the year of Kenyan independence, the legacy of colonial rule and its demands for gendered and racialized forms of labor had rendered Nairobi a thoroughly controlled, racially and sexually divided city. Nairobi continued in the postcolonial period to represent the dramatic contrasts of the colonial period, often with class segregation purporting to replace racial division. Its modern, upscale spaces such as the north and west suburbs that were low-density, high-income areas dotted with multistorey residences with large gardens and high fences continued to showcase Nairobi as a modern metropolis, even as its sprawling ghettos and slum districts in the south and the east such as Kibera, Pumwani and Mathare Valley grew exponentially, attracting Kenyans from all over the country with a promised share in the newly decolonized largesse as materialized in the capital city.

In the 1970s, the rate of urbanization in Kenya was far outstripping its largest city's social services, infrastructure, housing and employment capacities. But what the discourse of crisis often elided was the harsh material reality of neo-liberal economic policies of the new global players such as the International Monetary Fund and the World Bank, even as the representation of African urbanism focused on acute shortages of space and services, attributed typically to population "explosion" and to inherent cultures of corruption. The crisis was visually symbolized in the stark contrasts between the formal sector "geographies of affluence", to use Sarah Nuttall's phrase, being overtaken by the informal topography of sprawling shantytowns, unregulated workshops and make-shift kiosks sprouting up without logic and order. Eviction, harassment, insecurity and instability became the experiences of the everyday in the city for the unemployed, the petty traders, the shoeshine boys, the cab drivers and other poor. The backyards, alleys, slums and shantytowns constituted the city's margins whose residents were vilified as lazy and criminal. The influx of Somali and Ethiopian refugee populations over the years further gave rise to yet other sites of tensions about who rightfully belongs to the city.

Unreal State

Political theorists of various ilk have tried to make sense of the postcolonial state's re-inscription of the colonial il-logic of rule—bifurcated, unequal and consumed by corruption. The failure to institute a democratic polity in the postcolonial period is read by some as an implosion in the state's signifying capabilities as the dominant instrument of rule and order. Achille Mbembe's influential reading suggests that the African state is increasingly abstract and alienated from everyday life, and divested of any coherent logic of rule.[45] On Mbembe's account, the resulting breakdown of the postcolonial state constitutes a "regime of unreality" in postcolonial Africa.[46] In this view, state power takes on the features of a fetish; it is an empty ritual, form without content.[47] Ultimately, the regime of power takes on an "autonomous existence", and in the process of governance becomes "unaccountable".[48]

Mbembe's rendition of African politics of state and civil society as articulated in performative forms of power through the carnivalesque, the grotesque and the banal is meant to challenge the dominant frames of western rationality, Eurocentric political theory, and its understanding of the role of the state as a rational arbiter of justice and law and order. Mbembe's mode of apprehending the crisis of African modernity is through the positing of an African polis that is a fundamentally irrational place, a profound symptom of the failure of African modernity in the wake of postcolonialism. It is a failure that is nevertheless politically and theoretically productive as it exposes the lie of colonial governmentality as a civilizing mission.

Simon Gikandi has questioned the implications of such a mode of analysis that is premised on the devalorization of the subject and of "the regime of subjectivity" itself.[49] In this, my analysis is more allied with Gikandi's, as one of the key aims of this book is to restore subjectivity as a proper site of politics in the postcolonial city. In Gikandi's view, Mbembe and other postmodernist theorists of Africa are clearly working against the empirical work on Africa that dominated the academic and policy establishments throughout the 1950s and 1960s. Defiant of the social-scientific language of causality as embodied in the various projects of modernization, Gikandi points to the ways in which "living, experiencing and representing" happen simultaneously in the work of these postmodern theorists.[50] As Gikandi argues, on Mbembe's reading, it would be "impossible to apprehend Africa except through a figure of crisis". Crisis becomes both cause and effect of everyday life in Africa—it cannot be overcome by any appeal to reason, logic or structure.

But, as Gikandi illustrates, even Mbembe cannot entirely avoid using the figure of crisis towards an *explanatory* function. Concepts such as rationality and irrationality become performative functions, figural devices that provide "a grammar" for reading the magicalities and enchantments of postcolonial life without recourse to a broader and purportedly colonial concept of reason or subjectivity. Ultimately, Gikandi argues, Mbembe falls "back on the notion of an African mentality, a premodern epistemology in which there is no distinction between sign and the thing".[51]

So is Mbembe's view darkly pessimistic about the future of African civil society or is it naively optimistic about how irrationality itself can be empowering, as it allows subjects to circumvent the power of an illogical state? How can we think of autonomy of the self and its articulation with politics of resistance in this limitless empire of signs? And further, how can a politics of citizenship emerge from the detritus of the subject? These are the questions that are key to this book's project of elaborating postcolonial feminist citizenship and that remain elided in some of the dominant academic renderings of modernity in Africa.

One response to the question of the future of postcoloniality, typically centered on the city, has been the reiteration of politics as a struggle for survival that entails *local* appropriations of space. There is an attendant move here of an aestheticization of survival in the city that is nevertheless also a political strategy. The hasty borrowing of elements, a hodgepodge of things that have been thrown together, a practice of making-do, are seen to constitute the content and practice of daily life in the African city. The 2005 "Africa Remix" exhibition of contemporary African art at the Hayward Gallery in London reinforced this notion. Cramped into five small gallery spaces inside a building flanked by high touristic London as exemplified by the South Bank, the theme common among the artists represented there was this idea of provisionality, ephemerality and making-do with the detritus, the remains of high modernity (steel, weapons, art) in order to both make sense of a senseless reality, and in order to survive.

Further, some of the challenges of re-making the postcolonial city have led critics to question class and race as bases for understanding African civil society under neo-liberalism, even as the massive restructurings of the global economy persist in traversing older lines of division of class, race and gender such that the erstwhile colonial powers are still the beneficiaries of the new world order.[52] The erosion of state power has of course come not only on the heels of a tragic colonial history that shaped the inability of the postcolonial state to fully detribalize native society, and international pressures exerted through neo-liberal regimes worldwide that seek to bypass the sovereignty of African states. Whereas postmodernists see hope and potential in provisionally formulated urban forms of "pastiches, divergences and pluralities", or, as Mbembe and Nuttall put it, in the city's "leakages, its lines of flight, its borderlands and interfaces", Simon reminds us that most present forms of urbanism in Africa are in fact highly inequitable and unsustainable.[53] On this view, the breakdown of urban planning in African cities is not the by-product of a tragic process of modernization but the product of a struggle between different value systems and modes of accumulation—a top-down order of urban power versus a participatory and accountable planning process that might seek to redistribute resources from the rich to the poor.[54]

Ironically, it is the recognition of the complete breakdown of the symbolic and the signifying apparatuses of the state that has produced a renewed interest in urban civil society in recent years.[55] Focusing exclusively on the state, critics argue, tends to overlook the efforts of the poor and the marginalized to "create culture, sociality, and solidarity". The informal sectors and makeshift spaces of the urban are seen as examples of "that which coheres sociality outside the formal governance of nation states".[56] Much of the social science literature from a postmodernist bent has thus strategically reassigned marginality as a source of strength and focused on the creation of social spaces and social bodies outside the formal limits of the city. In turn, the notion of civil society itself has been expanded into a dynamic, complex and ambivalent set of relations between the state and society.[57] Partly in resistance to IMF-enforced Structural Adjustment Programs that have imposed spending cuts on welfare in already debt-ridden African states, and partly due to the inability of the national state to create a viable development future, the African city's informal frameworks and illegal networks are seen as instances of life where millions survive, often outside the grasp of both the state and of global capitalist institutions such as the World Bank and the IMF. As Frederick Cooper writes: "Capital's inconclusive assault on Africa created a guerilla army of the underemployed . . . The guerilla army frequently worked badly and cluttered up the city".[58]

Not surprisingly, then, one of the recurring tropes of the representational space of Nairobi is the idea of Nairobi itself as unreal space. The magical, inexplicable, often "illegal" devising of survival in Nairobi in spite of the incalculable chaos of the everyday generously lends itself to the experience of life itself as unreal. Nairobi is the space where officially sanctioned spectacle (such as sports events, political rallies, the Safari Rally, international conferences at the Kenyatta International Conference Center) collides with non-sanctioned, equally excessive spectacles of contortionists, evangelists, petty criminals, the lumpen proletariat and mobsters performing in public spaces such as parks, gardens and the street itself. The African "street", in particular has been seen as "the only space where a lumpen public can be seen and heard"; its children must survive through handouts and sheer wit, creating a new site where politics happens.[59] Among other sites of new political articulations in Africa, Hecht and Simone write of "popular neighborhoods" that are controlled through ethnic, religious or sectarian affiliations. These produce informal/illegal associations, alliances, strategies and practices that "provide an infrastructure for the community and a measure of functional autonomy" outside officialdom and bureaucracy.[60] Some of Nairobi's largest slums have been the subject of both a repudiation of the state and celebration of the sheer survival skills of the poor.

Thus the reigning affect in the city, as a consequence of the pervasive corruption of state politics, is one of cynicism, disillusionment and despair, jostling with scintillating battles of wit, verbal virtuosity and cultural innova-tion. The "'hum and buzz', the whispered, disguised and derisory words of the street" produce an orality that is distinctly urban, unlike the traditional orality attributed to *griots* in the countryside.[61] Nairobi's language *sheng*, which uses words from English, Swahili and other tribal languages to constantly invent and create new expressions, is itself an unreal language that can be appropri-ated by all citizens of its streets and neighborhoods. These informal networks of linguistic meanings and performances are pitted against the high discourses of illegality and legal citizenship, of law and dis-order.

There are two clearly visible threads in the discussion cited above. The first is a modernist approach that sees civil society in Africa in general as underdeveloped and marginal; the other is a communitarian approach that locates civil society within various communities in Africa that remain and flourish outside official and centralized institutions of public life.[62] The com-munitarian approach has often had both an anti-modernist populist aspect to it in the ways it has shunned law and order as modern forms of authori-tarianism, as well as a postmodernist angle that sees creative potential and political promise in unofficial discourses and practices of the city.[63] This tension between tradition and modernity, the contestations between state, civil society and community, and resistance within each of those social for-mations, forms the complex background against which I read the fictional-ization of Nairobi.

Fictional City

Roger Kurtz points out that novels and the city in Africa share "many of the same dynamics", as both are "ground for struggle" over identity; in fact, he argues that the city and the novel in Kenya are "inextricably linked".[64] Following on from Kurtz's formulation, I read Nairobi's fictionality through the postcolonial Nairobi novel that is a staging ground for the contestation between discrepant social spaces, and is an important site for debates over establishing an indigenous civil society and postcolonial identity in Kenya.[65] Bringing together questions of both the political and cultural economies of Nairobi in the nationalist period, I explore below how the postcolonial novel about Nairobi narrates the relations between the city and citizenship and the production of new urban African subjects that can inhabit and more importantly shape the city's modernity. Key to the ideological positioning of the Nairobi novel is a set of simultaneous moves from the rural to the urban, from the tribal to the national, from domestic to public spaces, and from peasant to worker identities. The novel stages the coming into modernity of a new Kenyan identity, and presents its own generic struggles as offering a glimpse into different modes of imagining citizenship. In fact, these novels themselves have been the sites of contestations over identity and ideology in postcolonial Kenya.

The articulation of the novel, city and citizenship is particularly complicated in the case of Nairobi, and not only for the city's deeply problematic location within contending debates about Kenyan futures and pasts. Whereas an influential critical approach to the postcolonial novel has been to read it as allegorizing the nation,[66] such a reading would reduce Nairobi to the frame of the national when in fact Nairobi is Kenyan (national), east African (regional), African (continental) and Third World (postcolonial) simultaneously.[67] The Nairobi novel is thus already a fractured site in debates over Kenyan national identity, linked to issues of neo-colonial extraction and urban bias in development planning as well as to projects of the nation as the basis for a hegemonic cultural identity and as the site of the intervention of global capital. Whereas writers like Ngugi wa Thiong'o have seen in the city neo-colonial patterns of the colonial extraction of resources and capitalist exploitation of the hinterland, others like Meja Mwangi and Marjorie Oludhe Macgoye have focused on the city itself as productive of the highly charged negotiations of postcolonial citizenship with local, national as well as trans-national formations.[68]

I would like to insert here a brief discussion of M. G. Vassanji's *The In-Between World of Vikram Lall* (2003) that approaches citizenship in the city from the perspective of subjects whose belonging is particularly precarious in postcolonial Kenya.[69] Unhomely in every sense of the word, Asians who chose to remain in postcolonial Kenya because it was home both temporally and spatially find themselves in an "in-between world", fated to play the role of middlemen between the African elites and a transnational class of capitalists including the erstwhile colonial rulers. Lacking a sense of emotional or moral rootedness, their sense of belonging to Africa is forever suspect. Vassanji's novel explores this crucial aspect of Kenyan postcolonial politics by plotting the life of its (anti)-protagonist Vikram Lall, a third-generation Asian African, from his innocent childhood in provincial Nakuru that was nevertheless shadowed by the Mau Mau insurgency and colonial violence, to his unwitting role in national corruption that is inextricably linked with his status as a disposable citizen. The grandson of a Punjabi railway man who along with other immigrant laborers built up the tracks of the East African Railway, Vikram grows up in the midst of a sprawling extended family that includes Indians such as his uncle Mahesh who have been displaced by the Partition of the Indian subcontinent, British colonial officers and their families, and African servants. Whereas the class and race lines seem utterly divided and harshly fixed, the everyday act of living in the small town community entails friendships with the white Bruces and the African Njoroge, grandson of the family gardener. It is a measure of the upside-down world of colonial Kenya that these friendships and solidarities while on the one hand seeming resilient and transgressive fall victim to the limits imposed by colonialism's strict social demarcations.

If at the end of part 1 of the novel, the move to Nairobi by the protagonist's nuclear family unit seems like a new beginning after the gruesome murders of the Bruces in Nakuru, the city it turns out offers only a perilous refuge from the uncertainties of the times. Even as it opens up new spaces of social and economic mobility, it forecloses other aspects of emotional and social life for its Asian inhabitants such as the Lalls. For the Asian African imagination, although London was always already a "Mecca" because "a visit there conferred status" (119), Nairobi was a city that was at least "half way to London" (122). In a moving episode where Vikram's father goes to a smart European tailoring shop in Nairobi to get a suit stitched for himself and is rebuffed by white customers, the city is exposed as a place where an Asian man could have only very limited access to European fashion, under-scoring the idea of self-fashioning in the city to be a highly dubious one, at least for some residents. Seen through the eyes of the young Vikram, colonial Nairobi during the nationalist period is both an emblem of modernity and savvyness as well as a place of racial difference, a ruin from which Kikuyu "terrorists" had been flushed out during Operation Anvil in the Emergency, "a sad, deserted place".

Part 2 of the novel opens in an independent Kenya, with Nairobi, "an Afri-can city now" (179), reflecting and encapsulating the new affluence and opti-mism of the times. It is also a newly politically charged space in which Uhuru Park is taken over by Mau Mau fighters seeking respect and settlement in the new nation. It is a "time of reconciliation and progress . . . a time of forget-ting the past, not picking at it" (180). This willed amnesia is embodied in the congregations of people in the city—at a fashion show, "the hall was packed . . . with people from all the races of Nairobi present. In that mixed crowd was the mood of happiness and all the hope and excitement, at least for the well-positioned classes, brought on by the rush of independence" (192).

Alongside the plotting of the precipitous rise and fall in the political and economic fortunes of Vikram Lall and his circle, the novel also plots the rise and fall of the city's Asian residents, whose right to apply for Kenyan citizen-ship was taken away in 1968. As postcolonial politics takes an increasingly communal turn and becomes riddled with corruption, the novel reflects the devastation of the Asian community in Nairobi: "Half the stores on River Road had new, African owners; from the remaining shops you would catch the vacant looks of owners expecting any time someone to walk in with an official writ ordering them to vacate the premises and hit the footpaths" (272). In just a few years from the hope and promise of a nation of open-ness towards all its people, the city is increasingly "compartmentalized", for "every evening from the melting pot of city life each person went his long way home to his family, his church, his folk" (311).

Central to the novel is Vassanji's insertion of a romantic plot of a doomed love affair in the city between Vikram's sister, the middle-class Asian girl Deepa (perceived by others as a typical "Nairobi girl—westernized, fashion-able and presumably free in her ways" [235]), and her childhood friend, the black African Njoroge. Even as the city's numerous public spaces—its cafés, restaurants, museums and shopping districts—enable the coming together of this inter-racial couple, Nairobi is still a city where such an inter-racial alliance is "not yet" possible. The affair is rendered illegitimate, forcing Deepa to run away from home and seek refuge in the down-market River Road. The novel shows the limits of freedom in the new capital city in that the only credible conclusion to Deepa and Njoroge's relationship is one of doom and tragedy. Unable to circumscribe their passion within the respective marriages they enter separately, Deepa and Njoroge meet surreptitiously in Deepa's family-run shop to re-ignite their passion, against the backdrop of increasing corruption and the evisceration of the hopes of liberation from neo-colonial chains. Their secret meeting place in the city is ripped apart by shame, scandal and tragedy when Njoroge is gunned down by a group of assailants and he breathes his last in Deepa's arms. As newspapers flash this last image of their final union, and the image circulates in the city with a vicious ferocity, the novel leaves the plot deliberately ambiguous about whether this was an honour crime against Deepa's infidelity or punishment meted out to Njoroge for challenging the regime.

Even as the affair begins to spin towards its doom, the novel opens up lines of relations between the individual fates of its protagonists and that of the capital city. Corrupt politicians flex their muscle and money power and dream of a Kenyan atomic bomb and the Olympic Games in Nairobi. Tall, big buildings sprout everywhere, "concrete giants that now dwarfed what remained of the squat grey stone structures of the colony that had housed its banks and showpiece library, its one Woolworths and its modest shops, and given the city its elegant tropical character" (331). These towering buildings are considered "a credit" to the country, "an example of the harambee work spirit of its citizens . . . proof that Africa was on the march" (330). In reality they are a source of profit to the politicians and the capitalists greasing the political machine. The city is turned into a gigantic capillary through which finance (and women) flows through domestic vaults to local banks to kinship networks to international clientele consisting of businessmen and transient European air-hostesses who double up as mistresses.

Vassanji's depiction of this corrupt world is as of a closed world from which there is no real escape. Even those characters who emigrate or who flee these conditions are haunted by the ghosts of despair and regret. The narrative belies any possibility of redemption from corruption as Vikram is thwarted by his attempts to plead guilty for his part in corrupt dealings by a regime committed to keeping a lid on the dirt and the illegal money that pours into its coffers. The novel offers only limited hope in the final image of a multicultural city as a figure of redemption: "The muezzin's call to prayer, then the street begins to fill up, the bustle rises to a crescendo and, to paraphrase the idols of my youth, I feel fine" (432).

Even as Nairobi's underbelly is chronicled in numerous Kenyan novels, the popular novel set in Nairobi that enjoyed a boom from the 1970s onwards became an important arena in which struggles based on class, gender and tribal differences over inhabiting the city were staged.[70] In these, two meta-phors have dominated representations of the city—Nairobi as a parasite on the body of the nation and Nairobi as a prostitute, a degraded body in itself. The idea of Nairobi as a parasite renders eating as a symbol of corruption, an especially poignant image in a context of poverty and underdevelopment in which food is scarce and often adulterated. In Leonard Kibera's *Voices in the Dark*, the main events take place on Etisarap Road, an anagram for "parasite". Meja Mwangi's portrayal of Nairobi's marginal spaces, its poor-est districts inhabited by people who are figured as "cockroaches" or as the "wretched of the earth", also plays upon the image of parasitism, albeit ironi-cally. The dour landscape of stinking back alleys, ramshackle dwelling, job-less youth, floating waste, corrupt officials, alcoholism, thievery and juvenile delinquency has led critics to talk of the "excremental vision" that dominates the horizons of so many African writers' view of the postcolonial African city. The evocation of foul odors, filth and grime, the dehumanized urban settings that are rife in these Kenyan novels recall Wole Soyinka's use of "voidancy" to critique urban Nigerian society in *The Interpreters* and Aye Kweyi Armah's depiction of postcolonial corruption in Ghana in *The Beauty-ful Ones Are Not Yet Born*.

Prostitution, like parasitism, dominates narratives of corruption and deg-radation in postcolonial Kenya. Though Kurtz argues that Kenyan potboil-ers use depraved scenes of rampant prostitution as an excuse for offering titillation and sensationalism at the cost of aesthetic principles, prostitution as already discussed has a long and complicated history in Nairobi that has to do with both questions of gendered belonging in the city and of its mate-rial underpinnings.[71] The city itself in the Nairobi novel has been figured as a prostitute. In most hegemonic nationalist discourses, woman's sexuality is deliberately erased, and contained within the domestic sphere, in need of protection from contamination by both colonialists and other agents of westernization. The figure of the prostitute on the other hand is consid-ered outside the economy of mother/land, both of which are central to the evocation of a masculinist patriarchal nationalism. Signifying moral decay and social decadence, prostitution is typically used to depict the disrup-tion of traditional structures of masculinity, family and community by the threat of African female sexuality in a modern colonial context. Deploying formulaic plots and clichéd endings in which law and order and social bal-ance are ultimately restored, the Nairobi novel depicts prostitution as both a pervasive social reality and a metaphor for the degradation of both the city and the women in it; it is a degradation that can and must be brought under control under the signs of state and society. In David Maillus's novels, for instance, women are corrupted both by the city and by modernity, a demonic interface that forces women into prostitution and uhomeliness.[72] Kurtz refers to such writings as "backlash literature", constituting a violent reaction to women in non-traditional roles and reflecting a curious mix-ture of crass commercialism and church-influenced conservatism. Kurtz's reading of women in the Nairobi novel astutely presents the social function of such "backlash" literature as both one of stabilizing fears and of titillating the popular imagination.

But such readings also implicitly draw upon African literary criticism whose sociological approaches have tended to focus on literary representations of the "roles" of women in society. Carole Boyce Davies draws attention to one of the first major discussions of women in African literature in G. C. M. Mutiso's essay "Women in African Literature" in which, Davies points out, Mutiso concludes that "the most memorable women in African literature are city types with loose morals and political roles who are free from the bondage of traditional mores but for whom this freedom is a mixed blessing".[73] Departing from such discussions about the role of the woman in Nairobi as a "type", my interest below is to look at the gendered political economy of the Nairobi novel, and at how the prostitute as urban woman comes to be marked as citizen.[74]

In the following sections I read Ngugi wa Thiong'o's *Petals of Blood* and Marjorie Macgoye's *Coming to Birth*.[75] Both texts narrativize the ideological and material contestations central to postcolonial Nairobi, although one has occupied a key place within Kenyan literary history as a manifesto and an epic of Fanonian cultural resistance, whereas the other is a largely marginal text in western discussions of Kenyan literature. Ngugi is of course the best-known writer from Kenya, famous not only for his substantial writerly corpus, but also for his outspoken views against the corrupt postcolonial regime in Kenya. His political positions have led to a series of detainments and long periods of exile. He also drew considerable attention when he publicly disavowed English as a medium for his creative writing, and moved to writing in Gikuyu, his native language. Macgoye, although known in Kenya as Kurtz claims as the "mother of Kenyan literature", is little known outside the country. An English woman who went to Kenya as a missionary and married a Luo doctor, she has presided over the literary urban culture of Nairobi for several decades. Her novel *Coming to Birth*, first published by Heinemann Kenya in 1986, won the Sinclair Prize the same year, and was re-published by the Feminist Press in 2000.

The radically different fictional accounts of Ngugi and Macgoye dramatize the contentious place of the city within Kenya's cultural politics, the postcolonial novel and postcolonial feminism. My interpretive frame approaches the salient questions about the complicated rural and urban axes of culture and development in postcolonial Kenya in the context of processes that are profoundly gendered in both these novels.

Swollen Center

A searing critique of neo-colonial driven underdevelopment, Ngugi wa Thiong'o's *Petals of Blood* presents a bleak portrait of postcolonial Kenya that is nevertheless interwoven with possibilities for a genuine African revo-lution.[76] "We took the wrong turning", says the Nairobi lawyer to the delega-tion of peasants from Ilmorog, voicing the loss of hope that is predicated on a certain teleology, a postcolonial road map as it were, towards a destination that has not only not been reached, but that is a lost object in the novel (165). The hope for freedom, for dignity, for equality and progress that had accom-panied liberation from British rule is rapidly replaced by the hard facts of economic neo-colonialism and a pathological national culture of corruption and greed. In this contest, independence is representable only as an "unreal" thing, a "gigantic deception" in which power has been transferred from the white rulers to African elites who are "eating the fruits of Uhuru" while the poor of the nation starve at its peripheries.

Simon Gikandi has suggested that *Petals of Blood* provides a powerful "framework for understanding the politics and poetics of underdevelopment".[77] In his book on Ngugi, Gikandi wishes to grapple with the ways in which Ngugi seeks to resolve the "crisis of representation" that emerged out of the seeming incommensurability of the aesthetic and political domains of his writings, the "politics" and the "poetics" of underdevelopment. Gikandi argues that in Ngugi's work art does not derive its identity from its ability to transcend its conditions of possibility, but in bearing "witness to historical experience", to enable the envi-sioning of a revolutionary future.[78] Gikandi tracks Ngugi's struggles with the very form of the novel—initially seen as an inherited bourgeois form preoccu-pied with individual consciousness and struggles of individuals to relate to the social—to its encompassment of the collective struggles of the Kenyan peoples. Drawing upon a Lukacsian reading of novelistic characters as "embodiments of historical forces which they must understand", Ngugi's fictional project is read as entailing a closing of the gap between the private and public worlds of his characters, such that the novel can represent a whole community trying to understand and come to terms with the articulation of a national and an Afri-can history that have been systematically repressed and debased. Writing from Cell 16 at Kamiti Maximum Security Prison in 1978, Ngugi himself wrote:

> Now my observation of how people ordinarily narrated events to one another had also shown me that they quite happily accepted interven-tions, digressions, narrative within a narrative and dramatic illustrations without losing the main narrative thread. The story-within-a-story was part and parcel of the conversational norms of the peasantry. The linear/ biographical unfolding of a story was more removed from actual social practice. (75–76)

Petals of Blood brings together both the historical development of peas-ant, anti-colonial consciousness as well as elements of social practice that represent the life-worlds of the peasantry. In his collection of essays, *Writ-ers in Politics*, Ngugi illustrates this point when he writes of literature as a "reflection on the aesthetic and imaginative planes, of a community's wrestling with its total environment to produce the basic means of life, food, clothing, shelter, and in the process creating and recreating itself in history".[79] It is in this vein that he writes of *Petals of Blood* as a novel in which "the Kenyan peasantry . . . was the real actor".[80] For him it was "a novel that explored and dramatized the inner lives of characters caught up in a historical development of underdevelopment".[81]

It is in light of such an articulation of the political meaning of his literary production that we can begin to see how, for Ngugi, the form of the novel inscribes the people's struggles as a historical struggle over *space*. Whereas critics have rightly noted the epic sweep of the novel that weaves together, in narrative form, thousands of years of peasant struggles against exploitation with postcolonial Kenyan disillusionments, it is the vast *spatial* scope of *Petals of Blood* that provides the novel something of a transnational form. This is of course crucially complicated in that spatially, the novel's most meaningful action takes place *between* the city and the countryside. It is a between-ness that signals several things at once—literally, it is in the journey *between* the city and the country that the space for a renewed cultural and political struggle of the people is produced, even as a rapacious neo-colonial regime produces a proliferation of other "between" or intermediary spaces, experientially blurring while materially reinforcing the distinction between the country and the city. But if the process of national formation is one of cognitive mapping, then the journey to the city maps out the contours of postcolonial Kenya in vivid and important ways. For the inhabitants of Ilmorog, whose children "knew no world outside Ilmorog: they thought of Kenya as a city or a large village somewhere outside Ilmorog" (109), it is the journey that makes visible the relations between space, community and the production of citizenship that is deeply linked to the development of capitalism both within and outside the national frame.

My interest here is to try to understand how and why the city is central to Ngugi's narrative of postcolonial disillusionment and disempowerment, and the ways in which it becomes the staging ground for narrating the complexities and struggles of postcolonial Kenyan identities. I will argue that although Ngugi sets out in this novel clearly opposed to the city, the representation of the urban becomes increasingly ambivalent and complex, underscoring the relations between city and country, between tradition and modernity, between tribal and citizen, in distinctly more dialectical than teleological or binary terms.

Nairobi in *Petals of Blood* is a city of "a thousand mirages" (110) to which young men and women are drawn, seeking escape from the drought and the impoverishment of the village. Like the alien il-logic of colonialism and neo-colonialism, the world of Nairobi in Ngugi's novel mixes "fact and fiction", creating a "surreal world" of the city that is in stark contrast to the countryside where the drought constitutes a "fundamental reality" (100).

But against the grain of much postmodern political theory (Mbembe et al.), Ngugi insists on a fundamental material reality that his fiction must make itself adequate to represent and encompass.

Ngugi's portrait of Nairobi draws on a nationalist populist tradition that could see the city only as inauthentic space. Such a populist approach contains two contradictory strains within it. One is a Left nationalist populism critical of the city's disproportionate use of resources at the expense of the nation's toiling and impoverished peasants in the countryside. In this view, the very form and nature of the city enables the concentration of power in the hands of African elites, and articulates itself with the new regime of neo-colonialism such that the capital city becomes a conduit for extracting Kenyan resources in the interests of a global capitalist order. African elites become insatiable consumers of foreign-manufactured automobiles and lifestyle, and act as middlemen signing away the economic sovereignty of the newly independent nation in pieces. It is this view of the city that leads Ngugi to figure the city as the "swollen center" of the nation's body. The concentration of capital in the city underwritten by unabashed greed creates a logic where people eat more than their own share.

Within a more culturalist and conservative populism, the city is seen as the symbol of moral and cultural inauthenticity, as a quintessentially modernist space contaminated by western ideas and values, and bereft of African tradition. In this view, even socialism is rejected as an imported ideology, seen as the source of seductive slogans rendered in a foreign language that is empty of meaning. Tradition is placed squarely in the countryside, and in tribal forms of community.

In Ngugi's depiction of populism, both versions are hypocritical and distorted and feed of each other. In his writing, a false discourse of tradition and authenticity is pitted against the empty manifestoes of postcolonial socialism. Both cynically deploy the idea of a return to the land and to one's roots, even as urban-centered development continues apace. Ruling the outlying agricultural provinces from an urban center of course replicates and reproduces the colonial legacy, while the new nationalism as articulated by the elites endorses western-style development models even as lip service is paid to old-style cultural nationalism expressed as Africanism. This would be Kenyatta's populism, as it is Nderi wa Riera's in the novel, the Member of Parliament who represents Ilmorog as "a government agent". For it is in the city where the educated, privileged elites such as Nderi wa Riera, Chui and Kimeria decide the fate of a primarily rural Kenya.

Critics like Gikandi have rightly read Ngugi's grasp of history as dialectical instead of Manichean, entailing a dogged refusal to romanticize the pre-colonial past, and I might add, the rural outpost.[82] Ngugi's challenge has always been to liberate the idea of culture from the colonial grip such that culture can work as an agent of liberation rather than of repression. The colonial legacy of casting native tradition as ahistorical is repeated with a difference under neo-colonialism that pushes through a forgetting or erasing of the distinction between capitalism and culture so as to enable the transformation of culture into a marketable commodity.

Ngugi writes his novel against the postcolonial developmentalist consensus of seeing the city as the repository of the developmental dreams of the nation. The novel shows us that not all urban dwellers enjoy privileges—there is a sharp division between those who inhabit the halls of power and those who live on pavements or in makeshift slums. The novel underlines the idea that there is no lasting promise in the metal roads and high rises that pass for development in an impoverished nation. Urban form is articulated with money form, as both are governed by a logic and structure that is exploitative and alien to African rationality. Thus, money is understood by the nation's poor as "glittering metal" imbued with evil power, while the call to the city is the veritable call of the devil, emanating from the city's tarmac roads and its electricity poles. The city's "metallic promises" are just that—mere illusions that mimic the form of reality. The critical challenge is to distinguish between the two. The proliferation of women in high heels in the city and its nesting of scorpion-like traders redefines gendered urban modernity and the city as a place where only the white man is at home.

But the novel is about much more than the production of Nairobi within nationalist, populist and developmentalist discourses. It is also a critique of the production of other spaces in the periphery, indeed of the production of the binary logic of centrality and peripherality that can be superimposed on the city-country dichotomy. Ngugi notes that the novel traces the "evolution of Ilmorog from a pre-colonial self-sufficiency into a colonial source of cheap labor and a postcolonial boomtown, that left more people even more deprived than before".[83] The task of survival is especially difficult as the "present" of Ilmorog in the novel is one of failed harvests and a looming drought that threatens to destroy the entire community. One of the novel's main questions then is to locate the "challenge of nation-building in remote Ilmorog" (54), an area that gets "not even a column-inch in the newspapers" (175). In contrast to the logic of exchange and expropriation that governs the city, the village embodies use-value, and a return to land in the village is likened to a return to self-knowledge.[84] Thus the novel attempts to set up Ilmorog, the forgotten village, as a locale of hope, only to dismantle the very idea by the end.

Ilmorog's tale of transformation from a "tiny nineteenth century village" to a "modern industrial town" is told in four parts in a non-chronological order: one part refers to pre-colonial Ilmorog when it was a self-sufficient community, "before imperialism came and changed the scheme of things" (6); the second is set in colonial Ilmorog when it was raided for its forests that served district towns like Ruwaini and the capital city (forests in turn are eaten up by the railways), reducing Ilmorog to a deserted homestead whose young men and women had either been captured for colonial labor, or were fleeing the poverty and hopelessness of Ilmorog (those refugees in Nairobi) in hopes of earning wages and joining the money economy. This was also the time of the Mau Mau resistance, an armed insurrectionary movement in the Kikuyu heartland that sought to overthrow colonial rule.

The third part, and the novel's dramatic core, is set in postcolonial Ilmorog ravaged by the legacy of colonial degradation, "still a kind of outpost of the Republic" (248), yet offering hope of escape to the novel's protagonists from urban-style exploitation (all of whom seem to be in search of "lost innocence, faith and hope", 46). Finally, there emerges the neocolonial Ilmorog to which "progress" eventually comes, but in a completely distorted way, and opens up the path for the complete degradation of community and traditions of resistance. Caterpillars, the monstrous "earth-eating machines" (265), replace the dogged labor of earthworms and tillers and herdsmen as peasants and farmers turn into wage laborers, all sacrificial victims to the nation's development. The Trans-Africa Road, a "monument to the hollowness and failed promises" of decolonization (263), makes Ilmorog a boomtown and within easy reach of exploitation. The values of the capital city—greed, reckless development and corruption—invade and destroy the old Ilmorog. The pervasive "spiritual drought" parallels the real one, leading to the death of the old crippled revolutionary Abdulla's companion, the donkey, even as the young revolutionary Karega departs to focus his revolutionary energies elsewhere, and the central female protagonist Wanja turns to prostitution.

The novel uses the satirical refrain "No Free Things in Kenya" to highlight the dissolution of the promise of socialism that is now forever located elsewhere, as in Tanzania and China. Thus the novel looks outside the national frame in order to locate the national story within an international system of capitalism and resistance to it. In fact, the novel consistently exceeds the frame of the national as the space of postcolonial citizenship. The Nairobi lawyer's experiences in western cities such as Chicago and Detroit, in the pre–civil rights era, reflect a feeling of internationalism in terms of racial solidarity that is inextricably linked to working-class solidarity, and recognition of gender oppression on a global scale.

It is the journey in postcolonial Kenya then that is positioned as the in-between narrative and territorial space between the city and the country. Its description as "epic", with all the accompanying characteristics of adventures, mishaps and accidental triumph, characterizes it synecdochically as encompassing the entirety of the novel and the nation itself as it is constituted spatially and temporally. Nyakinyua's song on the city sung along the way typifies Ngugi's mixing of folk and canonical evocations of the epic journey to the city. But the allusion to "epic" also reinforces the gigantic distance between the city and the country in postcolonial Kenya. The journey is described as the great trek and as part of "a new kind of war" (116). The military metaphor lends itself to the strategic struggle that must be waged by the landless peasants: "we must surround the city and demand back our share" (116). Stories of resistance told along the way—from Mau Mau to global justice movements—form an alternative history, one that has been repressed by those in power. The theme song of the journey becomes "Kenya is an African people's country". The song's simultaneous evocation of the national and the continental articulates Ngugi's vision that the struggle against exploitation has to exceed national boundaries, even as the nation provides an important and crucial site of resistance.

The novel traverses through the different geographies of the capital city, as do its characters that have been transformed into a collective. As the Ilmorog delegation glimpses the city's monuments, its shiny Hilton hotel and the Kenyatta Conference Center, the multicultural spaces of the Indian restaurants and the Khoja mosque, the well-guarded residential districts in the Blue Hills for Asians and Europeans in which these villagers can only be trespassers, they also see the slums and the back-alleys where the city's outcasts live. Moving uncertainly through the city's "jungle of vehicles, building and people" (184) the delegation arrives to wait in the famous Jeevanjee Gardens for the representatives of power to descend from the surrounding high-rise buildings. Whatever the physical and material challenges of this voyage, the outward journey from the country to the city has necessitated other inner journeys—the move to face the "terror" that is both outside and inside, to confront the fear of the unknown in the city and the familiar in the country (recall Jean Rhys's use of this motif as discussed in chapter 1). Through this collective movement, Ngugi presents a very different relationality of the subject to the city—it is no longer the isolated individual in search of a transient and fugitive modernity, but a collectivity in search of its place within the national urban imaginary that is also global in its hopes for justice.

"We Are All Prostitutes"

In this section, I want to specifically read the figure of the Kenyan woman in the city, and the ways in which Ngugi sets her up as central to the struggle over Kenyan citizenship. Scenes of Nairobi abound with African women in western-style clothes and high-heeled shoes serving beer to native and international business clientele, and of prostitutes serving the sexual needs of men adrift in the city. Signifying the city as the space of danger for women, the novel records how it is during the journey in the city that Wanja, the female protagonist of the novel, is raped by a former lover. Such an experience of violence and violation aligns with Nairobi's image as the space of sexual and moral corruption, one that turns young girls into barmaids and prostitutes. But the novel attempts to extricate the discourse on prostitution from a purely sexual and moral connotation and to link it to the neo-colonial exploitation of labor in general. Ngugi has written of how sexual labor is akin to wage labor; the novel represents them as imbricated. Women are "exploited as workers at home" and by "backward elements in the culture, remnants of feudalism" in the public world outside.[85] Such a conceptualization of women's reproductive and sexual labor has made Ngugi into an ally for leading feminist critics in their project of feminist literary criticism within African literature.[86] Ngugi's writerly imperative has been seen to "create a picture of a strong, determined woman with a will to resist and to struggle against the conditions of her present being".[87] The shift from a literary "type" of African woman towards the production of a feminist subjectivity is what marks Ngugi's work as distinctively political and oriented towards a project of postcolonial feminist citizenship.

The only woman among the novel's protagonists, Wanja (whose name means "stranger" or "outsider") is a Christian, English-educated city girl who first turns to prostitution as rebellion against her orthodox, petit-bourgeois parents who reject the village and embrace the city in order to become modern. In doing so, they leave Wanja's grandmother, Nyakinyua, in the village to carry on as the *griot*, or traditional storyteller. Wanja's experiences in the city are marked in a dual way by sexual exploitation and freedom from the prison-house of gendered social roles. For her, Nairobi is about both "salvation and shame". It is in the city that an older, married businessman seduces her—he takes her out to the Royal Cinema and introduces her to modern life in the city. But when she finds herself impregnated by him, he abandons her. She runs away to Nairobi's Eastleigh neighborhood, where work in bars is the only work available for school dropouts like her. Here Wanja finds herself in the company of many other women who come to Nairobi in order to escape a brutish life of domestic violence at home. Barmaids, like the chorus girls of the previous chapter, are more upwardly mobile than prostitutes. Their purported ambitions to gain social mobility and acceptance are consolidated via establishing economic and affective relationships with male customers. When the corrupt Kimeria promises Wanja that he would arrange for "a nice little flat in the city center" for her if she were to be his mistress, we get a glimpse into the ways in which women's sexual labor operates within the confines of modern respectability on the one hand, and sexual power, property and money in a postcolonial context on the other.

The city and country opposition is central to this drama of gendered exploitation within the context of postcolonial urban development. Exhausted by the endless cycle of degradation in Nairobi, Wanja goes to the village for renewal and for a more wholesome life, only to become part of an epic struggle against urbanization, which in Ngugi's terms is another name for neo-colonial exploitation.[88] Wanja's entry into Ilmorog is described as one where she intends to "make something of herself", an idea that is typically associated with the city. She enters Ilmorog dramatically—on a white matatu Peugeot loaded with modern things: a foam mattress, a pressure stove and her knowledge of cities such as Nairobi and Mombasa with its Arab streets, all signifying her modernity and cosmopolitanism, gifts of the city life she has lived so far. But it is in the village that Wanja finds sexual freedom in a sexual economy that is not one of exchange, at least not yet.

Wanja's return to the village, however, cannot be read as a return to any kind of romanticized past, although critics like Charles A. Nama read Ngugi's women characters as representative of traditional values associated with the land, especially in the way in which the novelist is seen to draw upon "specific conventions of traditional aesthetics".[89] The narrative does draw attention to Wanja's native beauty as well as her indigenous dress style that accentuates her distinctively "African" attractiveness and indicates her potential fecundity. She works alongside other women in the fields, nurtures Joseph, the adopted brother of Abdullah, and heals the politically and psychically wounded men—Munira, Karega and Abdullah—to transform them into agents of change. One can of course recall Kenyatta's description of the ideal Gikuyu woman within the framework of such traditional aesthetics. In a scene in which Munira watches Wanja and Nyakinyua planting seeds in the rain, the novel offers an image that has been central to gendered cultural nationalism. He likens Wanja to an "earthworm"; she is also a "maiden from the fields" (24). Her sweating body is both sexually appealing and the embodiment of agricultural labor. It represents women at one with the green land, but also working the land to produce communal survival and nourishment. It is when Wanja's grandmother Nyakinyua dances to an "opera of eros" that the image exceeds the frameworks of both traditional and modern modes of figuring femininity, sexuality and power, linking female sexuality and communal resistance in potent and potentially destabilizing ways.

Economic, political, cultural and sexual power are deeply linked in the novel—the circumcision ceremonies that had been banned during the Emergency, the Thengeta that had been outlawed by the colonial administration, the traditional fertility rites and communal ceremonies that had been rendered suspect—are all objects and processes of a cultural and communal reclamation that is profoundly political. The descriptions of Wanja as one with nature are similarly presented within the context of anti-colonialism, because the novel refuses to uphold Munira's vision of African femininity as passive, "earthworm"-like. In fact, Ngugi's version of the woman in the countryside is paradoxically predicated on a repudiation of the past, rather than based on a nostalgic recuperation of it, as some have suggested. As Wanja puts it, "sometimes there is no greatness in the past" (128). Critical of the village being treated as a church or sanatorium within African nationalism, Wanja eschews sentimentalism towards the land.

Wanja's eventual downfall comes with the arrival of full-blown neo-colonialism in Ilmorog. Women like Wanja and Nyakinyua must succumb to the economic exploitations of a new bureaucracy and of the privatization and commodification of community knowledge. Having inherited the knowledge of making *theng'eta* from her grandmother, a government ban meant to promote breweries owned by bigger businessmen forces Wanja to stop selling the native drink. In order to repay the bank threatening to foreclose on her grandmother's land, Wanja becomes a prostitute forced to now wear short skirts and make-up, transforming intimate or affective sexual relations into relations of exchange.

But when Munira pejoratively refers to Wanja as a prostitute, Karega, the young revolutionary, responds: "We are all prostitutes" (240). Such a rhetorical move is one in which prostitution is wrenched from its gendered significations and turned into a metaphor for neo-colonial Kenya. The trafficking in women in Kenya is of course linked to an expanding tourism industry, delineating the tracks of gendered globalization. Even as Wanja's body becomes a literal conduit for corruption, Kenya itself becomes a corrupt body. Both Wanja and Kenya must recognize that there are only two rules in the new global order—eat or be eaten. This is the pedagogical lesson that produces the new gendered citizen, Wanja, who survives by colluding with the exploitative economy of the new Kenya even as she traverses its new geographies that crystallize the uneven political and gendered development of postcolonial Kenya.

Having roamed the bars in Ruwaini, where women knew all the languages of Kenya, Wanja is made by the novel the gendered subject of a new version of postcolonial citizenship. Wanja's Somali lover is a long-distance truck driver who crisscrosses the continent, traveling to Zambia, Sudan, Ethiopia and Malawi. Criticized for going out with a "shifta", Wanja "liked the stories of all these places which he could make me see" (98). In the town bars, Wanja overhears men speaking of growing tribalization, even as the murals in the bar testify to the sense of a larger nation-space. It is Wanja's knowledge of urban spaces, gained through walking and working the city, that enables her to read exploitation, to understand it and ultimately to resist it. She is the one who moves with ease in both the city and the village—she is the new woman in Kenya. When the lawyer tells Wanja: "This city is no place for you . . . well . . . it is not a place for any of us . . . yet." (134), the novel defers the move to the city as the space of gendered citizenship and belonging, without actually repudiating it in its entirety. The novel's plot signals the dangers of reading Wanja (gendered subject) as a sign for Kenya's struggles against neo-colonial exploitation. Ultimately what is emphasized about Wanja in the novel is her transformation into a worker—self-sufficient and independent, and yet gendered in terms of the sexual economy that underwrites all forms of labor. But Wanja is also a worker in the making, an agent in the political sense in which the novel tries to mobilize resistance.

The novel however cannot escape the ambivalence undergirding the question of women's citizenship, of women as workers versus women as mothers. Wanja's destiny is ultimately one that involves fulfillment through becoming a mother. In the end she succeeds in becoming pregnant, recovers from the burn caused by the jealous and psychopathic Munira and reconnects with her once-alienated mother. She is now the carrier of a new citizen, and her child is the product of a willing union of love. The final narrative irony, however, is that she does not carry Karega's child, the untainted revolutionary, but the cripple Abdullah's. After all, Wanja's sullied past must not stain Karega's revolutionary purity. It is at this point that the novel reaches its limit of figuring a revolutionary citizen as female.

Engendering Revolution

The idea of the city as both the space of neocolonial contamination and of postcolonial education and politics is worked out through the figure of Karega. His education in the "university of the streets", as the novel puts it, imparts the disillusioning pedagogical lesson that the city brings no jobs or futures for men like him. All they can do is become road-boys, part of the surplus labor force of neo-colonial urbanization. The novel details the growth of the young revolutionary Karega, who also becomes the novel's chief ideologue, alongside the real historical emergence of Jomo Kenyatta as a leader of the people. Kenyatta's books find a significant place on Karega's shelves, preparing Karega to take on the mantle of imagining and materializing freedom. In doing so, Karega has to reject Wanja's acute analysis of life under neo-colonial capitalism: "you eat or you are eaten" as primarily a "static vision" of the future (303).

The very last scene of the novel has Karega looking into the future with a young woman beside him. It is a scene that signals his rejection of a romantic past of pre-colonial Kenya as well as the peasant vision of the Mau Mau revolutionaries. The new moment reveals that it is men's task to think consciously about the burden of colonial history and its implications for the history of free Kenya. Nation-building is "revealed", within the messianic tone of the novel, as a project among and between men. Karega's vision into the distant future does not include the young woman who has come carrying messages for him from the workers' party. She doesn't get a glimpse of this vision. The gendered realism of Wanja is countered with the masculine assumption of the nation's leadership in this last moment, underlining a struggle that is still ongoing in terms of the project of postcolonial feminist citizenship.

My reading of the last scene is nevertheless complicated by the novel's ambivalent concession that nation-building must be the job of both men and women, even if its visionary dimension belongs to men. After all, Ngugi's novel figures Wanja's hopes through her unborn child, in itself an ironic re-citing of the nationalist mythologization of motherhood as symbol of a nation's (physical) potential. Ultimately, both Wanja and Kenya have to make do with a less than perfect present.

Ilmorog is now irreversibly connected to the world. As Ngugi argues, "its grim picture of postcolonial Africa belongs more to the '90s and twenty first century than it did to the seventies . . . Hopefully the resistance envisaged in the narrative also belongs to the twenty first century".[90] Hope lies, the novel suggests, only in politics around work (in response to the proletarianization of Ilmorogians), and in eschewing tribal and religious differences towards attaining universal citizenship. The unborn child might still be the figure of this universal citizenship in a city yet to come.

Producing Citizenship

Marjorie Oludhe Macgoye's *Coming to Birth* (1986) ends on the eve of the demise of the Kenyatta era in 1978. This is also the time when news of Ngugi's arrest is furiously circulating about in Nairobi. In the novel, Martin Were sits down with a copy of *Petals of Blood* "to read it solidly, over long evenings with hardly a word spoken" (144). This scene of Martin reading Ngugi's book can be read alongside the scene of Karega's dreaming of the future at the end of *Petals of Blood*—Karega looks outward into the horizon of an African revolution while Martin contemplates the future within the frame of a revolutionary text. In both cases, Kenya's fate seems to be very much an issue that is between men. I want to interrupt this scene of Martin's reading of Ngugi's novel "solidly . . . with hardly a word spoken" with Paulina's words, and her act of self-making in the city.

If *Coming to Birth* closes with the scandalous event of Ngugi's arrest in 1978, it opens in 1956, seven years before Kenyan independence, during the time of the Emergency promulgated by the colonial British state in response to the Mau Mau insurgency. The novel chronicles the twenty-two years—from the nationalist movement to independence and elections to the decline of national aspirations, ensuing corruption, leading up to Ngugi's arrest—of postcolonial Kenyan history.[91] Throughout, the novel parallels the growing nationalist movement in both its colonial and postcolonial phases with Paulina's arrival, struggles and ultimate belonging in the city. In juxtaposing these two histories—Paulina's troubled entry, exile, and subsequent habitation in the city, and Kenya's struggle for independence in a real sense—Macgoye foregrounds the gendered imbrication of the city and the nation in postcolonial Kenya.

In reading the novel as such, I want to re-direct the more obvious critical gaze that would see in such a formulation a classic and perhaps uncritical and simplistic evocation of Jameson's "national allegory" in which Jameson writes with particular reference to Third World literature: "the story of the private individual destiny is always an allegory of the embattled situation of the public Third-World culture and society".[92] Following a particular line of criticism that understands allegory not in terms of a political unconscious but in terms of analogy, Joseph R. Slaughter has commented that in Macgoye's novel the idea of national allegory is "so heavy-handed" as to leave little room for "interpretive work", that the novel is too self-conscious in the ways in which it draws attention to its mode of representation.[93] Against this reading, my argument suggests that in fact the novel's self-consciousness towards its mode of representation is what allows for the gaps within allegory as a distinctive mode of political (un)consciousness to come into view. As such, its artistic failures nevertheless open up key questions about the modes of writing about women in Nairobi. Thus, far from Macgoye's novel being a straightforward and unimaginative transposition of a national story to Paulina's private predicament or the reverse, I see that Slaughter's own reading elides the complexities of the text in order to make his case for the novel as an example of a colonialist (likened to a "developmental aid loan"!) and modernist text.[94]

Whereas the "real" events of the Emergency ("an accepted fact") and of Ngugi's arrest bookmark the narrative, the central part of Macgoye's text narrates the "coming to birth" of the modern Kenyan woman, "a new woman", during the nationalist and post-independence struggles of Kenya (1, 139). To this end, Macgoye deliberately sets her story in Nairobi. For her, it is the city where citizens are made and where the nation is most legible in all its complexity. In this sense the novel reverses the spatial choices made by Ngugi for whom the city is a prostitute, selling its soul for greed, and turning into a parasite on the body politic.

Again, for a critic like Slaughter, Macgoye's spatial choice is nothing more than a reflection of colonial plans that sought to produce docile citizens through technologies of urban planning. Yet, I have shown in the first part of this chapter that whereas colonial rule might have produced the country-city dichotomy in particular ways that shaped racialized notions of civility and citizenship, Africans, and Kenyans in particular, engaged with those ideas in a variety of ways—from outright rejection to ambivalent approval to appropriation and re-signification—and from a range of different ideological positions—from populism and anti-modernism to a fervent belief in modernization. I read Macgoye's novel as intercepting these positions through the lens of gendered postcolonial urbanism.

Love and Belonging

In Macgoye's representation of the dominant city, the gendered spatial economy of colonial Nairobi is overwhelmingly masculine, in terms of the mobility and visibility accorded to its subjects. Lone women are as suspect as men potentially involved in political anti-colonial activities. Central to this narrative of gendered belonging to the city is then the native woman figured as a "stranger" in the city. The opening scene of the novel has Paulina arriving from the countryside by train, "the life-line of the country as he (Martin) had been taught at school" (1), into Nairobi.[95] The first chapter traces Paulina's initial journey through the city, from the railway station to her new home in Pumwani, one of the largest slum areas in Nairobi, her subsequent miscarriage and hospital stay, and then the dramatic episode of her losing her way in the city. Paulina is mistaken to be a prostitute or a beggar as she goes from house to house looking for Martin, completely disoriented in the city. As a woman "with no fixed address", Paulina is imprisoned in "protective custody", like other "lost" women who are housed in the mission homes for pregnant women caught in the curfew of Operation Anvil, an Emergency measure deployed to clear the city of Kikuyus who were seen as instigating the Mau Mau insurgency. On this view, Nairobi is a city where respectable women, including the newly professional women who are teachers and secretaries, are escorted around to avoid "the risks of Nairobi for a woman on her own" (16). What the novel clarifies at the very beginning is that the political repression by the colonial state is inseparable from the gendered repression of a layered patriarchy that is a deadly cocktail of colonial and native structures—both render the woman as a stranger to the city.

The most visible women in the city, especially in bars and public spaces, are of course the prostitutes and barmaids who abound, even as "in custom there was no place for the unmarried" in the city (16). The question of custom here exists in all its ambiguity—is it native custom that prevents women from belonging to the city, or is it the colonial state that translated native custom into a discriminatory legal apparatus? Calling her "slut! whore!" Martin expresses a common suspicion towards women in the city who are assumed to be prostitutes, as the city in turn is figured as a corrupt masculine client. It is in the city that Paulina finds herself confined by Martin to the home, a one-room tenement that is surrounded by stinking latrine blocks and neighbors speaking languages she did not know. A sympathetic neighbor generalizes Paulina's predicament and tells her how "Every wife who comes to Nairobi from the country has problems" (24).

Paradoxically, it is the city that provides the space of modern conjugal relations even as those relations are intensely mediated by the colonial and postcolonial state apparatuses, native social mores, the Church, and the expropriative logic of colonial capitalism. Macgoye shows how urban conjugality is underpinned by a distinctive Christian morality in which "the discipline of Christian marriage" is pitted against native authoritarianism and patriarchy in which wife-beating assures masculine mastery.[96] Christian marriage, on the other hand, introduces a different vocabulary of masculine domination, as well as entails subservience to an economic logic that involved "doing work and getting money" as important to the reproduction of family (56). The "educated, employed, married" Martin can "be a man indeed"; and it would be "in Nairobi (that) Paulina thought herself a woman" (26). Paulina's talent at crocheting and other domestic work is converted into a source of income, "contriving a profit from it". This supplemental income justifies Paulina's status as a Nairobi wife—she no longer needs to be sent home to bring in the harvest from the countryside. Such an arrangement not only re-shapes but in fact dilutes economic and social relations between the countryside and the city.[97] In setting up home in the city, in sharing a bed as husband and wife like Europeans did, Martin and

Paulina hope to become modern urban subjects, shedding their customary tribal assignations. Thus the still-to-come modern national state, emerging from the dark night of colonial rule, is therefore the pre-condition for such a relationship to be forged in the capital city.

Ethnographic accounts tend to emphasize how the colonial economy structured domesticity in very different ways from purportedly African conceptions of the home and the world. Roger Price, a London Missionary Society Evangelist, writing a report from Kuruman in southern Africa (dated December 12, 1896), had focused attention on the "semi-communistic ways" of Africans that needed to be sundered apart by the techniques for making citizens.[98] John Comaroff lists the wide-ranging ambitiousness of Western rule in Africa that included the imperative to help sever

> the "promiscuous" webs of relations that bound them together; by clothing them "properly", so that their bodies would be covered and enclosed; by persuading them to treat marriage as an ensemble of rights, a contract between two consenting adults, and to live in nuclear homes on fenced-off squares of land; by teaching their children to be disciplined and to improve themselves by dint of sheer effort; by encouraging each man to work on his own behalf as a wage-earner, thus to appreciate the virtues of money, the market and property; in short by ensuring that their would-be converts were biologically and legally self-contained individuals.[99]

The proliferation of Homecraft schools and Singer sewing classes for African women's education in housewifely duties and economic self-sufficiency that Paulina attends instantiate the links between colonial capitalism, ideologies of domesticity, consumerism and the concomitant sexual division of labor. "The neat house and the sewing machine" signal new forms of domesticity and social transformations that are difficult to recognize and grasp in the ferment of the anti-colonial period (70). But the struggle for women like Paulina is only indirectly framed as emancipation from colonial rule, and more directly constitutes a struggle with a native society that is represented and represents itself as existing in the grip of custom. The relationship between the two is the site of feminist critique in the novel. Macgoye in her narratorial voice of indirect free speech makes this struggle over home and the world very clear: "The home was pre-eminent in the lives of its people and since it had never been subdued it could not, either, be liberated" (60). The novel thus begins to plot the imbrication of gender ideologies in the tense negotiation of custom (heartily endorsed by colonial rule in an attempt to encourage authoritarian tendencies within native culture) and civic life in the city. Thus, far from representing Paulina's becoming a wife in Nairobi as fundamentally a product of the epistemic and material violence with which the customary self is exorcised, the novel reveals the complex and difficult negotiations involved in forging a different subjectivity that is neither wholly the product of custom, nor that of a colonially created individual, but of a new nationalist and feminist conjuncture. After all, Martin too, politically active in community and clan associations, "had hoped and prayed for freedom—no, not for freedom, Uhuru, which everyone knew in Swahili, but for loch, self-government"(77).

As a next step in the analysis, the aim of the following discussion is to wrench apart the opposition between proper gendered conjugality (predicated on capitalist development) and self-government, or the production of citizenship, from its assumed and overly saturated nationalist and colonial significations, towards a feminist project of citizenship.

Dislocating Modernity

Macgoye's novel reveals the contradictions between the techniques of citizenship deployed by the colonial apparatus in which to be modern Kenyans had to fabricate an urban, Christian, western self, and the colonial policy of constructing natives as ethnic, racialized subjects through the instrumentality of what Comaroff terms a "colonizing cartography".[100] Explicating this cartography in which "everything was designed to keep you out", Nairobi in the novel is a city rift apart by curfews and pass laws, barbed wire cordoning off African locations and armed Europeans policing African workers walking home.[101] As nationalist leaders are marked by their ethnic affiliations, Kikuyus for their involvement in the Mau Mau rebellion are singled out, locked up under suspicion and required to carry special passes to enter and move about in the city. Taking up extreme powers under the Emergency, the colonial state suspends civil society for the natives: "Curfew area—unrest over escaped prisoners—tribal mixtures—new workers replacing those in detention—political activity—all these factors required a firm colonial hand"(19). The city's topography provides a legible map for the city's ethnic and racial divisions. The struggles between "the powerful and the apparently powerless" presage their subsequent transmutation into postcolonial ethnic divisions within the space of the city.

Here to be noted is the fact-fiction mode deployed by Macgoye as a narrative strategy to contain the breathless pace of political events in the city. As even the space of the home comes under surveillance in the time of the Emergency, a clear connection between residence, ethnicity, and gender is established. After all, Paulina and Martin find home in the city in places from where, under the aegis of Operation Anvil, Kikuyus have been cleared out. In fact, the very presence of Luos such as Martin and Paulina is predicated on the extrication of Kikuyus from jobs and homes in the city. Thus the main actors in the narrative of resistance against colonial rule are denied home. In this sense, Martin and Paulina occupy a multi-layered spatial history of colonial rule and subsequent struggles over gendered postcolonial citizenship.

In contrast to the controlled and divided space of the native city, both inside and outside the home, is the space of the colonial city with its European homes, so new and neat but "exactly alike" (17). These residences are part of "the good order of the residential districts". For the Africans, this ordered affluence could only be glimpsed "where occasionally a gap between houses, a servant's shack under the trees, a shrub in flower or the high painted gates of an embassy took you into the fairytale world of the children's picture books" (131). To the native who is more used to a city full of stinking latrine blocks, and the stale air of the housing complexes that intensified when the rains came, as waterlogged shanties with airless polythene shelters become even more dank and stuffy, the sight of European order and affluence must have constituted a visual and emotional shock. The narrative underscores that shock by revealing the European city only through cracks and gaps that appear both physically and textually.

But the very same colonizing cartography that sought to keep the natives divided and separate also provided a cognitive map for resistance. Thus, the young white soldiers guarding the streets of Nairobi needed to police not just black bodies but "seething rumor" that miraculously emanated from "bush telegraph wires to every corner of the colony and beyond" (20).[102] Colonial rule provides native Kenyans with sharp political lessons—evening classes and trade union meetings in the Pumwani Memorial Hall are never held under the cover of dark! News of unrest on the radio spreads and disseminates in the air. Resistance networks take form in rumor and provide a new way of articulating contestations over space and citizenship, just as rebellious bodies unsettle the colonial spatialized and temporalized ("not after dark") logics of rule.

Benedict Anderson in *Imagined Communities* had suggested that the novel and the newspaper embody national form. Macgoye's novel links both those forms to the city, where there was always news. But the reportage of political events not only fails to keep pace with the real time of history, it presages other chains of events that haven't yet been reported, possibly because they haven't even yet happened. Although news filters through to the provincial outposts via rumor and radio, it is the city that is rife with the sense: "And yet you know that there must be a next event, and when the newspapers begin to report (the search for J M Kariuki) you know that in one sense or another the event has happened" (106). When this politician's mutilated body is discovered weeks after his murder, the expected event is realized, but "the real event was still not known" (107). J M (Kariuki) becomes a saint when the whole city grieves for him and the Kikuyu gramophone record mourning his death is banned.[103] The murder and the subsequent control of public mourning bring together poor people of different tribes. There is a profound irony as a distanced feeling from legislation and politics takes root in the thick of the postcolonial city. This double sense—of proximity and alienation—from the center of power in the city informs Macgoye's reading of politics in colonial and postcolonial Nairobi.

It is in this milieu of colonial/postcolonial state repression and its "colonizing cartography" that Africanism, as much as Kenya, becomes a palpable and powerful idea, as news of Ghana's independence from another part of the continent spreads and inspires anti-colonialists elsewhere. For Paulina, "Kenya was a hard enough idea to get hold of. Africa, to Paulina, was a name on a map. But perhaps before she went to Nairobi she would not even have recognized the map" (72). So it is the city that becomes the articulating space of local, national and global identities that exceed the frame of the nation and points to the limits of imagining freedom within it. After all, as Paulina learns, more Luo was spoken in Uganda so that "a Luo was a Luo and herself she was a new Kenyan" (75). The de-linking of ethnic, national and continental identities opens the space for postcolonial citizenship. As the then unknown future was to reveal, trans-continentalism was never a straightforward project. Postcolonial state violence in Uganda and the Kenyan exodus of Asians in 1970 were both instances of the instability of not just ethnic and national identity but of a larger East African identity.

Thus the novel's seemingly simple narrative of Kenyan nationalism is deceptive as it in fact works by destabilizing the conceptual categories within which the nation and the city have been typically read. The city is neither a synecdoche for the nation, nor the comfortable space of self-government and self-fashioning, but the space where the easy distinctions of city and country, tribe and citizen, sexual and wage work, organic seasons and manufactured news are troubled through and through. The novel's unevenness of language and its modes of address are what provide clues to its political commitment to the postcolonial city as a space jagged by history, especially for the liberation of Kenyan women in it, in as much as Ngugi's epic scale seeks to contain and narrate a people's history.

Return to the City

The central part of the narrative records Paulina's unraveling marriage to Martin and her struggle for independence. Paulina sets about making herself into a new kind of citizen, a process that parallels Kenya's postcolonial history. The traumatic personal events in her life coincide with the struggle for the nation's freedom as the narrative underscores a certain strain of liberal feminism that could be accommodated with the *realpolitik* of nationalist politics as situated in the city. It is in Nairobi that Paulina can think: "I can make a home here now that I am alone" (87). A surprised and estranged Martin says to Paulina: "I did not think . . . when I first brought you to Nairobi, that there would be ever a time you would feel safer here than at home" (87).

The novel complicates the relationship between the personal and the political as theorized in the national allegory formulation: "In fact she didn't have much time to ponder over her personal relationships *because* the election was coming up and she was worked off her feet" (97; emphasis mine). The causality attributed to Paulina's remaking of herself as citizen belies the formula of reading the personal as the political within the Third World text. It is not so much that the personal stands in for the political, but that the political intercepts the personal, in the task of nation-building. The narrative voice bursts through Paulina's consciousness that increasingly imbricates domestic work with the ideological production of the nation: "There was challenge in the air, not to say scholarships to America. The least one could do was to learn to bake cakes in a real oven and sing Swahili songs" (41). It is not a case where the personal is fused or sublimated in a collective self, but one where the personal is tested against the limits of political subjectivization.

When divested of all familial trappings, Paulina becomes a "proper" working woman in the city. She takes up the job of housekeeper with a wealthy Kenyan politician in the posh "Upper Hill" end of Nairobi. The "blessed anonymity of the big city" (86), the air of "detachment", like that of the Turkana watchmen she sees, provides her with the space to make her life anew. Basking in the scenes proffered by Cross Street, "the immense vitality of the district" with "every little shop front spawning new business, enterprises taking shape on the pavements, the young and the old thronging corners", Paulina rejects "the languor of small towns streets, their ponderous slowness and paucity of conversation" (130). For in the city there is "the continuous change of spectacle, the bustle and the hard-learned possibility of belonging" (90–91).

Nairobi's cosmopolitanism is evidenced in the Indian saris and Masai *shukas* fluttering from railings, evoking "the presence of something sophisticated and immeasurably old" (130). The postcolonial city is thus the product of not merely a colonial ideology but of a pre-colonial history as well. As the postcolonial gendered subject walks the city, the experience can only be an ambivalent one: "She did not mind dealing with the new things, but there was an emptiness where some of the old things ought to have been" (118). The simultaneity of the old (even as an absence) and the new in the city defines the very experience of modernity, a juxtaposition that male modernists rendered in terms of shock and anomie. The colonial myth of conjuring urbanity out of nothing is belied by the persistent presence of the old. The passages quoted here evoke the long history of cosmopolitan belonging that the small town woman discovers in the big city. This older history is of course also marked by a resilient patriarchy such that going back to the village or the provincial town, where she had needed the dignity of a husband just to get a job, is no longer an option for her.

This simultaneous sameness and difference of urban spectacle, and the concurrent sense of the old and the new, becomes the quintessential

experience of the capital city, in both its commodified and phenomenologi-
cal forms. Changes in habit are predicated on material developments and
provide a different sense of being in the city. The key to becoming a modern
citizen is to also become a consumer of goods, to improve what is known
as "standard of living"—in Nairobi people expected meat once a week and
used toilet paper and soap for improved hygiene. The wearing of modern
dresses, including the brassiere, registers not just a material fabrication, but
by extension a new body within which the modern urban self must find a
home. The description evokes Pierre Bourdieu's concept of habitus: a structuring structure that limits but does not efface individual agency. The structure can also be translated as a predisposition. For instance, to the working
woman the wearing of a watch enables her to keep track of the time of industrial urbanism even as she becomes subordinated to it. The dominance of
wage labor entailed a conquest of both space and time. Macgoye's narrative
records these microscopic changes that are material and everyday, but that
also signify vast shifts in the existential and material experience of urban
modernity. The fabrication of a new citizen whose activities include going
to the museum, the theater and the cinema; the figure of romantic couples
in the city; of women dressed scandalously; the leisurely act of gazing into
the windows of big shops to look at expensive clothes; of walking into the
City Park where rich people lived are all part of the everyday spectacle of
the city and of experiencing a new self that is always and already haunted
and marked by racial and gender difference that is forever in the process of
being commodified. These activities also mark a stark delineation of work
time from leisure time.

Commenting (in)directly on life in postcolonial Nairobi, the narrative
voice tells us how each resident:

> became absorbed into the multiple rhythms of everyday life . . . For in
> Nairobi you get dressed whether you have clean clothes or not, you eat
> whether you know where the next meal is coming from or not, you do
> work, whether the work is a compulsive progression from dustbin to
> dustbin, from one employment office to the next, or whether it is a ritual
> with scales or paper clips to dress out someone else's fantasy. In Nairobi
> you withdraw when someone threatens your personal space, you ma-
> nipulate the calculations necessary to crossing the road almost without
> accident, you recognize by a shrug or a lifted eyebrow the appropriate
> stations of men and gods. So you cannot be said just to hang upon the
> next event. (106)

The emphasis on a machinic rhythm in the city accompanies and comple-
ments the fabrication of the new citizen who must manipulate, improvise and
insert claims to citizenship within the postcolonial city, even as it marks a
critique of the distortions of capitalist development in which laziness, indisci-
pline and illegality loom as threats to the stable notion of a worker.

In this the novel also evokes the ideological work required by and of postcolonial urbanism. Paulina's visit to the bank underlines "the new officialdom of towering buildings" (120). On the celebration of Uhuru day, Paulina takes her sister out for sightseeing—they go to see the Parliament building and the post office. The dance performance that Paulina goes to watch is hybrid, composed of new elements. The performance itself produces a "national" audience of "people of all shapes and colors" (117–118). New Kenyans included

> brown teenagers who spoke Luo and brown toddlers who spoke little else than German and black children with foreign mothers (or not so foreign) who seemed to speak only English. And you did not ask of these people where they belonged or where they would marry, you only asked it in English and Pumwani. (117–118)

Language once again interjects the space of multiplicity in the city as "the strident music, Hindi or Congolese, . ., the shouts across the street in one language or another which always seemed, half-caught, to contain a word or two of your own" (130). To learn Swahili, "one of the measures of unity of the intertribal group" (28) and by itself a deeply controversial project, whether through new editions of the New Testament or Sunday Swahili services, or by spending time with neighbors, or through navigating shops and the vegetable market, was to learn to belong to the town (not to mention the nation state), to inhabit it by having a voice in it.

But the limits of the idea of the national language (efficacious for a project of national citizenship) come up against the demands of intimacy in the city. For Paulina, "mourning was something you ordinarily did only in the mother tongue and had to be rethought if your sympathies lay outside" (111). The city, then, paradoxically, provides the space of self-making while foreclosing certain elements of intimacy and tradition and a sense of the past. The question that the novel poses is: does the new self emerge from a re-articulation of the old (tradition) aligned with the forces of capitalist colonialism and postcolonialism (modernity), or is it something profoundly and altogether new that is produced?

Reproducing Work

The novel reconfigures domesticity as national work as it weaves the everyday and the ordinary with the monumental and the political in the postcolonial city. As Kenya's postcolonial politics continue to be in turmoil, Paulina feels "the months came and went, cleaning, washing, minding children", work that is experienced as seamless and never-ending (88):

Perhaps women's work was like that—the word for creation was the same one you used practically for knitting or pottery. Men's work was so often destructive—clearing spaces, breaking things down to pulp, making decisions—and how often did the decisions amount to anything tangible? Words in the air, pious intentions, rules about what not to do. She was glad that a lot of her work lay in making and mending things. This was more satisfying to her than those nebulous women's meetings where you were expected to keep your hands still but weave and work your mind laboriously through a tangle of words. (129)

As the nation's politics became more complex in the nationalist, anti-colonial period, more opportunities opened up for women, especially in the sphere of education. Paulina's entry into Homecraft Training School in Kisumu to obtain vocational education is shown to parallel the nationalist movement. The training school for women serves as a refuge from the extended family, while husbands labor in Mombasa or Eldoret. New roles for women proliferate as sewing and nursing schools for girls and women open up in Nairobi, in keeping with notions of women's work and its place within the familial, and by extension national, economies. Now new figures emerge on the scene: the modern girl, the absentee wife, ayahs from Indian and European homes and young midwives seen in different parts of the city.

Paulina's employer Mrs. M is herself a trained secretary. With her begins Paulina's political education about "women's place in society". In Mrs. M's circles, Paulina becomes an example of "a person who had achieved a balanced and contented life without the blessing of children", one who possessed "great usefulness to society though she was not competing directly in any man's field of achievement". The passages in Macgoye's novel that gloss women's development in postcolonial society must be read as part of the dominant sociologically inflected arguments that shaped women's lives in Third World nations in the period of decolonization. It is here that the novel skirts the boundaries of sociological discourse most closely and where the limits of exploring citizenship through overlapping official and academic discourses are encountered.

The politicization of Kenyan women in the postcolonial period, from "different professions, tribes, communities", crystallizes in the campaign to save Chelagat Mugtai, a woman Member of Parliament who is imprisoned for inciting a crowd to violence (112). Although Paulina thinks such politics is not her business, yet: "Chelagat, a strapping young woman and single, was within her comprehension, cut off from friends and constituents, humiliated in the cell . . . (111), appears as an imaginable double on the political horizon. A still politically innocent Paulina "did not claim to understand it all, but worked" (110). Mugtai becomes the figure on whose predicament all the complaints of woman in a man's world could be condensed, especially on issues "which she dared not relate to her own commonplace experiences" (110). As Mrs. M works on a women's petition for her release, there is the shared political knowledge that "even if it failed, women might become politically conscious by making the attempt . . . no one in these non-Emergency days could arrest thousands on thousands of women" (112).[104]

Highlighting popular struggles in the city that seek a just postcolonial society, the novel culminates in Paulina's discovery of a new urban community of street children that consists of the little boy wearing oversized University of California T-shirt and the boy named Che articulating "the fellowship of the down and out", betting and begging in the shanties. For Paulina, the work of adopting and helping these child vagrants becomes part of the process of "learning in Nairobi" (136), however dismissively her boss, Mr M declares that "palliatives" for the street children don't help" (139). Although Paulina's picture appears in the papers for her work with them, she knows that it is the street children that are the new citizens of Nairobi. After all, "the future was for everyone" (82). In spite of the dereliction of dreaming and hoping, the delegation of squatters that visits Mr. M, recalling the epic journey made by Ilmorog's peasants in *Petals of Blood*, endorses the horizons of a postcolonial city "yet to come".

The novel concludes with reconciliation between the public act of adopting street children and the private one of bearing a child, representing, within the scope of the dominant narratives of gendered nationalism, "a very great hope" (150). The preceding discussion of the articulation of women's work, political agency and the question of motherhood (Paulina, even before conceiving biologically, adopts the street children) is meant to relocate the question of rights as an attribute of labor, especially of gendered labor, in both its affective and productive forms, even as the novel carves out a complicated and often ambivalent relationship to the ideology of motherhood as an entry into national citizenship.

In an earlier moment when her first-born child is killed during a political demonstration on the visit of Kenyatta to Kisumu, the incident signifies the death of East Africa's aspirations (coinciding with Idi Amin's overthrow of Milton Obote in 1971). After losing her son, Paulina thinks of the Luo expression "the country had eaten its people" (84). But the very fact that she was a childless mother means that "she could not be excluded. Had she not lost a child?" (106). Motherhood as a claim to citizenship is seemingly re-inforced (through the metaphor of sacrifice) just as nurturing (literally and politically) as national production becomes an important ingredient in Macgoye's gendering of citizenship in the novel that ends with hope for new futures.

We see how state/postcolonial/gender ideologies intersect in this ending that has another variation. Paulina's friend from the slum district, Amina, adopts Joyce, the daughter of an ayah and a white man, and opens a maternity home that distributes family planning material. She not only engages in a different relationship to mothering and child-rearing, she also becomes an informal agent of the postcolonial state's simultaneously Utopian and repressive mechanisms of shaping the family within the nation. Thus the novel belies the readily available forms of reading the articulation of motherhood and citizenship in the final instance. The personal is not superseded by the political; rather the two emerge as interlocking spheres of postcolonial citizenship.

Macgoye's choice of Nairobi, the capital of the country, of course is most fitting, as it is in Nairobi that the problems of tribalism, corruption and economic development are rife, complicating the very issues of citizenship and gendered belonging. For Macgoye, the city is the space of politics, a door to Africa, to the world, to Che. After all, "there seemed to be no end to what one was supposed to learn and be interested in" (29). And whereas ostensibly the novel seems to mimic the standard urban narrative of African fictions—where women are raped or sexually exploited in the city, and are ultimately redeemed through motherhood—it also offers different modes of figuring hope in the city: through pregnancy, through the street children's futures precariously perched on the fate of the city, and through the mixed-race children who might yet inherit the city still to come.

Peter Osborne assesses the task of the novel as modernizing everyday experience and then representing it. In this sense, we can read the modernity of Macgoye's novel as legitimized by gendered decolonization and represented in the uneven and jagged aesthetic of Macgoye's fictionalizing project. If, for Ngugi, the city is the site of colonial and neo-colonial extraction from the countryside that might yet be redeemable for a postcolonial future, for Macgoye coming to the city means coming into a complex modernity. In terms of resistance to dominant ideologies that situate the capital city in an exploitative relation to the countryside, Ngugi's novel posits hope in a workers' revolution. For Macgoye, reclaiming identity as gendered citizens is the pre-condition for a genuinely postcolonial city. In both accounts, the "unhomely women" of Nairobi can no longer be only represented as unauthorized, temporary residents of the city, but as belonging to it.

3 Uncivil Lines[1]

Different Mumbais existed earlier. But the gaps between them have
grown . . . All in all, (Mumbai is) an explosion waiting to happen.

—P. Sainath

This chapter looks at the representational history of Bombay, a city that,
like Nairobi, was a product of colonial rule but whose contours evoke a different set of contestations and negotiations concerning postcolonial urbanity and gendered citizenship. If in the previous chapter I had argued that
the idea of the postcolonial city was a key site of resistance and authentifi-
cation of postcolonial national identity, in this chapter I examine the ways
in which Bombay articulates the idea of the postcolonial city with multiple
processes that range from local identitarian movements to those of globalization in the contemporary moment. In doing so, I elaborate on the ways
in which the postcolonial city can be understood as a specific conjuncture
of the present. As throughout this book, my interest in this chapter is in
locating a postcolonial feminist project of citizenship within the postcolonial city as conjuncture.

Bad Copy

Triggered by events such as the Partition of India in 1947, famines and other
"natural" and political disasters that brought millions of villagers to cities,
Indian cities became "bloated receptacles" in the postcolonial era, stretching
their resources and spaces to their limits, and came to represent the uneven
development of India's economy.[2] A constantly deteriorating urban environment in subsequent decades was met with a generalized sense of inevitability
in terms of diminishing resources and increasing social tensions, considered
to be a necessary consequence of Third World industrialization. With economic liberalization unleashed in the 1990s, purportedly as a reaction to the
perceived failures of state socialism and centralized planning, the spatial and
political unevenness that characterized Indian urbanization became more
visible than before.[3]

Today, a burgeoning population of middle-class Indian "consumers"
(the size of the entire population of western Europe), trans-national bank-
ers and brokers reside in India's big cities cheek by jowl with slum dwellers,
poor migrants and the homeless, all contesting the space of survival as

"citizens" of new Indian modernities. In this milieu, concepts of centers and peripheries that structure analyses of the global system and of global cities seem increasingly inadequate to explain the dizzying pace of political and structural transformations surrounding and producing the contemporary Indian city.

The signifying power of the postcolonial Indian city as the unstable locus of the modern is said to have roots in its colonial history where cities were "instruments of cultural change in India, providing a theater for the demonstration of European architectural and planning concepts", and by extension of the inherent superiority of those ideas.[4] Thus the older colonial city became the palimpsest upon which postcoloniality inscribed itself. On this text, postcolonial Indian urbanism emerges in significant tension with its "past"—repudiating it as oppressive, nostalgically preserving it through history and memory, pessimistically seeing it as shaping a distorted future (a bad copy), and indicating, ultimately, the hegemony of modernity itself as embodied in the colonial history that is impossible to erase.

The many-layered, palimpsestic quality of the postcolonial urban foregrounds the history of decolonization, allowing India's urban spaces to be read as what David Harvey calls a configuration of "social inventions . . . that seek to generate new meanings of possibilities for social practices".[5] In the space of the postcolonial city, colonial modernity shatters into what many cultural critics think of as myriad alternative modernities. The city provides the space where "natives" become "citizens" by virtue of experiencing firsthand the contradictions and the gifts of freedom and liberation from colonial rule. It concentrates hopes for a progressive future in its capacity as a container of all sorts of ethnic, caste, class and regional differences, even as colonial rule produced these differences according to its own logic of rule. At the same time, the city is also always already the source of contamination of an authentic national identity, even as it becomes the instrument for the articulation of communal and other differences.

Historical and contemporary scholarship on postcolonial urbanism in India expresses a deep-seated ambivalence towards the city. This goes as far back as the nationalists in the era of the freedom struggle. Whereas some critics point to how the "valorisation of the metropolitan milieu in India" can be seen as "coeval with the formation of a national consciousness", others note a profound distancing from the idea of the city in nationalist thinking and politics.[6] The "valorization" of the urban is evident in the literary and political narratives of liberal nationalism. In these accounts, the village is presented as a cesspool of caste, class and sexual exploitation, and as therefore an object of the projects of emancipation and development.[7] Within more romanticized versions of liberal nationalism, village folk might appear as caricatures with flattened subjectivities, as hapless victims of urbanization or as artifacts of a lost way of life.[8] In the language of national policy, the city came to symbolize the culmination of postcolonial "development", constituting the dominant economic "sector" of the nation, lending itself to state-directed planning and to the production of a national culture in a concentrated form. Providing visible and material access to centers of power, finance and culture, the city offered hope of citizenship and belonging in an era of Third World development and increasing globalization. Even as it formed an important node from which the network of international capital and culture was made accessible to Indians, the city still retained its national identity and contained furious contestations of it.

The primacy of the city within national imaginings of citizenship is evidenced in the ways that popular discourse distinguishes between recent arrivals from the village as objects of urban humor—seen as backward, primitive and unsophisticated (in Bombay lingo the term used is *ghati*, in north India the word is *dehati*, literally meaning "from the village", both used as pejoratives) and those who are *shehris*, or the modern, sophisticated citizens of the city. The resilience of this view of the village is evident in the paradoxical theme-parking and commodification of the rural in contemporary Indian cities—a posh and expensive restaurant in Bombay is called "the Village", and in Delhi's "Pragati Maidan" (literally, "Progress Park"), a village is recreated in which urban folk dress up and enact scenes from Indian villages. These rural spectacles allow the urban Indian to claim roots in tradition while enjoying the benefits of progress and urbanity.

At the same time, romanticization of the Indian village has been an important constituent of national consciousness, albeit emanating from a metropolitan milieu, and for metropolitan subjects.[9] Critics have noted that

> unlike the numerous innovative and passionately ideological projects to either preserve or transform rural India, the period of nationalism produced little fundamental thinking about the desired Indian city of the future. The paradox is indeed very curious, because the place of colonial modernity in India in the nineteenth and twentieth centuries was obviously the city and that is where India's nationalist elite was produced.[10]

Within romantic nationalist discourses, the city is already marked as western and foreign whereas the village becomes a symbolic referent for the nation's pre-colonial history, the site of the origin of Indian culture that needs to be reclaimed against colonial degradation. Gandhi emerges as a central figure in this ideological mobilization against the city, as a "stern censor of the modern city".[11] Indian nationalist discourse relied heavily on such an articulation of nationalist identity and Gandhi's celebration of village India as the repository of true Indian values was only its most eloquent pronouncement. In the context of Bengali literature Dipesh Chakrabarty notes that from the 1880s onwards, writers like Bankim Chandra Chattopadhyaya and Rabindranath Tagore were creating "new perceptions of the countryside" through the construction of a "powerfully nostalgic and pastoral image of the generic Bengali village" that was "for and on behalf of the urban middle-classes".[12] Roshan G. Shahani remarks that in post-colonial Indian literature "the need for 'Indianness', of tradition, found expression through a valorization of the Indian peasant and of the Indian rural landscape".[13] On this view, migration to the city by peasants is repre-sented as a form of trickery, in which the innocent villager is cheated by the false attractions of the big city.[14] The figure of "the stranger to the ways of the city" comes to bear the potential for an ethical order amidst the moral degradation of the city. The village, in contrast, is presented as providing an alternative, purer and better model of postcolonial citizenship.[15]

Pitted against Indian tradition and values more generally, the city stands in for the modernity that enacts an epistemic violence on native and tradi-tional peoples, destroying their ethic of community, replacing it with the rapacious individualism of modernity. The city becomes the space of alien-ation in which *popular* culture with its commercialism and hybrid western-ization corrodes *folk* culture's authenticity and innocence. For some cultural theorists, the resurgence of Hinduism as a political and spiritual force in late-twentieth-century India can be attributed to a populace lost and with-out direction in an alienated urban economy.[16] For such critics, tradition is necessarily anti-modern; it is the source of resistance to modernity's indi-vidualistic and anti-nature tendencies. In such a view, the city is rendered as a threat: the site of a dangerous contamination in opposition to the rural that is seen as the locus of true subalterneity and traditional culture. The power of this view finds endorsement in the suggestion that for most Indians the big city has remained "a deeply profane place, corrupted by money and commerce and littered with dangerously seductive amusements".[17]

The deep ambivalence summarized above might explain the absence of a theory of the city as both material and ideological space in Indian historiog-raphy and radical theory. For sure in recent years there has been a plethora of monographs, edited volumes and journal articles on the subject of the Indian city, constituting what Gyan Prakash terms "the urban turn", but what is still needed is a proper theorization of the postcolonial Indian city.[18] For many, the persistence of rural ties, even for middle-class urbane families, is understood to have thwarted the emergence of a proper bourgeois urban subject. The same is considered to be true for the absence of proper working-class identity in Indian cities. Chatterjee argues that the "persistence of pre-bourgeois modes of sociality in factories and slums impaired the ability of workers to act as a class".[19]

This specifically Indian debate between the country and the city opens up a number of other questions for the future of Indian cities in the twenty-first century. How have globalization and the embrace of neo-liberal economic policies shifted the terrain of such debates such that the older certainties of city and country as categories of belonging have been comprehensively eroded? How have the new social movements, of middle-class residents in big cities campaigning on issues of consumption of resources, distribution of public goods, security and law-order, of environmental sustainability (waste disposal), of religious and caste identity, articulated new domains for urban politics? And what about the purportedly "older" working-class and trades-union politics? What about the politics of the dispossessed: the refugees, the rag pickers, the illegal migrants, the urban poor, the unhomely women? Whereas some of these questions are beyond the scope of this chapter, the new political formations of the urban (in terms of both material space and social subjectivity) in contemporary India must inform any ongoing reading of the postcolonial city.

Contesting Citizenship

There has been a constitutive elision of the interconnectedness of the urban and the rural in the discourse of both nationalism and postcolonial development. This has entailed a further elision of how the village and the city occupy overlapping spheres in contemporary India and structure the material bases of each. In a bid to maintain a binary and absolute distinction between the rural and the urban, there is both a de-historicization of space and a theoretical and political occlusion of the process of the production of that difference itself. Crucially as well, there is an erasure of social agency, of how it might negotiate social change and articulate new spatial forms.

Sometimes an answer to the conundrum of city versus country is sought in yet another position in Indian postcolonial discourse that finds in the city means for theorizing the hybridity of postcolonial identity, because the city by definition is perceived as heterogeneous and as a signifier of "difference".[20] The complexity of the city provides a way for theorizing a multi-cultural nation. The plurality of cultures inhabiting the city is seen as more reflective of the diversity of India as compared to its more homogeneous rural communities. Further, the city precipitates a rupture between backwardness and progress, and becomes the space of negotiation between a national identity and a larger global one.

Whereas many progressive critics have derided the urban bias of postcolonial planning, they have acknowledged that the historical reconfigurations of class and identities around such issues as housing, environment and employment, leading to what are known as new social movements, have also taken place in the postcolonial city.[21] The city's spatial locus is where the asymmetries produced by what Edward Soja calls "the changing mosaics of uneven regional development within the capitalist state" and "the various configurations of the international spatial division of labor" are negotiated and new political subjectivities and communities created.[22] Riddled with the contradictions of the homogenizing effects of global capitalism and the polarizing structures of global capitalism's unequal diffusion and distribution, the city becomes the space of new forms of sociality and citizenship based not on common land ownership, ethnicity or caste and occupational homogeneity, but on the materiality of the shared experience of living in the city. Sunil Khilnani writes:

> All the enticements of the modern world are stacked up here, but it is also here that many Indians discover the mirage-like quality of the modern world. This experience has altered beliefs, generated new politics, and made the cities dramatic scenes of Indian democracy: places where the idea of India is being disputed and defined anew.[23]

Using a slightly different terminology, Partha Chatterjee ascribes and traces the "urban turn" within Indian social theory to the formation of what he terms "political society", in which state agendas of rule and development come together and impinge on notions of citizenship. In this political society, the urban poor emerge at odds with the demands of citizenship that is typically understood as the domain of middle-class consumers whose demands pertain to property rights and rights of the individual against polluters, encroachers and criminals. Whereas the move of demanding the city back for its citizens might include demands for the resettlement and rehabilitation of the urban poor, Chatterjee interprets the move not as an "extension of citizenship to the poor" but as one that is predicated on "a careful conceptual distinction . . . between citizens and populations".[24] If citizenship carried "the moral connotation of sharing in the sovereignty of the state and hence of claiming rights in relation to the state", Chatterjee argues, "populations do not bear any inherent moral claim".[25] Such a distinction forces a reconsideration of the very definition of citizenship in the contemporary postcolonial Indian city.

For Chatterjee, then, the task of politics is to "mold the empirical discreteness of a population group into the moral solidarity of a community".[26] It is community then, as opposed to citizens, whose "vernacular resistance" can take on global capitalism's "global designs" and address the challenges posed by "the material as well as the imaginative forces of the new regime of globality".[27] But what does "community" mean in the current conjuncture? How can we think of it, as Chatterjee here proposes, as an unmediated good that can take on global capitalism when community itself has been the site of gendered and communal violence, and has been mobilized to evict others from shared space? And what about the framework of law within which struggles for citizenship, for a proper right to belong, have been fought and won?

These questions animate not just the analysis in this chapter but also this book's overall project of inserting a postcolonial feminist project of citizenship in contemporary theorizations of the city. I now turn to the specific question of women in the postcolonial city, its unhomely women, in order to substantively assess the claims of community, solidarity, citizenship rights and the emancipatory potential of the postcolonial city as a site of resistance.

(En)Gendering the Citizen

The postcolonial city, whose normative subject has historically been torn between nationalist and nativist roots and a global cosmopolitanism, has been remarkably male in orientation. The modern projects of nationalism and citizenship have only reinforced the patriarchal contract in which often "the question of the 'new woman' was . . . formulated . . . as a question of coping with change".[28] The male nationalist, concerned with the new requirements of life in the city where ideas of emancipation and progress were rife, was typically engaged in the production of a rational and urbane self, able to disentangle itself from rural and "backward" origins, associated with, and the site of, traditional Indian womanhood.

In story after story of modernizing Bengal, the modern Indian male sends letters to his innocent wife in the village as a means of her education.[29] Within the scope of these modernizing narratives, the city woman is painted as inauthentic, typically at the cost of a whole urban underclass of women workers and slum-dwellers. Thus, one of the key points of exploration in this chapter hinges on the question of how the woman in the city is constituted as a problem for the representation of postcolonial Indian citizenship. After all, questions of authenticity invariably center around the issue of "woman" in which the urban and westernized woman in the postcolonial city appears as an anomaly because she fits neither the mold of the authentic subaltern located within rural and domestic spheres, as the west's absolute Other, nor the mold of the hybridized, trans-national woman in the western metropolis.[30] The woman in the city, the archetypal new woman, is both a sign of modernity and its radical other. She represents the moral dangers of modern life as embodied in the figure of the prostitute, or the potential of a partially realized, decolonized Indian subjectivity in the figure of the modern housewife. Both figures constitute a key site of debates over the urbanization of society and culture.[31]

The postcolonial state for the most part reinstated elements of an older, colonialist patriarchal compact through a nationalist project in which women provide a peripheral backdrop to "the essential procedures" of the nation.[32] Thus postcolonialism could be understood as resituating women from the margins of the public sphere to subordination within it. As the project of citizenship remains lodged in the interstices of a masculine order even as democratic procedures offer nominal equality to women, the urban Indian woman remains central to the erasure of the concrete gendered subject in favor of the abstract subject of postcolonial Indian citizenship.

In the process, a powerful politics of cultural metaphors has come to fetishize the city and women in it through a proliferation of discourses on modernity and tradition that in fact mask fundamental questions of justice and equality, especially in gendered terms. In this, the imagining of a pristine rural India is intimately tied to a notion of women as carriers of tradition. Even as critics have derided the denial of agency to rural women, the latter have continued to be the archetypal subjects of oppression. Modern urban women, on the other hand, have embodied the very threat of westernization and an erosion of native patriarchy, even as they have been marked as containers of liberal experiments with the idea and the materiality of the modern.

The twenty-first century's global economic compact—consisting of structural adjustment deals, trans-national production of flexible citizenship, international circuits of information and capital—insinuates itself into nationalist projects, creating new conditions for the marginalization of women. We see new forms of gender oppression emerging in the context of weakening labor and environmental laws under new global trade regimes, the sexual trafficking of women and children, and the increasing exploitation of women's labor in both the home and outside it. It is within this new imperium that a project of postcolonial feminist citizenship must be forged in order to challenge and intercept it.

The Dream City

The idea of the postcolonial city as a conjunctural site of gendered citizenship is explored below by looking specifically at the representational space of Bombay within discourses of postcolonial urbanity in India. I situate a study of the representational history of Bombay within (a) the contending nationalist and postcolonialist discourses on the place of the city in Indian modernity; (b) the feminist debates on the postcolonial city and its gendered subjects; (c) and the fictions of Bombay as sites where the city is imagined in terms of gendered solidarity and belonging.

Historians have pointed to Bombay's pre-eminence as a metropolis and as India's financial capital from colonial times.[33] Located on the west coast of India, Bombay provided the British with a harbor, and its ethnically mixed population perpetuated an air of cosmopolitanism that encouraged trade and cultural exchange with the West. Sujata Patel has argued that "the requirements of British commerce and British industry . . . determined the selective recruitment to the city of merchants, artisans and labourers" as well as "clerks and petty officials" from various ethnicities and regions.[34] Bombay's pre-eminence as the quintessential modern Indian, even Asian, city is based on facts such as it was the first Indian city to have modern waterworks, and it is Asia's oldest stock-exchange market. But Bombay's past also implicates it in a complex colonial history of spatialization and urban planning. Several urban historians locate Bombay's twentieth-century standing as a modern and cosmopolitan metropolis to its origins as "a quintessentially colonial city" in the nineteenth century that served as "an open gateway for the exploitation of its hinterland and, indeed, the country as a whole".[35] Anthony D. King asserts that "the norms of London, Manchester, and Leeds (such as 'the Sanitary Idea', health and density statistics) were used to shape the forms of Bombay (such as sewage systems, urban layouts, and civic space)".[36] Statistics on nineteenth-century Bombay reinforce the idea of the colonized city as a laboratory and exemplar of urban planning. "Facts" such as Bombay's lower mortality rate as compared to that of London's in the 1860s and its better health and hygiene record than that of the colonial metropole point to Bombay's special status in the colonial imagination concerning urbanity.[37]

Both popular and academic accounts trace a trajectory of Bombay's transformations from its colonial status as a cosmopolitan center of trade, commerce and bourgeois nationalism to a postcolonial dream city of the possibilities of enterprise and industry. The city's promise of civic order and efficiency had attracted the nation's poor, the disenfranchised, and "unproductive" members of the educated class who arrived there to become productive citizens of the nation, making it India's most populous city in the immediate decades around and after independence.[38]

The representation of Bombay as the signifier of Indian modernity relies on a paradoxical attitude towards this colonial past or heritage. Bombay is seen as being "modern" in a western sense of the term, and yet, as Rao puts it, its modernity of sensibility "fails to find an objective correlative in the reality of experience".[39] This disjuncture between its sensibility (westernized, outward looking, cosmopolitan) and its "reality of experience" (shortage of space for housing, everyday struggles to find work, ethnic strife) is typically attributed to Bombay's spatial history. Bombay was, after all, a group of island fishing villages that was transformed into localities that continue to express their "native flavour" even as it became India's pre-eminent cosmopolitan city. On this analysis, Bombay never really achieved a definitive break from its rural and pre-colonial origins—its nativist roots co-exist alongside its cosmopolitan energies.

It is ironically the city's colonial history, however, that enables the metropolitan Bombayite to become the model national citizen, transcending colonial categorizations of the provincial because he or she has had historical access to metropolitan norms and forms. The distinctions of caste and religion are subsumed in the city's uneven spatial formations (and by extension in the nation) through the very nature of its simultaneous containment of ethnic identity within neighborhoods, and its role in forging a larger national identity through an ethic of free enterprise and hard work. In this, Bombay's sensibility, Rao argues, radically differs from that of India at large, even as it simultaneously mirrors the nation's constitutive contradictions. Rao points out how "the sanctity of self is challenged by the heterogeneity of caste, class and religion that makes up life in Bombay".[40] Salman Rushdie writes of the heterogeneity of Bombay as if it has some vital link to "the nature of Bombay, a metropolis in which the multiplicity of commingled faiths and cultures curiously creates a remarkably secular ambience".[41] Bombay, insofar as it represents what Arjun Appadurai calls the global "ethnoscapes" of contemporary globalization, purports to de-territorialize ethnicity, as also inhabiting it are those populations that have only a tangential claim to territory as signifier of belonging.[42]

A key idea that animates the image of Bombay in the national imagination is that of the city as a space of survival against all odds. Survival, in fact, constitutes a dominant mode of belonging in the city.[43] It requires not just grit and determination, but a transcendence of communal roots and an embrace of radical heterogeneity. The act of producing a new self that is the proper subject of the city is itself an act of survival in the city. Some of the popular cultural representations of the city, as in the Bombay cinema, testify to such an assessment.[44]

Thus one of the key contradictions at the heart of Bombay's popular and canonical representations has been its simultaneous presence as "the quint-essential India",[45] and its very unreal status as "more like a movie set than the real thing".[46] The challenge for a chronicler of the city involves the difficult task of both representing its complexity as well as taking into account the impossibility of doing that. A central question explored in the discourse remains that of the possibility of being and becoming Indian in a hybrid public sphere such as Bombay.

The question is even more charged in gender terms because to be a woman from Bombay is already to occupy an especially tenuous position of (in)authenticity. For it is also in Bombay that women are said to enjoy greater freedom because of the anonymity and the indifference of others. One writer describes Bombay thus: "Like the streets of New York, the streets of Bombay abound with women". Further elaborating this image, she writes:

> They are out shopping or doing errands; they are pouring out of trains and buses and hurrying to work . . . Walking in the city streets, you will step around a woman cooking supper on the pavement . . . Waiting for the bus, you will be able to study women scavengers . . . In the smart boutique, at the taxi stand, in the pastry shoppe at the five-star hotel . . . Standing in a packed bus, conversing in the post office queue, visiting their offices or their living rooms, you can gather impressions of the lives of women over a spectrum that, in Bombay, is about as wide as it can get.[47]

Whereas it could be argued that such an "experience" and view of Bombay is predicated on Bombay's discursive power in imagining a women's world in the city, sometimes having little truck with its masculinist and provincial realities, the city also realizes this discursive construction through the constant struggles waged on its terrain over issues of gender. The public world in the city—of Bollywood (in which many women actors have achieved freedom and prosperity), of bars and restaurants, of the mills and offices, of politics in general—while constituted as male-dominated, is unable to eclipse the "other" spaces inhabited by women such as homes, brothels and streets. Thus it is that in Suketu Mehta's much-acclaimed auto/biography of Bombay, *Maximum City*, the writer starts off on a personal journey to make sense of the city and swims in its world of cops, businessmen, underworld dons, real estate mafiosi and Hindu extremist gang leaders, only to take on, unwittingly, the role of the protector of Bombay's bar girls.[48] Whereas dominant accounts of this sprawling book see it as brilliant reportage of a city bursting at its seams, the book also emerges as Mehta's love affair with Bombay's most vulnerable women—the bar girls who are constantly under threat from domestic and public violence. In the end Mehta is unable to do anything for these women as he returns to the comforts of his upper-middle-class cosmopolitan domesticity and his role as a reporter, the limits of figuring women in the city as agents of their own destinies is exposed in a stark manner. Following a very old trope, the Bombay bar girl comes to allegorize all the seductions and the vulnerabilities of this great city.

Bombay is of course deeply enmeshed in the narratives that aim to grasp "difference" itself—gendered, religious, class and ethnic—within the general urban geography of postcoloniality. Bombay's multi-facetedness, its mind-boggling plurality, its stunning contradictions and distasteful polarizations, condensed evocatively in Suketu Mehta's idea of the "maximum city", make it a rich ground for examining the material bases of postcolonial modernity and its relationship to questions of citizenship. After all, Bombay's physical constraints make more complex the politics of class in the city. Whereas roughly half of Bombay's population lives in slums or on footpaths, the rich swan around in expensive cars commuting between their expensive real estate in high-rise buildings, spacious clubs and expansive shopping malls.[49] Drawing specific attention to the relationship between space and class, Khilnani writes: "Bombay's congestion makes it impossible for the rich to flee the poor", rendering the contrasts of wealth as "vividly adjacent".[50]

Thus the representation of Bombay as the boundless space of enthusiasm and promise, "India's Capital of Hope" as *The National Geographic* puts it, needs to be linked more generally to late-twentieth-century Indian capitalism. As India's commercial capital, Bombay has historically been the haven of free economic enterprise and cosmopolitan culture.[51] But free-market reforms from the early 1990s onwards reinforced Bombay's image as resister of state-directed and bureaucratized planning and economic control; Bombay continued with greater vigor to be represented as "propel"ling India into modernity and development.[52]

Some analysts have in fact tied Bombay's ethic of tolerance towards difference with its ethic of the free market. Such an argument of course assumes capitalism as the panacea for ethnic conflict, when in fact capitalism's uneven development has typically exacerbated struggles over ethnic differences in the city. The failure of the famous textile strikes of the 1980s effectively broke the back of working-class solidarity in the city. The organized work of the Shiv Sena, a right-wing Hindu supremacist political formation that gained political force in the 1990s, has focused on mobilizing support not so much in the workplace as in the slums where the urban lower-middle classes and poor live. This has redirected the locale of political mobilization from productive labor to reproductive labor generated in the slum and the street. But more significantly, it has brought the spatial struggles in the city into the domain of politics proper.[53] In the closing sections of this chapter, I will return to the issue of postcolonial Bombay as a conjunctural space that allows for a more complex reading of feminist postcolonial citizenship and its imbrication in contestations of space, commerce and rights to the city.

A Rupture?

Much of the recent scholarship on Bombay has emerged in the wake of the perceived dissolution in the 1990s of Bombay's iconic status as the nation's cosmopolitan center. The dissolution was marked violently by the riots of late 1992 and early 1993, in which thousands of Muslims were massacred and about a quarter million of them fled the city. The targeting of Muslims, who account for some 15 percent of the city's population, led some observers to comment that these were not "riots" but in fact acts of genocide carried out against a minority community. State forces such as the police and the bureaucracy, meant to provide protection to all citizens, reneged from such duty, and revealed themselves as violent and prejudiced members of the majority community.

In the early 1990s the promise of a postcolonial dream city was violently transmuted into the nightmare of an ethnically cleansed city in which Maharashtrians and Hindus became Bombay's only legitimate citizens. This has caused a serious rupture in the image of Bombay as India's capital of hope both for many of its own residents and for those living in less cosmopolitan parts of the country.[54] This thoroughly divided city, far from being a model for the secular Indian imagination, now seems to be emulating a different model of nationalism that is rooted in provincial and exclusionary identifications.

The origins of what Arjun Appadurai has called the "decosmopolitanization" of Bombay, or what I call its "provincialization", are most often situated in the rise of the right-wing party Shiv Sena that was formed in 1966 but really gained political hegemony in the 1980s and 1990s.[55] The Shiv Sena was the main engine of the unleashing of the violence in 1992–1993. The violent project of cleansing the city of all "foreign" (read Muslim, but also Bihari and Tamil) elements has continued a decade later, most recently in the form of vicious attacks on poor migrants from the more backward states of north India. The party's ideology promotes regional chauvinism (in which Bombay belongs to Maharashtra, the state in which it is located, and thus to Maharashtrians), and Hindutva, or Hindu supremacism (in which Bombay is part of the sacred geography of a Hindu nation and Muslims are "outsiders").[56] A key political goal of the party has been to fix an ethnicity on to Bombay itself, such that it can be translated as Hindu and Maharashtrian.[57] Traditionally popular among the poor, migrant labor from the Maharashtra valley (the state in which Bombay is situated), the Shiv Sena grew in strength throughout the 1980s and 1990s and came to command a key constituency among the middle classes as well as the lower and poorer sections of the city. This popularity stands in an awkward relationship with the perception by the upwardly mobile wealthy Bombayites of Shiv Sena's nuisance value in the ways in which their popular mobilizations tend to disrupt the smooth operation of business in the city.

Accounts of the rise of the right-wing party usually link the growth of ethnic chauvinism to struggles over economic resources in the city. One popular theory suggests that the 1993 riots were in fact real estate scams in which the mafia mobilized communal divisions to raze slums that existed in prime property areas so that they could be transformed into more lucrative shopping and office districts. Thus, far from papering over differences, Bombay's embrace of free-market economics seems to have exacerbated them. Appadurai's theorization of de-territorialized ethnoscapes of globalization then has to be studied in conjunction with a simultaneous rise of ethnic and religious fundamentalism in the city and the decline of other forms of solidarity.

Feminist Responses

Bombay has thus become the site yet again of hotly contested political debates around the role of urban space in the political imaginary of citizenship, particularly on the question of gendered belonging. In 1993 it became clear that underneath the supposed tolerance characteristic of the city was lurking a growing rapaciousness and unwillingness to share the city with those that the majority felt did not belong there. The conflict between Hindutva and cosmopolitanism after 1993 was no longer describable in older terms of class and gender identifications. Not only did India's English-speaking elites embrace right-wing Hindutva, among the unusual things that marked the riots in 1993 was women's participation in the communal violence, even as the violence itself was gendered in terms of a virile masculine Hindu identity seeking to right a historical wrong perpetrated by Muslims.[58] Thus, ethnic violence that was earlier associated with the working-class and lower middle-class districts of the city, as well as with men as its primary agents, now engulfed the whole of the city's body.

In retrospect, my own shock at women's turn to fundamentalism in Bombay was part of this notion of Bombay—that Bombay women were somehow free of the burden of partisan hatred and distrust, of the encumbrances of narrowly defined loyalties. As I sat in Chicago and my dossier on the Bombay riots continued to bulge all through 1993 and much of 1994, I read with dismay accounts of women's participation in the riots, and of the Shiv Sena's open exhortation to men and women from the Hindu community to play their part in the annihilation of India's minority Muslim community. It was easy to recognize the toughness of life in Chicago as an Indian woman but harder to imagine what it was for the minority, for the outsider, for the villager, for the non-Hindu back home. The dismay and incomprehension in the wake of the 1992 riots led me to examine not only my assumptions regarding women's relationship to urban life, but also to contextualize these theoretical endeavors within the framework of a very real "crisis". In this section, I use this moment of crisis to open up a way towards thinking about gendered subjectivity and political agency in the postcolonial city.

Liberal feminist discourse has typically blamed the violence on tradition and unreason whose primary purveyors and beneficiaries are men. But the active role played by women in communal violence has demystified the notion of women as representatives of community and social harmony. Studies on women's participation in Hindu fundamentalist movements have shown that women define community in as exclusivist terms as men, and that community, contra Chatterjee's suggestion, is not an adequate or politically efficacious site for mounting a resistance to either local or global projects of domination.[59] In the riots of 1993 Hindu women participated in substantial numbers in killing and assaulting Muslims. Madhu Kishwar, a well-known feminist journalist, gave the following account:

> Women and young girls avidly looting shops along with men was a common sight in Bombay during the January riots. I heard accounts of how Hindu women dragged Muslim women and children and joined the men in stoning them and setting them on fire.[60]

In her account of the violence, the historian Tanika Sarkar points to an underlying irony:

> In an ironic inversion of women's former invisibility in the domain of public violence, large numbers of women have been extremely active and visible, not only in the rallies and campaigns but even in the actual episodes of violent attacks against Muslims . . . The complicity has also involved an informed assent to such brutalities against Muslim women as gang rapes in December '92 and January '93 . . .–informed, because these episodes had been widely reported and publicized and there was no way that these women could have escaped knowledge of them.[61]

Accounts such as these prompt Sarkar to remind feminists that

> in fact, the politicization of right-wing women involves a painful surrender of a cherished article of faith about the relationships between

women and violence. In most studies of communal violence in India
women have been predominantly conceptualized as victims and heal-
ers—a position that is generally considered representative of their roles
and experiences in society as a whole . . . We now need to modify and
enlarge the possibilities of the political role of women.[62]

Because communal riots have become a disturbing feature of urban life in
postcolonial India, whether in small townships or in big metropolitan centers
like Bombay, it is necessary to examine the production of urbanity in terms
of violent struggles over belonging, including on the question of gender.[63]
The roots of Shiv Sena's appeal lay in its exploitation of the urban crisis of
space articulated as a question of women's needs as consumers, mothers
and citizens.[64] The Sena's activism over issues of housing and other civic
amenities held out the promise of social and political agency to women, even
as it superficially countered the religious right's reputation for being retrograde and chauvinistic. By manipulating gender politics, the right-wing party
attempted to occlude the fact that women are the worst victims of riots, both
in terms of physical vulnerability but also in terms of the very possibility of
economic and cultural survival.

Progressive feminists have also located women's reactionary involvement
in the communal violence as a characteristic feature of the gendered politics
of the middle classes in urban India. Sarkar asserts that "for a section of affluent upper-castes and middle-class urban women of northern Indian cities and
small towns", the Hindutva mobilization "does provide a public political identity and a limited, yet real sense of empowerment".[65] Thus upward mobility in
gendered terms is predicated on maintaining class and caste privileges.

But whereas such a misappropriation of women by the religious Right
shows the salience of women—as vote banks and as agents of cleansing the
national community from foreign elements (the Muslim)—it also points to
the complex subjectivity of women within the postcolonial city who increasingly participate in the political realm as constituted by both the Left and the
Right. Rather than interpreting women's participation in religious violence
as an instance of false consciousness or "plain fear" as Kishwar suggests, a
postcolonial feminist theory of the city must attempt to understand women's
complex agency in cities that leads to their political mobilization as (hateful) citizens. Liberal feminist discourse tends to represent women as victims
and dupes of violent machismo who need to be rescued, but a materialist
reading involves examining the process by which women's subjectivity as
communalists and as hateful citizens is created, even as a project of feminist
citizenship must be forged, enmeshed within the possibilities of social justice
in the postcolonial city.

For the Shiv Sena Bombay has to be reclaimed from the Muslims and
the non-Maharashtrians, and women from a specific articulation of modernity that renders them vulnerable to contamination and corruption by

purportedly western notions of feminism and secularism. Such a project is of necessity selective in its delineation of tradition and modernity—thus whereas it is acceptable for Hindu women to mobilize the community against an imagined enemy and to participate in physical exercises that would prepare them for militancy like the men of Hindu Right-wing cadres, any expression of the above mobility and public participation in the rhetoric of feminism is construed as a western import, and as inauthentic. Thus the very duality within the discourse of the Hindu Right, between its vision of the Indian woman as the supreme figure of purity and sacrifice who forms the backbone of a militant Hindu identity, and that of a modern and activist woman who can take to the streets for the cause of her nation and religion, problematizes issues of women's agency and their role in urban space. Ultimately, it is necessary to point to the limits of women's agency as liberatory when it is constrained within a deeply divided city.

The city plays a crucial role in feminist politics in India in the ways in which gender and community are articulated. In the contemporary political context of resurgent fundamentalisms of varying religious orientations, women's identities are being presented to women as one of self (privatized) versus community (private and public). Ironically, secularist and multi-culturalist ideologies have had a weakening role in the public sphere of the city in the ways in which they have created as opposite and separate a secular public sphere and an autonomous private sphere where individuals make their own choices regarding religious practices.[66] Responding to the wave of Hindutva that dominated Indian politics in the 1980s and 1990s, Sucheta Mazumdar argues for the construction of a radically secular public sphere that can transcend "class and caste interests" and take on the patriarchal-communal-capitalist nexus unleashed in modern India where violence has erupted as an epidemic against women and minorities.[67] In the absence of radically secular coalitions, Mazumdar fears a contaminated public sphere that unwittingly sanctions violence against women and minorities. Thus, Mazumdar's ideal of an "unoppressive city", to use Iris Marion Young's term, is predicated on a disavowal of religious and cultural markers of women's identity.

Picking up on these contradictions, the media plays out gender struggles, such as the anti-Sati campaigns of the late 1980s or the anti-dowry protests, as a conflict between small rural or small-town communities fighting for tradition against urban, westernized women from the cities, preaching western ideas of equality and secularism.[68] Recent social transformations in India however belie such easy distinctions between rural and urban women. To describe women primarily as victims of the ideology of religious supremacy elides the possibilities opened up by political mobilization, even a conservative and reactionary one, to produce political consciousness.[69] Right-wing women have devised means from within Hindu patriarchy to claim spatial mobility and freedom from the accouterments of gendered roles. Much of urban women's popular culture is taking the form of several new, commercialized forms of religiosity. The deployment of high-tech media to modernize religious practices, while still claiming access to tradition, has also been a significant feature of women's politicization in cities.[70] Women have attained a great deal of visibility and voice in communal politics, and by extension, in national politics.

But whereas it is true that these new cultural forms and political formations provide avenues for women to come together in urban areas, the underlying ideology of such politics is strongly capitalist, patriarchal and communal. A critique of these reactionary formations must be attentive to the ways in which the Right wing has appropriated the rhetoric of women's liberation and indigenized it, while divesting it of its political efficacy for a critique of Indian patriarchy. The complex web of gendered political identities makes visible the contradictions within women's lives in the postcolonial city in India. Against the backdrop of economic liberalization and large-scale urbanization that has had what Appadurai calls "deterritorializing" effects on national identity, women have come to bear the brunt of male violence in the context of shifting spatial and political formations. The honor of women provides a "new arena for the formation of sexual identity and family politics", a "surrogate for the embattled communities of males".[71] Gita Sahgal and Nira Yuval-Davis note that "women, their roles, and above all their control, are at the heart of the fundamentalist agenda. That they should conform to the strict confines of womanhood within the fundamentalist religious code is a precondition for maintaining and reproducing the fundamentalist version of society".[72] In the process, it is reproduction that is de-territorialized, radically intertwining the locales of "home", family, work and survival.

These new configurations of social, economic and political relations offer a theoretical challenge to feminist theory and to its conceptualizations of citizenship. To understand the city as a site of both conservative and progressive feminist organizing seems to provide a more fruitful approach to analyzing the centrality of urban space in the construction of women's subjectivities. Such a position points to the conjuncture of economic and the cultural realms and opens up space for a feminist appropriation of the city, enabling us to both come to a better understanding of gendered political consciousness and agency, and to help articulate a broader social agenda where gender, class, religious and ethnic differences are "taken into account" in the construction of a socially just city.

The disjunctions between competing feminist versions of a radical democracy are revealed in the above discussion, but they also provide an opportunity for a productive engagement with the postcolonial city. Many readings of women's politicization do not adequately understand the postcolonial city insofar as they tacitly exclude multiple ways of expressing and experiencing the gendered self and its relation to community/city/ nation. Whereas progressive responses call for a reassertion of gender as a primary site of identity for recognizing women's subordination within the family, community, economy and the state, the Right-wing attempts to locate women squarely within the community, and within the idea of the nation as a community. Further exacerbating the issue, the state responds by non-gendering minority women, subordinating their gendered identity to a larger communal one. These conflicting conundrums call for a necessarily materialist, feminist and postcolonial reading of the contemporary city. Thus, my analysis differs from the general consensus as voiced by Radha Kumar that for the feminist movement in Indian cities, political space is getting "curtailed by identity politics". In my view, new forms of identity politics offer new critical challenges and even open up new spaces for feminist movements to articulate a vision and a project of feminist postcolonial citizenship.

The Silent City

In the following sections I seek to open another front—the ground of representation—to think about Bombay as the site of postcolonial urbanism and of new feminist subjectivities and political agency. Whereas the introductory sections of this chapter pointed to some of the ideological and cultural moorings of the postcolonial city as the space of citizenship in India, the following sections consider how some of Bombay's literary texts create a set of representations in productive relationship with material transformations in the postcolonial city. My main argument in the following sections then has to do with the assertion that Bombay is readable not only through its fictional texts, but as a fictional text in itself that lends itself to the protocols of literary readings.

The widespread ambivalence about Bombay as a city that is simultaneously counterfeit and representative of something real, as a city that is a microcosm of India and radically different from it, has informed its dominant representations in the first sixty years of Indian independence. Postcolonial Bombay of course has had many brilliant chroniclers, from the poets Nissim Ezekiel and Dilip Chitre to Namdeo Dhasal and the Dalit Panther poets, from novelists Salman Rushdie, Kiran Nagarkar and Rohinton Mistry to the many illustrious writers in Marathi and Gujarati in both fiction and journalism, not to mention the prodigious artistic and popular output of the lyricists and script-writers associated with the Bombay film industry. Indeed cinema has dominated what in effect has been called a "cinematic city", underscoring the city's complex imbrication in material reality and imaginative constructions.

In this chapter I want to focus on a group of texts that represent important moments in the constitution of the imaginative languages in which Indian modernity, linked inextricably to gendered urbanity as embodied by Bombay, is shaped and produced. Thus, I read them not only because they narrativize the gendered "experience" of living in the city, but because they emerge from a specific cultural and intellectual formation of Bombay. They thus both fictionalize Bombay and offer Bombay as a fiction. The texts I consider are Shashi Deshpande's 1988 novel *That Long Silence*, written before the outbreak of the communal violence in the early 1990s but after the catastrophic textile strikes of the 1980s, a short story called "Shakti" from Vikram Chandra's 1997 collection *Love and Longing in Bombay*, set in the Bombay of the mid-1990s, after the 1992 riots and the neo-liberal reforms introduced in the preceding decade, and Thrity Umrigar's *The Space between Us* (2006), set in the Bombay of the early twenty-first century.[73]

Novels such as Deshpande's *That Long Silence* have remained largely unnoticed in the emerging canon of urban postcolonial writing in English from India dominated by male writers such as Rushdie, Seth and Mistry.[74] The novel's realist, stripped-down, interiorized narrative style differs from standard literary evocations of Bombay as a cacophonic, polyvocal space of difference and "excessive" postcoloniality (its realism describable primarily as magical as in Rushdie's fiction), but also from the populous tragic-comic urban vision of a writer such as Mistry. Whether Bombay has lent itself, in its metaphorical plenitude and robust assertiveness to masculinist renderings of urbanity is a separate although related question. Here I want to begin by focusing on Deshpande's text as it poses the question of women's relationship to urbanity in general, and to Bombay in particular, in a central way.

Rao has noted that much of the poetry on the city of Bombay by women focuses on the theme of isolation and loneliness.[75] Such a reading aligns itself with a general sense of Indian women's writing as largely inward looking and focused on domesticity as the proper domain for postcolonial feminist agency. Drawing on the tradition of isolation, albeit obliquely and critically, Deshpande's novel articulates the isolation of women in the postcolonial city with their political marginalization. The novel makes visible an affinity between the spaces inhabited by women in the city and the spaces that exist *between* the women themselves. The "silence" of the title thus speaks of an intensely "private" alienation with the nation, civil society and the city, and the failure of various dominant narratives in accounting for women's agency and their constitution as political subjects.

The novel's voicing of silence, in the contradictoriness of its gesture, challenges the city's gendered subjects to imagine a different social narrative. As Jaya, a middle-class housewife married to a corporate executive, Mohan, is caught between the private act of creating a home (in which her family's presence becomes "a burden" on the solitude she treasures and that enables her self-expression [68]), writing her diary, and the public act of writing her life story in a magazine column (that also becomes the novel), the experience of alienation emerges from both the public and the private milieu.[76] To break that silence is to transgress the codes by which women's "public" identity and sexuality are subordinated and domesticated within the postcolonial city.[77] It is this framing of the text within a middle-class woman's consciousness (saturated with Hindu tradition's patriarchal script) that has prompted the critic Rajeswari Sunder Rajan to judge the novel as a mediocre and ultimately limited evocation of Indian feminism, in its individualized and family-oriented solutions to the crisis of Indian womanhood.[78] In the following discussion, I attempt to problematize the political stakes of feminist literary criticism and its unease with resolving the very resilient binary of private and public spheres into a singular feminist postcolonial project in and for the city.

In the novel Jaya comes to associate the act of writing with "the fear that I was losing control over my own body" (3). Writing here is both de-linked from the body, in that it happens seemingly independent of the body's condition, and is intimately connected to it as a mode of embodiment itself. Writing also has a crucial spatial dimension—it becomes a way of creating a space in the city, a sort of a room of her own where Jaya records the ennui, the feelings of displacement, disorder and quiet insurgency as a middle-class housewife in Bombay confronting an alienating and vexing city. It is through her writing that "the picture of a life spent on such trivialities" (70) emerges and provides a critical perspective on her class and gender location. Thus, contra Sunder Rajan, the novel from the very outset points to the limits of individualized solutions, as the materiality of space confronts its ideological but always tenuous divisions of public and private. In its critique of middle-class women's implication in caste and class privileges, the novel dramatizes the complex negotiations of Indian feminism with the spatiality of modern life in the big city. Ultimately, as I discuss below, Deshpande's novel elaborates the terms within which a critical postcolonial feminist subjectivity can reach out towards a more collective feminist subject. In other words, the novel is oriented *towards* and *with* the city, rather than against it.

Deshpande invents her own mode of urban realism through a combination of the conventions of social commentary and modernist autobiography. Throughout, the novel is undergirded by the tension of genre, and the narrator devotes the epigraph to this tension. She writes:

> Perhaps it is wrong to write from the inside. Perhaps what I have to do is see myself, us, from a distance. This has happened to me before; there have been times when I've had this queer sensation of being detached and distant from my own self. Times when I've been able to separate two distinct strands—my experience, and my awareness of that experience. Can I do this with our story? Do I have the necessary ruthlessness? . . . I had found myself agonising over what I could write, what there was in my life that meant something. Finally, when I had sifted out what I had thought were irrelevant facts, only these had remained:
>
> I was born. My father died when I was fifteen. I got married to Mohan. I have two children and I did not let a third live. Maybe this is enough to start off with. I can take off from here. (2)

The opening section points to the fragility of what might at first seem merely the narrative of a self-absorbed middle-class housewife, expressing a subjective and unreliable "experience" that is vulnerable to the critical questions of narrative form and social meaning. The very genre of the diary situates the literary project as episodic, selective and fragmentary, and engenders a space of expression where the subject can be "true" to herself, however incoherent her subjectivity might be. Yet in its negotiations with its discursive challenges to women's "place" in both the material and representational realms, the diary destabilizes the categories of public and private, and more interestingly, of spatialized perspective. The story makes sense only if it can be viewed from a distance, yet gaining distance is impossible within the space of a diary. The struggle over perspective is what allows the story to open up the problematic of the temporal and spatial distance encountered in narrating experience.[79]

In her study of modernity and biography, Veena Das notes such a "double articulation" in which "we see a stable narrative of the female life cycle provided by tradition" as well as "certain moments of rupture".[80] Jaya's writing performs a similar function with regard to the social text in which women's bodies are rendered as sites of hysteria, and their subjectivity as doomed to a veritable unhomeliness even as they are trapped in domesticity. This negotiation in the novel between the public and the private self, the social text coded as tradition and the always-present rupture, produces a series of "private" crises that are propelled by what happens in the city, even as the city shapes the experience of the private itself. Thus, whereas the 1993 riots discussed above brought to the fore a very public violence in postcolonial Bombay, *That Long Silence* records the invisible violence of the postcolonial private (in marital relations, in caste and class differences) such that both spheres can be seen to mutually constitute each other. I thus read the novel as constituted by a singular production of postcolonial spatiality, especially postcolonial urbanism, against the resilient frameworks and modernist categories of city versus country, of public versus private that occlude the project and politics of feminist postcolonial citizenship.

New Metropolitan Forms

My analysis suggests that Jaya's awakening to the silent crises engulfing her life is inextricable from her experience of the city of Bombay. The city spatializes her desires and anxieties, her sense of self and her solidarities with others, in very specific ways and towards particular ends. Deshpande constructs a narrative in which consciousness of space is achieved through the act of writing, enabled through the trope of mapping objects in the room, in the city, and in her consciousness. The three levels of spatialization—self, home and city—pave the way for a re-mapping of her life in both its daily iterations and its political articulations. Thus *That Long Silence*'s narrative of a modern urban woman's life is intimately mediated by and intertwined with postcolonial India's urban forms.

The novel evokes many different urban spaces and forms emerging in postcolonial India, with the protagonist's journey through these spaces reflecting as it were the somewhat jagged trajectory and uneven formation of urban development in India. However, Jaya's memory of "other" places can only be evoked from her situation in Bombay; the memory of place necessitates the presence of proper perspective provided by the metropolitan city. She recalls her parents' home on the outskirts of the town of Saptagiri. There Jaya grows up into a young woman, imbibing the small town's pastoral and seemingly complacent air, encompassing spaces not-yet urban, but existing on the outskirts of the adjoining provincial town where Jaya's relatives lived their narrow and depressing lives. Their shabby homes stand placidly along the narrow by-lanes that emanate the putrid odor of a backed-up drainage system. Towns like Saptagiri seem forever caught in a space of in-between-ness in the national urban project, assuming all the demerits of urbanization—the filth, squalor, perverse lack of planning, overcrowding, lack of economic opportunities in a distorted development regime—and none of its merits of hope and possibilities. Deshpande's dry tone only intensifies the sense of dullness and aridity evoked by these places. In other words, they seem to be spaces where the metropolitan ideal is still indecipherable or even unimaginable.

What needs to be underscored here is that this indecipherability in terms of the urban is a view from Bombay, the city that has dominated the imagination of urbanity in India. The symbol of that indecipherability is Crossword House in Saptagiri, the name itself a bizarre protrusion of supposedly western codes of cultural literacy in the backwaters of the small town. Yet the name also projects the purportedly incommensurable juxtapositions of the modern and the non-modern within postcolonial urban spaces. For it is in Crossword House that Mohan first encounters metropolitan modernity in the figures of the English-speaking women who visit it. If Mohan's engineering degree could provide a passport into urban modernity, Jaya's degree in English literature would provide the couple with cosmopolitan credentials. Austen and Trollope, writers who evoke a dying but idealized pastoral realm in the context of industrializing Britain, become symbols of the English literary tradition and its ersatz modernity as played out in provincial India. Jaya becomes a living symbol of Mohan's middle-class desires—providing access to a specifically postcolonial kind of westernization, while still performing the "traditional" tasks of an Indian wife.

Whereas the escape from Saptagiri's provinciality first comes from the imagined power of Crossword House, Mohan finds material freedom when he lands a job in Lohanagar (or "steel town"). Characterized by its uniform, drab houses and giant industrial plants, Lohanagar stands in for an archetypal postcolonial Indian modernity based on ideas of progress, industrial growth and prosperity. Such a modernity is predicated on socialist ideals of the benevolent state, providing decent wages and creating utilitarian spaces such as dwelling houses, parks for recreation, factories for working and schools for the education of the workers' children. These Soviet-style urban formations, often literally built with Soviet collaboration, appeared in stark contrast to the more feudal and older towns where the gap between the rich and the poor, the upper castes and the lower castes, was made evident through distinctive architectural representations and spatial distinctions. The new urban formations of the industrial steel town, in their uniformity of style and content, provide a vision for a new kind of life for the country and for the people, in which its engineers would build a modern economy, and where new nuclear families would be forged in the image of a modern nation. Khilnani suggestively refers to this phenomenon as a new "provincial cosmopolitanism" that emerges in the context of postcolonial development and industrialization and away from the big city.[81]

The novel plots how Mohan's search for greater economic mobility through hard work and dedication to the factory takes him farther away from his small-town roots and into the big metropolis. And then this novel, like so many novels before it, records what the new arrival to the city finds there—"nothing but grey, uniform ugliness" and the "endless rows of looking-exactly-alike, ramshackle, drab buildings", dashing the provincial's dream of the moment of arriving in the big city (54). Economic mobility turns out to be only a mixed blessing—Mohan's thirst for bourgeois comforts and status symbols is thwarted when he finds himself embroiled in a financial scam and is suspended from his job. The novel narrates how corruption in the public world of officialdom and private sector capitalism destroys the sanctity or the purported autonomy of the private. Forced to leave the company flat in Churchgate, a posh Bombay locality, the couple moves to a flat that belongs to Jaya's family in "a drab building in the heart of Bombay" (7), in Dadar, a sprawling middle-class district of the city. Here the passageways show trails of garbage, and the flat itself "reeked of mildew and rot" caused by the unhappy mixing of "the fetid stench" with "the closed-in monsoon mustiness" (12).

The shift to the flat in Dadar, while registered as a spatial dislocation, signifies a destabilizing of Jaya's marital relations that were based on the clear-cut spaces of the patriarchal bourgeois family and on bourgeois economic values. With Mohan's career spiraling downwards, Jaya's "career" as wife also falls in jeopardy, for: "wasn't he my profession, my career, my livelihood?"(75). After all, Jaya had sought fulfillment as "a woman who had scrubbed and cleaned and taken an inordinate pride . . . even in a toilet free from stains and smells" (13). The monsters of housekeeping, the "gadgets, glassware . . . mahogany elephants" inhabiting their carefully furnished Churchgate home suddenly seem to loosen their hold on Jaya. The juxtaposition of modern implements and traditional artifacts, the controlled placement of objects, and the dominant ethic of orderliness that characterize her middle-class existence are now radically displaced and disoriented.

The glossy commercials spreading across the screen in the city's cinema halls had faciliated Jaya's internalization of her role as a dutiful and happy mother and wife. "Those cosy, smiling, happy families in their gleaming homes" (3) produce motherhood and wifeliness as consumable commodities in the big city. The advertisements, preceding the cinema's popular and raucous music that had once been prohibited to Jaya for being too "wicked", aim to create the effect of normalcy for the middle-class viewer, while seeking to ascribe agency to the act of making consumer choices. The strategic sequencing of the advertisements enables a bracketing of the more unruly content of the feature films to follow, and represents the distinctions between public and private, high and low culture, as relentlessly re-iterated but equally subject to destabilization in the swirl of images that make up the city.

Thus the ideological effect of keeping up appearances emerges as crisis, reflected in the uneasy and unstable equivalence assumed between economic success and the ability to keep one's home clean, for instance. Mohan's "passion for neatness and order" (12) fuels and marks his desire for upward mobility and metropolitanism, even as it ironically exposes the corruption that makes such success possible. On the other hand, the disorderly and unkempt homes of Saptagiri define a provincialism that is saturated with its own set of moral connotations that camouflage actually existing economic disparities. For India's middle classes, whose children abandon the city for American suburbs, flattened into a uniform image of "bacteria-free, prosperous suburbs" (42), the familial code is rearranged or broken up by these new migrations as new economic and social relations are forged in Bombay with those coming in and those going out.

What is also to be noted is that in response to the dominant construction of the home as the space of bourgeois values anchored in consumption, spatial order and social reproduction, the narrative appeals to a fading nationalist discourse that rests on a repudiation of commercialization and economic aspiration. In contrast to her husband's consumerist fantasies, Jaya recalls the slogan of the Gandhian era—"Simple living and high thinking" (60). Those words are from an irrecoverable era. Figures of corruption now pervade the institutions of postcolonial India—union officials thrive on bribes from industrialists and corrupt business deals finance a new geography of "bungalows that have mushroomed on the outskirts of the city" (23). But most importantly, there is the shadow of corruption within her own home in the figure of Mohan. It is this moment of political, economic and social *transition* that the novel so effectively captures—from an idealistic nationalist period that nevertheless seemed to stabilize gendered social roles and the rural-urban divide, to the presaging of a new economic, ethical and social order in which a corporate man is the figure of corruption and his wife the source of new gendered anxieties—that allows it to be read as a properly feminist articulation of the postcolonial city.

Threatening Classes

The novel narrates how private spaces of the home and the street are both sites of constantly negotiated social relations and self-making. The "diverse" sounds of Bombay and its "magic(al)" street sights of "teeming life . . . the mobs, the brawls, the drunkards . . . processions" (54), of beggars and of refugees, "those sad, defeated people who poured into Bombay from the barren countryside" (72), produce a "sense of being invaded, not just by sounds, but by a multitude of people and their emotions as well" (56). The novel emphasizes not only the movement of sight and sound—of the light and the dark of the city, of the precarious shuffle of migrants and refugees—but the movement of "emotion" itself that allows for the possibility of something like collective solidarity. The city thus exacerbates both the singularity of individual feeling (isolation, alienation) as well as the shared emotion of belonging to the big city.

The novel juxtaposes the state realism of the images in the newsreels (state-sponsored documentary films that preceded the projection of feature films in cinema halls in the decades after independence)—of road constructions and other development "works" that ultimately end in "nothing achieved but statistics in files" (74)—with the ungraspable, unassimilable messy reality of Bombay that consists of never-ending upheavals experienced as strikes, riots, migrations and movements. In a move typical of the novel's plot, the failure of the state to establish control of India's civic spaces is presented through a personal analogy. This is narrated as a disjunctive moment in the story of middle-class mobility and comfort. Jaya's family, ensconced in their car, finds itself uncannily threatened by a beggar on the street. The threat reveals the precariousness of all their possessions, but also the volatility of the class divide in the city. But the beggar never speaks in the scene, only looks. The look of the beggar, like the look of the native in Fanonian terms, destabilizes the power of the middle-class position, if only momentarily.

As the novel plots the unmasking of the bourgeois family (with provincial roots nonetheless), there are hints of violence breaking out in different parts of the city that evoke other memories of what the middle classes term "trouble" in the city. The areas of Lal Bagh and Parel become out of bounds for a woman of Jaya's status.[82] Avoiding these trouble spots involves re-routings and new traffic arrangements. Crucially, the omnipresence of trouble in the city recalls the figure of the striking workers in Lohanagar. What is significant, however, is how differently Jaya and Mohan remember the strike in the steel town:

> But I knew, when Mohan spoke of it, that in Lohanagar that time, unless my memory was playing me false, I had not been frightened. On

the contrary, there had been, as far as I could recall, a peculiar exhila-
ration. It had fascinated me, the thought that there was only a sheet of
glass between me and the shouting, gesticulating, menacing-looking
men I could see through the windscreen of the company car. I had
watched them with a curious detachment. It had been the C.E.'s wife
who had panicked and Mohan who had urgently cried, "Driver, don't
stop, go on, don't slow down, go on". (76)

The car, as object and as space, in both scenes is simultaneously public and
private. The motif of Jaya, the middle-class privileged woman sitting behind a
thin sheet of glass, separated from supposedly violent men (beggars, striking
workers), is one that is re-cited more than once in the novel. It is a decidedly
gendered image in which Jaya is problematically tied to her class position by
being placed in a car, that ultimate symbol of bourgeois mobility and power
in the city, yet one that also sets limits and imprisons in terms of gender.
Yet, instead of remembering fear and horror, Jaya recalls "detachment", an
affect that nevertheless signifies a certain mode of privilege and disconnec-
tion simultaneously. The irony of these repeated scenes unmasks the fact that
the masculinity of the mob, in the prevailing political and economic order,
consists of merely the powerless in terms of class.

The Bombay of *Silence* is thus a simmering city, bubbling with communal
and labor unrest and threatening the city's representational status as the
space of upward mobility and unencumbered freedoms. Jaya's feelings of suf-
focation in the city, however, are predicated as much on the masses of people
who band and disband in tumultuous ways, as on the polarizing effects of
those groups: their emancipatory potential as well as their chauvinistic and
exclusivist agendas. But above all, in her rendering of the postcolonial city as
a conjunctural space, neither the public/outside nor the private/inside can be
hierarchized or superseded.

Solidarity Out of Bounds

For women the very impossibility of separation between the outside and the
inside creates new limits and possibilities. The city stages and creates encounters between women from vastly different social and economic classes. In
particular, it is the story of Jeeja, the domestic servant who is beaten up daily
by an alcoholic, ex–mill worker husband, that provides the larger writerly
challenge for Jaya than the lives of "all those happy women with husbands
in good jobs, men who didn't drink and beat their wives, those fortunate
women . . .—they were of no use" to her (52). Her friendships with women
of her own class consist of exchanging trivialities and are never more than
pretences, never "probe(d) deeper" (48). In contrast, Jaya's affinities with the
domestics and the working-class characters, with whom she shares a gendered position in spite of the class divide, are worked out with painstaking

self-consciousness. It would be easy to dismiss her understanding of affinity and solidarity as an impossibility or as an expression of middle-class liberal guilt, given the constraints of class and status that circumscribe her movements in the city. But my reading suggests that the novel's aim is to precisely work through the challenges of figuring gendered solidarity in the city across and between class and religious divides that have been foundational to modernist and postcolonial understandings of cities.

The issue of gender solidarity is also worked out through the question of political affiliation within the polarized space of the city. In doing so, the novel attempts to articulate political "identities" with private "subjectivities". Thus when her son Rahul asks of his parents' political affiliations as the family watches a street procession, Jaya's reply of "nothing", she suspects later, becomes the cause of her son's teenage cynicism (50). For Jaya and Mohan it was important that: "we did not speak of what we had seen", of "the vague disquietude of the afternoon", and the slogans of total revolution (55). Whereas the novel does not provide specific details of the particular procession the family witnesses, it nevertheless locates it in the turbulent decade from the late 1970s to late 1980s. This was the decade of a radical shift in Bombay's political and social economy, marking the end of trade unionism and political mobilization around questions of industrial labor. The social fallout of the new conjuncture is experienced as catastrophe by both Jaya and Jeeja—Jaya's husband is embroiled in a financial scandal and she ends up losing her family, even as Jeeja's husband vents his frustration as a jobless worker on his wife's body.

The novel deliberately eschews both the narrative of a return to normalcy (the scenario of Mohan coming back to his wife's arms and regaining respectability as a proper citizen of the nation), and a narrative of total destruction (in which the female protagonist commits suicide or faces death, as is the case with *Voyage in the Dark*). Jaya returns to the streets of Bombay for signs of hope and regeneration. Although she recovers her voice in the end, ending "that long silence", it is not the singular, authentic voice of the artist triumphant over all odds. The voice is that of a woman who has come to an understanding of her city and her situation, of the new maps she needs to draw in order to make sense of its gendered social reality. The novel acknowledges the incompleteness of affiliation and solidarity, and the limits of those when it is imposed through the liberal will of a middle-class woman. Jaya remarks that in the end, it is the servant's daughter, Manda, who emerges as the true "child of Bombay" (164), thus articulating a different kind of belonging to the city, one in which a poor servant's girl can make, if only still symbolically, claims to home and citizenship.

The novel represents Bombay as thwarting any understanding of its space in terms of nostalgia for an unreconstructed home and city. A few years later, in real life, Bombay would witness a total conflagration of sociality as religious identities and social localities got violently entwined, producing a most uncivil drawing of boundaries between the city's inhabitants. In the wake of the 1993 riots, Bombay's pluralities emerged as its incongruities and its catastrophes. Ultimately, the political and social space of Bombay in this narrative is already a "scandal", an increasingly inhospitable territory that has nevertheless to be claimed for a politics and a narrative of difference and belonging.

That Long Silence interrogates the ways in which urban space is constitutive in literary representations of postcolonial identity and citizenship. By staging the (im)possibility of community, solidarity and of women's agency in a deeply fragmented Bombay, the novel presses for rethinking the postcolonial city. In not ultimately necessitating the return of the postcolonial male to the woman/home/nation that remain stable and fixed, the novel both mocks that ending as false and points to the fissures in imagining the contemporary city as a controllable and essential space of masculinity and modernity. What it offers instead is an imaginative space in which women can inhabit the postcolonial city by forging difficult modes of sociality and solidarity.

Articulated Lives

Vikram Chandra offers his reading of the gendered class divide and the politics of solidarity in Bombay in a very different register in his short story "Shakti". Rendered through the semi-anonymous male storyteller and the various strands of gossip that circulate in the city, the story tells the tale of two women who exist across a vast class divide, but whose lives become inextricably linked by and in the city itself. The story of Sheila Bijlani, the beautiful daughter of an ordinary shopkeeper, a refugee of the Partition from Lahore who dares to dream of wealth and power in the big Indian metropolis, and of Ganga, a working-class woman who does part-time house-work for Sheila and who dreams big dreams in the big city, too, is enmeshed in the transformations taking place in the city itself. Both their lives, although framed within the limits of family, class and gender difference, are marked by a dogged determination to push these frames into unfamiliar territory and to query the possibilities of fashioning a new feminist subjectivity and solidarity within the space of an increasingly neo-liberal and chauvinist city. Ironically, a globalizing Bombay both makes that sense of a new political subjectivity possible and inhibits it. Chandra's Bombay is a city of the 1990s, in the aftermath of the 1980s' textile strikes and mill closures, and in the present of a rapid globalization of the economy and a simultaneous communalization of city politics and social identities. This radical shift from the Bombay that Deshpande describes is analyzed in greater detail in the last section of this chapter.

The logic of global finance that imperceptibly pervades the city is pitted against the set of "rational" choices available to the individual women in the story who have to negotiate family and community pressures. Sheila is the figure in the city that embodies a collective desire for success and material enrichment. The narratorial voice that assumes a collective "we" tells us: "We used to see Sheila then in a flash as a car roared around the curve on Teen Batti, and we would sigh because somewhere there was a life that was perfect and wonderful" (34). Sheila's life story then is not just that of an individual but the story of the community and of the city.

The sense of aura around Sheila exists in direct proportion to the ease with which she climbs the ladder of success; it has the effect of drawing out "the venom up and down the coast of Bombay" (36). Her ferocious political will and ambition rides roughshod over the petty jealousies and rivalries of the aspiring classes and of those in possession of old money. So when Sheila settles in marriage for the rather plain-looking Bijlani with an engineering degree from the not-so-cosmopolitan Utah, she confounds the social calculus of marriage, desire and upward mobility. But the choice allows Sheila to begin to remake him as a highly successful industrialist, starting him up with her own money saved while she worked as an airhostess. The magic of their economic prosperity in globalizing Bombay is not noticed as unfolding over time: together "they suddenly reappeared with an enormous flat on Malabar Hill" (35), one of Bombay's poshest and most expensive areas.

The social milieu of "the hill" resisted the overnight appearance of Sheila, clearly viewed as an upstart, a woman out of place, tells the narratorial voice that is both distant and intimate with the city simultaneously (36). The rivalry between Dolly Boatwalla and Sheila Bijlani takes centerstage in the "masala-grinding" of the community, unraveling "histories of friendship and betrayal" (51). Chandra hones in on the particularities of the social signs of this particular class of Bombayites in which class pretensions must trump all other forms of social affiliation. In the face of Sheila's sharp wit and her new status, Dolly's old money and the confidence of serving "soggy" sandwiches without self-consciousness, her "careless imperfection" that "had nothing to do with perseverance or intelligence" but "took generations" to achieve (41), are threatened. After all, the Boatwallas' land had been bought when land cost nothing, whereas the Bijlanis' new wealth is the outcome of sheer grit and business acumen in the context of loosening state control over real estate prices and commerce. Dolly Boatwalla's physical height and her ruthlessness, her way of commanding a room, the "delicate way she patted her pursed lips with a napkin after she ate pastries" (37), as well as her cruelty towards those less sophisticated are pitted against Sheila's sharp features, her firm and crisp closing of the door after the women leave her company, and, most crucially, her ability to relate to Ganga, the domestic servant, who provides a mirror to Sheila's own desires and aspirations evoking the sense that "something had started", something new and sinuous and infinitely improvised that would unsettle older relations and modes of belonging to the city.

The story cuts between the rarefied world of the Hill residents to that of Ganga, a short, wiry woman who

> worked, as nearly as Sheila could tell, in another dozen houses up and down the hill, and she sped from one to another without a pause the entire day, after which she stood in a local train for an hour and fifteen minutes to get out to Andheri, where she lived. It had taken Sheila six months to get her to eat lunch, which she did squatting in a corner of the kitchen and holding a plate directly in front of her face for greater efficiency. (42)

The frenetic pace of Ganga's working day is detailed here, in which every moment is internally clocked, rationalized and accounted for. Spatially, she traverses the homes of the rich and the powerful, even as socially she is an outcaste, taking backdoors to work invisibly inside the big mansions and lavish apartments of her employers. Ganga's clipped speech, her tightened *dupatta* around her waist, the way in which she "smoothed her hair once in a single movement, tucking back and tightening all at once" (47), her manner of eating with the plate close to her mouth, all indicate the temporal and spatial economy that structures her life. The storyteller tells us her life in surprising detail, given his own class position that like Sheila's would likely be ignorant of the precise location and materiality of a servant's life. Widow of a Marxist mill worker who was killed in a union fight, Ganga works hard to make a living and struggles to imagine a different life for her child. Her own movement in the city, when not working in the affluent districts, presents a different plane of upward mobility—she moves with her meager belongings from a single room shack on a narrow lane, surrounded by neighbors from the same village in the Ghats near Poona, to a plot of land two stops up on the Western line, where she builds her own *kholi*.

Chandra's story attempts to narrate the possibilities of friendship and solidarity between such differently located women in the city, who are brought together initially in a relationship of employer-employee, but whose desires to exceed their social situation run like parallel lines. The relationship itself grows in unexpected directions and ways: "For the first year that they had known each other, Ganga had been courteous but dry, her face always expressionless and impossible to read" (42). In fact, the story makes no attempts to invade or inhabit the private mental spaces of either Sheila or Ganga. What is revealed is a particular outward affect that seemingly springs from a voluminous inner life that seeks to survive, gain control of and make self in the city.

The terms of this impossible relationship between Sheila and Ganga are explored through the metaphor of a loan, underscoring the ways in which economic relations structure all other relations in Bombay, the city of capital. When Ganga takes a loan from Sheila, it is given without a fuss but its terms are clearly laid out—it is to be paid back in monthly installments.

This contract is a co-authored one. But the loan exceeds the terms of the written contract and the logic of an economic calculus. For what cannot be subsumed in this logic is the gendered social relationship crisscrossed with class difference, as the impossibility of fixing value on what is exchanged between the two women remains central to the narrative. In return for the (in)calculable loan that Sheila gives Ganga (incalculable because its effects could not be easily or only measured in terms of costs and benefits), Ganga gives an unreturnable loan when she delivers the business secret to Sheila, a secret that would make Sheila's position unassailable in the social hierarchy of Malabar Hill and provide her unquestioned superiority over her most threatening rival, Dolly. The loan then is best returned through the sharing of a secret sisterhood that is nevertheless materially entrenched. In this encounter, we see the tremendously precarious nature of loan and gift when understood in terms of relations between women of completely different social and economic classes.

The idea of the loan and its analogue the secret provides us with a different way of reading the question of feminist solidarity in the story. It is no longer a question of empathy or liberal guilt that might be seen in Jaya's experience of Bombay in *That Long Silence,* but one where the economic realm becomes the site of both the most violent inequalities and of the possibility of freedom from earlier divides of gender and class.

The story makes clear, however, that the economic realm is always already articulated with the social and the political. It explores the various, unstable meanings of money and wealth—as currency, as real estate, as metaphor, as structuring relation—and its imbrication in the very form of the city and the social relationships made possible therein. For Sheila, the metaphor of "liquidity" for cash was a

> strange phrase, because money was, if anything hard, impersonal. But now she saw how it could be like a stream, unpredictable and underground, and she was going to turn it into a torrent that would flow up the hill instead of down, crumbling the bloody Boatwalla gate like paper. It was going to burst out of the hillside under the mansion like a fountain from the interior rock.(62)

Money here is imagined as intertwined in the landscape itself, having an underground source, dark and invisible, but that can be forced aboveground, as a torrent promising to wash away weaker adversaries. But if money can be imagined as a force of nature, then it is also imagined as having magical qualities that exceed the terms of nature and culture. The hard world of numbers in account books assume metaphysical qualities, as in the evocation of *shunya* or zero as symbolizing a simultaneous nothingness and infinity. The accruing of capital is both at the same time—the source of infinite power and of metaphysical meaninglessness. In Bombay, where the power of money was always magical, a globalizing finance capital regime produces its own mysterious narratives based on speculation, secret, rumor and trickery.

The Gift of Friendship

The tale culminates in two marriages even as it began with one (Sheila's), providing the story with an air of narrative continuity and social repro-duction understood as a continuous cycle as both female protagonists have their offspring settling down in marriage. The imbrication of mar-riage in culture and tradition as much as in the capitalist economy of the city that spans both acts of survival and of endless accumulation is central to this story of love and be-longing in Bombay. Ganga sells her *kholi* to finance the long-dreamt-of (as in Bollywood) big wedding for her daughter Asha. The wedding symbolizes the culmination of a lifetime of desiring social status and dreams of making it in the city. Ganga's custom-ary gift to Sheila at the wedding (a return gift traditionally given to all close family and friends) finally seals the friendship—it is no longer simply describable in terms of patronage and clientelism; the gift in fact seeks to unsettle social hierarchy as a permanent or natural state of affairs.

Meanwhile, the narrator notes that another wedding has been orga-nized—the ceremony for lovers Roxanne Boatwalla and Sanjeev Bijlani crystallizes the reconciliation of not just business rivals, but of religion and community, of love and longing. As Dolly and Sheila walk hand in hand at the wedding party, there is "a great moment of silence when nobody knew what to do with each other" (74). The story of this union between the offspring of erstwhile social rivals is ultimately just one more story in a city dominated with news of business mergers, loan scandals, the fall of one government and the rise of yet another politician. After all, what seemingly matters most and least simultaneously in Bombay, the class divide, seems resilient.

As love seals business, we also learn that in spite of all the expenses incurred in her daughter's wedding, Ganga eventually buys a large shed in Dharavi, Bombay's largest slum colony, where she plans to set up a cloth reclamation factory. Ganga's story ends with her transformation from worker to an entrepreneur in her own right, a right that is also a claim to belonging in the city.

It is at this point that the narrative self-consciously withdraws from a full-fledged public comment about what was to follow in the city. The narrator encapsulates the oncoming ravaging of the city by the 1993 riots and genocidal attacks on Muslims as: "and what happened after that we all know", "but that's another story" (74). Meanwhile, what Ganga and Sheila's story has allowed to surface is the simultaneous precarity of social relations in the city, predicated as they are on ever-turbulent tides of global capital, and of the possibilities and limits of gendered solidarity that might offer a different mode of citizenship in the postcolonial city.

Widening Spaces

If both Deshpande and Chandra conclude their stories on a note of ambivalence that strikes despair and hope simultaneously on the question of feminist solidarity in the city, Umrigar's more recent novel *The Space between Us* delivers a somewhat more sobering view of the possibilities of such solidarity in neo-liberal Bombay. The crisscrossed patterns of gender and class relations in the big city that are elaborated in the novel are products both of older social and political relations of patronage and welfarism and the new drive towards individualism, self-sufficiency and globality. Departing from the conventions of the middle-class feminist novel such as Deshpande's *That Long Silence*, Umrigar's novel narrates the story not from the perspective of Sera, the upper-middle-class widow who is one of the novel's two protagonists, but from that of her sixty-five-year-old servant Bhima. Even as the novel's ideological milieu seems resiliently bourgeois, it boldly delves into and deftly constructs the consciousness of its subaltern protagonist to whom belongs the story as a whole. Thus narratorially at least the novel seeks to undo the class asymmetry of the archetypal servant/mistress story.

Umrigar's novel self-consciously presents a poor, illiterate woman's relationship to the city not merely in terms of its literal cartography, of the smells and the sights of the city's sprawling slum districts, of the social relations that mark life in the slum (where caste and religious divides hold strong) and produce it as life lived in the city, but through a complex emotional engagement in which the external, material city becomes the emotional landscape of Bhima's inner life. Even as the representational space of the city contains Bhima's everyday life, its mind-numbing tedium ("the trials that await her today and the next and the next", 5), it also registers dissonance in the ways in which the city also enables her to eke out some "free" time, time that Bhima spends at the beach, alone, with her family in happier times, or later with her grand-daughter Maya. Thus both kinds of times co-exist not only in the elite world of its prosperous inhabitants, but in the world of the subaltern as well in the city. It is "free" time, at home or in the city, time that is not entirely encumbered by work hours that imbues the world of subaltern existence, its bare life, with social and political consciousness. Bhima's sheer exultation in experiencing the city—"she misses the pageantry at the seaside . . . Bhima had loved leaving behind the grim isolation of her hut in the basti and melting into this amorphous, fluid crowd" (297)—belies the notion that the city as a place of pleasure is a distinctively elite one. This stands in stark contrast to her husband Gopal's disappointment with the city that is "mistress to many, wife to none . . . this harlot city" (249), one that leads him to return to the village with his son.

Such a consciousness of time and social relations is distilled most sharply in the relationship between Bhima and Sera. Bhima wonders:

Do the rich think like this? . . . She is acquainted with Serabai mostly through her actions and routines, Bhima now realizes. She knows that her mistress likes her tea light and milky, that she doesn't like starch on her laundered clothes. (307)

In a key scene that underscores the everyday as the site where class and gender relations are reproduced, Sera experiences considerable difficulty in peeling onions for cooking breakfast, the most mundane of activities in an Indian kitchen. She is of course put to this task in the first place because Bhima is late for work. But Bhima is not only adept at this routine cooking task, she knows how to keep Sera's house in order. What unsettles this seemingly settled social order of the home is Bhima's unwitting access to Sera's emotional trauma as a victim of domestic violence. Bhima's knowledge of Sera's pain is not gained through words, but understood through the dampness she finds on Sera's pillows and the half-concealed bruises she glimpses on her body: "this unspoken language, this intimacy that has developed between them over the years" (17) does not however mitigate Sera's physical revulsion towards Bhima's slum living that taints not only Bhima's body and the spaces that surround it, but also threatens to contaminate Sera's own pristine existence:

> It was one thing to drive past the slums that had sprung up all around the city. It was another thing to walk the narrow byways that led into the sprawling slum colony—to watch your patent leather shoes get splashed with the murky, muddy water that gathered in still pools on the ground. (113)

But as the narrative proceeds it is made clear that it is not only the patent leather shoes that get muddied—the stench, the poverty and the degradation of poor lives haunt the lives of those who seem to be above it all.

The drama of Bhima and Sera's complex friendship across the class divide and their solidarity as women who have suffered emotional tribulations takes place as part of the larger tableau of lives lived in the neoliberal city. Bhima muses:

> In the old days, at least the women were spared the elbowing and the jostling that occurred each time a bus appeared like a mythical beast at the stop. But in today's Bombay, it was everybody for himself, and the frail, the weak, the young, and the old entered the overflowing buses at their own peril. Bhima felt as if she barely recognized the city anymore—something snarling and mean and cruel had been unleashed in it. She could see the signs of this new meanness everywhere: slum children tied firecrackers to the tails of the stray dogs and then laughed and clapped with glee as the poor animals ran around in circles, going mad with fear. Affluent college students went berserk if a five-year-old

beggar child smudged the windows of their gleaming BMWs and Hondas . . . It was as if the city was mad with greed and hunger, power and impotence, wealth and poverty. (92–93)

The city with "gleaming BMWs and Hondas" is clearly the city that has embraced neo-liberal capitalism in the aftermath of state sponsored welfarism. It is also a city where a generalized anti-Muslim feeling is rife, and Bhima is not immune to such prejudice. As Sera reads accounts of the horrors of communal violence in which the city's Muslims have been targeted pointedly, she also educates Bhima into the liberal values of secularism. Bhima's solidarity with "an entire breed of Bombayites (such as the balloonwallas and the earwax removers and the rag collectors)" who "clung to the promise of this great metropolis by the skins of their teeth" (98) is what ultimately allows her to embrace the secular ethic on her own terms, from her position of deprivation.

The novel best exemplifies this in the cameo role it gives to the Afghan balloon seller whose loneliness in Bombay resonates with Bhima's own sense of alienation. In a moving moment towards the very end of the novel, the balloon seller transmutes for Bhima into a figure of the god Krishna, his "brown fingers" that ran down "the slick bodies of the swollen balloons, like Krishna's fluid fingers as he played his flute" (314). But he is also a man who has few worldly possessions: "Empty handed, he had built a world" (314). Bhima's story also concludes with this sense of possessionlessness in the city. Having picked up her meager belongings from Sera's home and placed them in a cardboard box, Bhima decides to leave the box so that "someone else can pick through its contents" (312). This is the novel's final repudiation of the globalizing, materialistic, frenetic neo-liberal Bombay, in the grip of classes such as the affluent business executives like Sera's son-in-law Viraaf, who has seduced and impregnated Bhima's grand-daughter, and who, in a bid to maintain honour through secrecy forces Sera's hand to dismiss Bhima from her service to the household.

But like the other two novels under consideration, Umrigar's narrative also ends in hope that is displaced on to a young woman. For Bhima, too, will face "a new day. She will face it tomorrow, for Maya's sake." (320). In the teeming, gigantic metropolis, tomorrow is of course both "a promise and a threat" (321).

From Bombay to Mumbai

I want to close this chapter by signaling some of the major transformations that have taken place in the city since the heady days of independence when Bombay was the "dream city" of the nation, but also more specifically since Deshpande's fictional rendering of a post-Nehruvian Bombay, to its current practices and politics of representation as registered by Chandra and

Umrigar. These shifts and transformations indicate the possibilities and the limits within the project of the postcolonial city that this book set out to explore and analyze. They also pose a series of challenges to the question of postcolonial feminist citizenship that must be integral to the project of the postcolonial city as a site of justice.

The Shiv Sena government that came to state power in the 1990s officially changed Bombay's name to Mumbai in 1995 after a long popular campaign to indigenize the city. Many believe that the city has hit upon hard times since Shiv Sena's rule and has experienced a subsequent decline in the larger political sphere. Once the financial capital of India and the center of its cosmopolitan modernity, Mumbai in the twenty-first century is a city facing a downward trend in real estate, with economic figures indicating that there is now more "official" money in circulation in New Delhi than in Mumbai. Global finance capital has also found other sites for investment in cities such as Bangalore (now known as India's Silicon Valley), Pune (once a back-water to Bombay's finance industry) and Hyderabad (unofficially referred to in high-tech circles as Cyberabad), and, as Achin Vanaik points out, "production has either ceased or shifted to the lower-cost towns of the hinterland—Nagpur, Aurangabad, Nasik".[83] Even the output of films in Mumbai, the center of the Hindi film industry popularly known as Bollywood, declined in the mid-1990s as more films were produced in Madras (Chennai) and Hyderabad.[84]

Various factors are attributed to this downturn—the attractiveness of other more disciplined yet flexible sites of the global economy, Mumbai's decaying infrastructure, its growing ethnic chauvinism, the breakdown of "law and order" in the city, and the growing strangle-hold of Mumbai's underworld mafia that saw a "spectacular rise" in the aftermath of "the collapse of the Mumbai textile industry in the 1980s and the urban despair it caused".[85] Ironically, the Mumbai mafia has produced its own forms of globalization by establishing transnational networks involving a variety of illegal enterprises through smuggling, piracy, narcotics, prostitution, construction, real estate, politics and Bollywood, that nevertheless have had very specific local effects and have caused generalized panic. The mafia uses multiple strategies of extortion, protection rackets, abductions and contract killings, and uses *hawala* or illegal money transfers to circumvent the official economy of the city.

The horror of the massacres of Muslims in the 1992–1993 riots that destroyed the older cosmopolitan Bombay was followed by a series of bombings in the heart of the financial district of Bombay, including at the Bombay Stock Exchange that killed 250 people. The bomb attacks were thought to be the "retaliatory" work of a transnational group of Muslim gangsters led by Dawood Ibrahim, who is based in Karachi and Dubai, and is rumored to be in cahoots with Pakistan's Inter Services Intelligence Agency. The city's underground network of criminal gangsters was once considered to be secular, but after the 1992–1993 riots it seems to have been split along religious lines and provincial loyalties (many of these gangsters are from small towns in north India), even while it has become increasingly transnational.[86] These transnational syndicates are seen as having "far-reaching consequences for national security", with the state tending to prefer Hindu dons to Muslim ones![87] This underground world of crime that includes politicians (who use the mafia's money and muscle power to ensure electoral victory for their supporters and for themselves) and builders in the construction industry (who use the mafia's violent tactics to secure land deals, facilitate evictions, etc.) has close links with Bollywood, as well as with the cricketing world.[88] These particular corruption links extend from Mumbai to London to Johannesburg to South East Asia and New York City.

Bollywood's commercial reality is that it has seen an unprecedented financial downturn in the last few years—in fact, movies that actually make money have been few and far between.[89] These losses have been attributed to the rising cost of film production, the onslaught of cable networks, television serials and pirated DVDs, and to the stunning criminalization of its financial transactions. Filmmakers who have been losing money have thus borrowed money "unofficially" from the underground mafia that is flush with cash.[90] In return, top film stars and producers pay hefty amounts in protection money to the mafia in the wake of famous, daredevil murders of key figures in the film industry.[91] The underworld bosses now dictate the cast and plot lines of many films.[92] This relationship with Bollywood has been a blessing for the underworld gangsters who use investments in films to convert a part of their wealth into "white" money.

Although upbeat numbers at the Stock Exchange every now and then open up an avenue for Mumbai's incorporation into the Hindu Right's now defeated slogan of "India Is Shining", the fact is that Mumbai is no more the source of that light. The flight of capital to India's new high-tech cities, and the flight of culture and cosmopolitanism into provincialisms due to routine attacks on artists, accompanied by the burning of books and banning of films, all indicate that Mumbai is the crystallization of the right-wing culturalist and political agenda to provincialize the city.[93] The moment of provincialization is thus the latest moment of Mumbai's modernity.[94]

Ironically, it is only now that Bombay is being considered seriously as a global city.[95] Comparisons with Singapore and Shanghai are routine in the mediatized national discourse. A further irony is well-noted by Achin Vanaik in his account of the meaning and significance of the decision to host the 2004 World Social Forum in an "indifferent" Mumbai, a city already committed to neo-liberalism even while struggling to deliver the goods promised by that project.[96] As theorizations of the global city have linked the demise of nation-based trajectories of development to an opening up of possibilities of citizenship through the introduction of non-state actors (as evidenced in the "joint presence" of new corporate global actors alongside refugees and immigrants, none of whom can be subsumed under nationhood), this link is supposed to have facilitated the formation of a new kind of politics that cuts across the old North/South divide.[97]

But in Mumbai, we see that the globalization of capital has unleashed contradictory forces of provincialization. Globalization is no longer the necessary pre-condition for cosmopolitanism. Far from unbundling nation-state and territory, we can see how the nation-state is being defined in more exclusivist and territorial terms. Periodic resurgent movements to expel north Indians from Bombay further signify that within the nation-state itself territory is being defined in exclusivist terms. Of course this too can be explained at least partly by the fact that the Bombay street has become more cosmopolitan and by extension more national than ever before, thus raising anxieties and fears of the local or native Maharashtrians. This is undoubtedly a subaltern cosmopolitanism consisting of street vendors, hawkers, informal laborers in the construction industry, taxi drivers and others who bring their own accents, cultures and modes of survival to the city. P. Sainath outlines a world that consists of a ferocious struggle for survival at the very bottom of the social scale for the over one million migrants who came to Mumbai from outside the state in the last decade alone, even as employment in the state in both public and private sectors fell and agriculture is in ruins.[98]

Whereas contemporary postmodern and Left analyses of the city maintain a binary opposition between the city and nation, and maintain as well an enduring faith in the progress narrative (the idea that things are in general becoming better as they become more global), we see how the state and nation are articulated with urban form in both provincial and transnational networks. Recent struggles that have involved the forced eviction of poor migrants from Bombay highlight the unevenness of economic development, as well as the national site upon which political struggles are waged. Both of these are glossed over within the commodified celebration of global cities. Indeed, global capital has been all too eager to embrace the idea of the global city.

All this goes to show that the "case" of Mumbai does not exactly fit the global city narrative. Attendant with this discrepancy is the tendency to gloss over the overlapping colonial and neo-colonial histories of cities such as Bombay, histories that opened them up for economic and cultural exploitation from the North, and that unleashed the contradictions emerging from uneven development within globalization.

Contemporary forms of global capital and citizenship—articulated in the space of the postcolonial city—are offering different challenges to our very being in the city. Capital's visible, tangible, material forms, and its invisible, speculative, mysterious flows through the space of the city (crisscrossing between the multiple layers of the official and the unofficial economies) exist in productive tension with each other and with citizenship in terms of who belongs, moves into and through the city, in both official and unofficial capacities. Crucially, both capital and citizenship are dependent on intersecting economies of representation. The materialization of value in bodies, property, money on the one hand, and the anxious gap between reality and image, legal status and non-status, use and speculation on the other, produce contradictions that have become key to the constitution of the global cities of the South, releasing great uncertainties about the direction this particular political moment is going to take. What we see in the transmutation of Bombay into Mumbai is an example of such a contradictory articulation in which the globalization of capital confronts the provincialization of citizens within the postcolonial state.

If the urgent political task is to make sense of how both the Hindu Right and transnational capital have achieved a necessarily incomplete hegemony over Bombay's image and reality, it is equally urgent to construct alternatives. The somewhat hasty fabrication of an earlier universalism (as in Deshpande's narrative) needs now to be refashioned in the context of an ever more careless celebration of the global marketplace. Our work, both political and intellectual (and across that potent divide), too, must answer to the new political configurations of our times which do not allow either for the easy recuperation and celebration of the older socialist and nationalist Utopias, nor for an outright rejection of the possibilities of decolonization and global solidarity (as in Chandra and Umrigar's narrative).

Finally, and at the center, there is the question of women in contemporary globalized/provincialized Mumbai. What must be the stake of postcolonial feminism in urbanizing globalization? On the one hand, there is the need for a rigorous critique and opposition to ever new global restructurings of capital and labor, in which women's labor, whether in sweatshops, as domestics, or in sexual trafficking, is being subjected to new forms of exploitation, even as resurgent conservative patriarchies seek to drive Bombay's "bar girls" out of business. On the other hand, there is the necessity of keeping the question of universality and global solidarity alive. Fictional spaces, such as those created by Deshpande, Chandra and Umrigar, certainly allow us to at least begin to imagine a feminist postcolonial city that is a conjuncture in terms of both crisis and transformation.

4 Conclusion
Situated Solidarities

London, Take Two

With 7.2 million people, 33 boroughs, 250,000 businesses and a £116,444 million economy, London has extraordinary potential. Regeneration and innovation are at the heart of London's future.

—London Development Agency's "London Pride" advertisement (2003)

In a piece that Monica Ali, author of the much-acclaimed and popular novel *Brick Lane* (2003), wrote for *The Guardian Weekend Review*, she narrates her attempts to re-trace the footsteps of her predecessor Virginia Woolf's walks in London in the 1930s.[1] If Woolf's view on the Thames Walk, the site of the docks that were the nerve center of British imperial trade, had been marked by domes, church spires and factory chimneys, Ali's perspective on the twenty-first-century city is emptied of those traces of twentieth-century industry. No longer are there the images of men (porters, merchant seamen) working—lifting, loading, and hoisting goods and things (timber, iron, grain, wine, sugar, paper, fruit) gathered from the peripheries, "the plains, from the forests, from the pastures of the whole world"; instead, the figures dominating Ali's view are tourists, joggers and commuters zigzagging alongside and in between "gleaming office blocks" and luxury apartment buildings. Even the sound of the city is starkly different—in place of the industrial "roar" that had engulfed Woolf's auditory senses, there is the "new, noiseless commerce" of men in suits talking interminably into their mobile phones, and overheard fragments of conversations about deals made and thwarted. Now the workers come from all over the world, but they work mostly invisibly in hotels, restaurants and office buildings, in the ever-expanding service industry that underpins this city of global finance capital.

Ali's London is multi-cultural in the bodies that populate it as much as it is in the goods it has historically swallowed up from and spewed out on to the rest of the world. Perhaps it is this new sense of a city in which difference becomes yet another good (human beings as capital) that prevents Ali from ever offering a remark on her own gendered (female), ethnicized (British Asian) and classed (upper-class) body walking about in London. Establishing a direct lineage with Woolf and her meanderings in high imperial London in the early decades of the twentieth century, which also provided the starting point for this book, Ali traverses a postcolonial, post-imperial and global city that affords a kind of "flexible citizenship", to use Aihwa Ong's term, to the city's global elites who crisscross national boundaries with relative ease while those who are forced to flee across borders to find a home exist in the unseen but policed spaces of the city. In both cases, lives are built around mobile homes, or homes that are not tied to the contingencies of older notions of belonging.

On the eve of the release of his film *Dirty Pretty Things* that documented and narrativized the lives of new (il)legal immigrants in the underbelly of London, Stephen Frears had remarked on how London's contemporary anxieties about its identity and status in a globalizing world have "nothing to do with empire".[2] On this view, the imperial geography of an earlier period no longer provides obvious clues to the pathways traversed by twenty-first-century migrants. New, ever more eccentric routes emerge in the wake of such historical transformations as those unleashed by decolonization and the landing of the Windrush that brought the first wave of migrants from the Caribbean in the middle of the twentieth century. More recently, the reconfiguration of a new Europe has resulted in some borders that are opened up even as others are closed off. The latest inflow of Eastern Europeans as sex-workers and domestic workers, as decorators and builders, as taxi drivers and corner shop assistants, or as underworld millionaires emerging from capitalism's erstwhile peripheries, is attributed not to the earlier outposts of empire, but to the newly constituted centers and margins of Europe itself.

For Ali the history of empire might not be so easily erased: instead it provides a productive contradiction in the ways in which in London "the weight of history lies heavy, and in an instant is cast off". In the twenty-first-century global city, history is experienced as simultaneously weighty and light—a palpable burden in one instance and a mere wispy imagining in another. In either case, for Ali, as for Woolf in another time, colonial history operates as an ever-present spectral double of post-imperial London, even as the very idea of the postcolonial city provided an earlier imperial city with intimations of both mortality and reinvention.

From London to Londonistan

"London got its groove back", declared *Vanity Fair* in its March 1997 issue, indicating that the city was ready to take on the global imagination with a vengeance in the new millennium. It underlined the idea of London's return to pre-eminence, of getting "its groove back" after at least two decades of economic and social crises. Such a sense of return necessitates a reading of London's long history as the site of imperial capitalist accumulation and as the container of the racial, ethnic, class and gender differences produced and congealed in the course of that history, one that this book set out to address.

London's assignation from at least the 1980s onwards as a city that exemplifies multiculturalism, defined broadly as a set of state, civic and popular practices that involve surviving, belonging and creating forms of citizenship across racial, gender and ethnic differences, must further be read alongside the geographical unevenness of global capitalism, indeed of neo-liberal capitalism, its latest formation as materialized in the space of the twenty-first-century city.

The declaration of London being "cool" (as expressed in the "Cool Britannia" phenomenon) coincided with the purported demise of Thatcherism and the end of a long period of Conservative rule in Britain. In actual fact New Labour's Third Way was premised on a historic compromise with the Thatcherite commitment to neo-liberalism. The Third Way entailed an emptying out of the political into a management-oriented, hyper-mediatized celebrity culture concentrated in a constantly escalating race for consumerism and high living in one of the world's most expensive cities. Thus living in London in the opening years of the twenty-first century has been akin to living in a bubble that floats dangerously above the more brutish reality of regions peripheral to the meanderings of global capital both in and outside the city. Irrespective of political orientation, London administrators aggressively pursue Indian and Chinese business in the interest of London as the quintessential capital city of the world. The upcoming 2012 Olympics to be hosted by London is a significant part of the project to secure the city's place in the new global imaginary, not to mention the arguable economic gains (business, infrastructure, transportation) to the city that will accrue from the hosting of the games. What typically gets elided in the mediatized discourse are the new structurations of urban space (new rail links, neighborhoods linked and de-linked, increasing unevenness of real estate prices, environmental costs) and social relations across class, race and gender lines. As the long drawn-out economic upturn and the late 1990s housing boom is subject to new pressures in an unprecedentedly globalized urban economy, new anxieties about London's future are now being articulated. London's over-dependence on an economy of finance has made it especially vulnerable to the mortgage crisis, speculation and disappearing capital.

This is also the moment when London's governing principle of multiculturalism has turned wobbly. Typically, the divergent narratives of multiculturalism, emanating from state, popular culture, and media discourses, all converged on the question of how it might be possible to survive in, and belong to, the city. In these discourses, London is simultaneously an asylum for the world's beleaguered, an English city coming to terms with a post-imperial world, the world's capital city, and the cultural hub of an increasingly cosmopolitan world culture. But in its most recent re-incarnation as Londonistan, in which the city is imagined as the hub of Islamist extremism, the consensus around multiculturalism is finally seen to be unraveling.[3] On July 7, 2006, on the first anniversary of the London bombings now known as "7/7", the Arabic station Al-Jazeera beamed a video suicide note by the Aldgate station bomber Shehzaad Tanveer. In the video, an unidentified man uses his finger to circle an area on a map of London. Referring to the cross-formation of the 7/7 attacks—north, south, east and west of King's Cross station, Ayman al-Zawahiri's voiceover makes the point that the bombed stations were chosen because they "held symbolic spiritual significance for the crusader west".[4] Al-Zawahiri, reputedly the second in command to Osama bin Laden in the Al Qaeda network, articulates here a counter-imperialist fantasy to rewrite the secular geography of an older empire with a religious one. The Right in its multifarious formations (Islamist; neo-imperial; neo-liberal; ultra-nationalist) articulates different versions of this attempt to occupy spaces of secularism within the contemporary global city and infuse them with legible differences that can nevertheless be assimilated within specific racialized projects of domination. The Christian Church has controversially also supported the view that religious rights should be treated on a par with human rights in the new multicultural nation. Whereas the Islamic Right's project attempts to transform the erstwhile imperial city into a religious one, saturated with religious markers that proclaim Islam as a universal ideology, the ultra-nationalist Right draws attention to the defiling presence of Asians, especially Muslims, on European/English soil, dangling the specter of what Niall Ferguson has termed "Eurabia" as the future of English London.[5] At the same time, the anti-war Left and other departments of the multicultural state, such as the British intelligence agencies, warn against an "encroaching secularism" that is swallowing up the spaces of legitimately expressed, "moderate" religious identities. Multiculturalism is now recast as multi-faithism by the liberal responses to the perceived crisis of multiculturalism in London today.[6]

Asian Women Write London

London's status as a global city is both unquestioned and subject to the tensions besetting the British state in its attempts to tackle, by stabilizing, marking and naming religious and cultural differences in the city within a dominant framework of English national culture and free market capitalism. In the discussion below I offer a reading of the ways in which South Asian women in London (part of the oldest and most visible minority population in the city) have opened up critical spaces for the insertion of the question of postcolonial citizenship within what has historically been the world's pre-eminent imperial city and what has now become the site of contestation of not just different ethnic and racial identities, but of a broader question of what constitutes a right to live in the multicultural city and who has the right to do so.

I want to briefly return to Monica Ali, this time to a scene from her novel *Brick Lane*, in which the protagonist Nazneen, a young lower-middle-class

Bangladeshi woman emerges from her public housing estate in the East End of London and confronts official, high capitalist London.[7] This is how Ali describes Nazneen's first encounter with the city/City (London's financial district):

> Nazneen walked . . . She sensed rather than saw, because she had taken care not to notice. But now she slowed down and looked around her. She looked up at a building as she passed. It was constructed almost entirely of glass, with a few thin rivets of steel holding it together. The entrance was like a glass fan, rotating slowly, sucking people in, wafting others out. Nazneen craned her head back and saw that the glass above became dark as a night pond. The building was without end. Above, somewhere, it crushed the clouds.

In this classic evocation of the moment of the immigrant's arrival in the city that re-cites previous encounters of the gendered subject from the periphery confronting the dizzying sights and sounds of the city (like Anna Morgan in early-twentieth-century London or Paulina in mid-twentieth-century Nairobi), Ali offers a stark instance of the ways in which global capitalism is figured in the shape, texture and color of the building in the City. The building is simultaneously machinic and natural, a monstrous outgrowth of the surroundings while also possessing both the vulnerability and transparency of glass and the indestructibility and opacity of steel. It is both a landmark and a space without end. It reduces to insignificance the human life it swallows up or looks down upon. Human relations, too, are subsumed within the all-encompassing logic and presence of capital as symbolized by the building.

Hywel Williams has written of "a peculiarly fetishistic quality to the way in which the English have looked at the City in their midst—so awesome, secretive and ritualistic". He attributes the imbuing of the City's capitalist machinery with magical qualities to the 1980s deregulation of financial services that severed capitalism's connection to state and social control.[8] Operating according to its own internal, purportedly supra-rational logic, capital becomes de-linked from social relationships and social purpose. It is in this context that capitalism's supra-rational operation appears to be magical, only the latest incarnation of a much older process of what David Harvey has called "accumulation through dispossession", such that London's hyper-capitalist present is a reiteration as much as it is a successor to the City's accumulating imperial past.[9] Williams writes: "Britons nostalgic for the age of empire need only visit the City to find the heirs of Clive of India seeking the plunder and dividing the spoils. Here is the great mercenary army of our time, the most achingly modern and frighteningly efficient of Britain's imperial institutions".[10]

So it is in this context of global London that the novel tells us about how the writer sees Nazneen seeing the city:

Every person who brushed past her on the pavement, every back she saw, was on a private, urgent mission to execute a precise and demanding plan: to get a promotion today, to be exactly on time for an appointment, to buy a newspaper with the right coins so that the exchange was swift and seamless, to walk without wasting a second and to reach the roadside just as the lights turned red. Nazneen, hobbling and halting, began to be aware of herself. Without a coat, without a suit, without a white face, without a destination . . .

But they were not aware of her . . . They knew that she existed . . . but unless she did something, waved a gun, halted the traffic, they would not see her.

In this remarkable scene that holds echoes from Woolf, the novel presents the imbricated nature of cultural difference and neo-liberal capitalism as ideologies that nestle together within the space of London as a global city. Capitalism's rendering of culture as a form of commodification is exposed in the ways in which Nazneen's cultural difference is rendered invisible ("they would not see her") precisely because it is superfluous to the calculus of commodity production, even as her awareness of difference is mediated by the geography of high capitalism.

Jane M. Jacobs writes, "contemporary urban transformation is far more likely to engage consciously with the local character of an area than rapaciously obliterate it" such that the mobilization of heritage becomes "part of the legitimating framework of contemporary urban transformation".[11] The long history of the contending territorial claims of the immigrant communities of Brick Lane, in the borough of Tower Hamlets, one of the poorest of London boroughs, and of speculative high capital's constantly expanding spaces in the City, is illustrative of capital's selective use of cultural difference, in which "immediate and intense encounters" can opportunistically transform into indifference and even exclusion.[12] As the City concentrates and channels global capital through gentrification and redevelopment projects, a majority of Brick Lane's residents suffer from high unemployment rates and subsist on sweatshop work or work in the down-market retail and restaurant sectors that offer a lowbrow experience of consuming "curry" in the city.

It is here, then, on the edges of the City, that Ali's ethnographic fiction of life in the Tower Hamlets for poor and culturally marginalized immigrants is set. Brick Lane has of course been one of the key sites in the narrativization of London's long immigrant history.[13] More recently, it has also emerged as a pathologized site of Islamic extremism—images of girls in headscarves being pushed into religious schools and radical mullahs controlling the local council abound in the media and the public imagination—and that Ali's novel directly references through its depiction of the radicalization of Tower Hamlet youths in the post-9/11 context. Nazneen seems to be only inchoately wary of the kind of communal politics being mobilized in the context of global capitalism, white racism and the war on terror. The novel suggests that it is her awareness of her lover Kareem's involvement in increasingly radical politics that precipitates the end of her extra-marital romance. The narrative refuses a romantic ending in which Nazneen's choice of London over Dhaka would in reality be a choice between her loving but older, secular, less attractive husband Chanu, who decides to go back to Dhaka when his dreams to succeed in London as a postcolonial subject fail, and her dashing lover Kareem, who seeks to reclaim London as the space of radical immigrant alterity as signified through Islamic radicalism.

The novel does not fully reveal the motivations behind Nazneen's choice of making London her home. It could after all be read as the triumph of her desire for individual empowerment and self-making. But there is also another potential site of personal engagement that is not entirely reducible to the private. Her work as a sweatshop worker stitching garments for London's fashion industry connects her not only with other women in her community, but also with her sister in Dhaka who also works in a sweatshop supplying garments to the world. Exploitative and unfulfilling as this work is, the novel pulls the domain of women's work into its still invisible articulation with the global economy. Ali's novel is an attempt to fictionalize both the experience of such work at a microscopic and intimate level (the sorts of relations it destroys and others that it produces) as well as its linking up with a transnational sisterhood. But whether Nazneen would go on to participate in any kind of feminist or secular politics that could challenge the dominant neo-liberal and increasingly unsecular global city is of course a question that the novel's plot does not accommodate, even as its discourse opens up these questions to critique.

Alongside this narrative of individualized, even localized empowerment within a consciously global setting, I want to place the work of Southall Black Sisters (SBS), an activist group that emerged in the context of anti-racist and feminist politics of London of the late 1970s and 1980s. Established in 1979 "to meet the needs of Asian and African-Caribbean women", the group's work has laid bare the contradictions within both anti-racism and multiculturalism as politics, ideology and state policy in Britain. Whereas its immediate aim was to provide a safe refuge for women fleeing domestic violence in the city, SBS's work was extended towards legal work in the context of discriminatory immigration regimes, and towards working with the state's labyrinthine welfare policies as they related to black women. SBS's biggest contribution and its biggest challenge have been framing these struggles of women and immigrants within a secular, pluralistic, democratic framework, a task increasingly difficult within the context of the war on terror and a neo-liberal economic regime seeking to drastically curtail social welfare and privatize the city.

If migrants and women have given SBS a transnational character, SBS's work has also been crucially framed by its location in Southall, a pre-dominantly Asian settlement in west London. Commenting on its complex location and positioning in the city, Chetan Bhatt has characterized Southall as representing "a cultural cauldron located in the city', a place "whose dense ecology acts to distance it from genuine metropolitan belonging".[14] Southall's uniqueness lay in the fact that its locale and its history of settlement had rendered it to be a highly mixed borough, and as a consequence, a secular space that represented every major religion of the Indian subcontinent. Sukhwant Dhaliwal notes how "this early period of settlement was also characterized by local workers' strikes that gave the struggles of Southall a clear class perspective".[15]

Southall placed itself firmly on the map of progressive politics in London when in 1979 Asian and African-Caribbean immigrants allied with white anti-racists and socialists to demonstrate against a meeting of the National Front, the ultra-nationalist white supremacist party, at the local town hall. It was at this demonstration that Blair Peach, a white anti-racist activist who was demonstrating against the NF, was killed in a terrible instance of police repression. The protest came to be seen "by locals as a proud moment of unity against racism, fascism and police brutality".[16]

It was in this context of a politicized anti-racist working-class identity that SBS was formed to address the internal contradictions that beset the anti-racist struggles, in which women's issues were often subordinated to the purportedly higher cause of community cohesion. The formation of SBS was part and parcel of a larger rise of Asian women's organizations and their campaigns and activities around immigration laws, racial and gender violence, civil rights, religious fundamentalism, policing, and generalized state repression in the 1980s. Within trade union politics, class struggles were typically pitted against cultural identity, even as factory owners exploited the lack of legal status or low social status of immigrant workers.[17] Campaigns around these issues were fuelled by a secular commitment to human rights, civil liberties and civic citizenship, and with the goal of achieving social and economic justice and radical social transformation. SBS was thus an integral part of what Bhatt has referred to as "an independent black political sphere" that was sustained well into the 1980s".[18]

Crucially, SBS must also be understood as part of the project of black British feminism that emerged in the late 1970s and early 1980s as a critique both of the post-war, post-imperial British state, as well as of the Left, anti-racist and mainstream feminist movements. Black British feminism became a recognizable political movement and critical entity in the intensely racialized terrain of politics during Thatcher's conservative rule (1979–1990). The politics of anti-racism and the work of forging black-white alliances against the racist practices and rhetoric of both the state and of popular politics provided the background to the articulation of a black British feminist agenda that sought to understand black experience in Britain, particularly in the cities, through gender difference and to forge a politics of gendered racial justice.

Such an agenda faced a major challenge when the local state in many instances (based in city councils) adopted what seemed like then a radical policy of multiculturalism against the onslaught of Thatcherite nationalism and economic privatization. Whereas the Thatcher government openly promoted its xenophobic and racist view of Britain through its immigration policy and its erosion of state support for immigrants in general, progressive local authorities such as the Greater London Authority (GLA), where black Labour councilors had played an important role, attempted to tackle issues of institutional racism and to forge multi-racial politics.[19] The practice and rhetoric of multiculturalism was thus paradoxically incubated within the logic of Thatcherism. Over time, the "municipal anti-racism" of local authorities became too formalistic, and privileged cultural differences over issues of economic and social justice. It rendered non-white groups into "ethnic minorities" (forged always in relation to the dominant white mainstream), promoted culture as a way of celebrating identity, and saw gender equity as a private matter to be left to the community. It was in these troubled sites of official multiculturalism that black British feminism made important and transformative interventions in at least three inter-related fields—the British state's immigration policy, multiculturalism as a political ideology, and struggles over work and the right to welfare in the city.

Issues such as domestic violence, so-called honor killings, and forced marriages in the Asian community more generally have highlighted the British state's problematic construction of gender rights as subordinate and even antithetical to its policy of multiculturalism that treats tradition as sacrosanct. Viewing cultural differences as inherent and immutable, the state installed men as the natural spokespersons of their communities. Paradoxically, such "exotic" practices as arranged marriage and the use of religious markers of identity are marshaled as evidence of the need to rescue black and Asian women from illiberalism by imposing progressive ideologies such as secularism, sexual freedom, and individual choice in marriage, seen as exclusively belonging to the West.[20]

Looking specifically at the work of the SBS, Gita Sahgal points out how the main challenge of SBS was to provide a secular space to women who were victims of domestic and community violence so as to enable them to express the multiple sites of their struggles and the contradictory locations of their affiliations. She argues that responding to calls of a community in danger from racist assaults, anti-racist politics moved away from a socialist orientation and "became intimately bound up with questions of ethnic identity".[21] In its more dangerous form, it took the form of attacks on women who were seen as challenging tradition, and thus endangering community identity in the face of a racist white British society. Paradoxically, the contradictions within the state policies of multiculturalism, the colonialist impulses within white feminism (or "imperial feminism"), and community-oriented anti-racist politics have created new spaces in the city for a critical black British feminism to intervene in and to re-formulate itself.[22]

But there are fresh challenges ahead. Southall itself has become an intensely communalized terrain, reflecting the fears and anxieties of Londoners at large. Dhaliwal chronicles the way in which the secular geography of an earlier Southall is being reconstructed as "religious buildings occupy prime sites while voluntary groups have been decimated", as festivals and religious processions proliferate—"the commodification and promotion of religious identities" mark a "new consciousness" in the borough. Women, once again, are at the center of these new political tendencies. The fear of wayward women and girls has resulted in the area becoming awash with leaflets exhorting Muslim men to convert Hindu and Sikh women by marrying them, and offering advice on family, on child-bearing and on minimizing personal contact with non-believers, even as Hindu women are taught to fear all Muslim men as dangerous. Radio stations transmit the defense of sexual harassment in the community, blaming it on overly westernized South Asian women. As Bhatt puts it: "Real or perceived insult" from a culturally or religiously different group imagined as the enemy now provide "points of mobilization", inculcating popular vocabularies of victimhood, siege, militancy and thereby strengthening the sphere of "illiberal religiosity" that seeks to place itself above and beyond scrutiny and that positions itself against a deracinated cosmopolitanism of the earlier moment of a secular and working-class solidarity.

If the most fantasized and manipulable figure in Brick Lane today is a hijab-wearing Muslim schoolgirl, from Southall emanates news of honor killings such as that in which Samaira Nazir, daughter of Muslim greengrocers in Southall, was killed by her brothers for loving a man from another community whom she had met on the very streets of Southall. The Old Bailey termed this killing "barbaric" in its judgment. As Samaira was dragged and mercilessly beaten by her own family, neighbors report seeing Samaira's bloody hand emerge from the front door, in a last ditch effort to escape her home. For those instants, the world outside must have seemed a far safer place to her. Samaira's case is just one among the many that SBS often has to take up. It foregrounds the critical politics of the private sphere, of "home" in the context of a "world" in which the war on terror, Islamo-fascism and Islamophobia, and an ever-expanding neo-liberal agenda that directly affects the work that SBS does (new laws arrayed against immigrants, funding curtailments, privatized housing).

Towards a Conclusion

Against the brutalized backdrop of an honor killing in Southall, London, are also visible the marks of the much cited apocryphal graffiti inscription in Southall: "We are here because you were there". The parameters of the "here" in the sentence (an erstwhile imperial London) necessitate an understanding of the "there" (the postcolonized periphery), and indeed of the reconstituted "here" (postcolonial London). How the two locales become terms of at least linguistic equivalence and more is a question that lies at the very heart of the postcolonial city.

What this book has argued is that the postcolonial city can best be understood as a conjunctural space where imperial and postcolonial histories collide and create new political subjectivities and forms of citizenship even as disenfranchisement and struggles to inhabit the city against all odds remain part of reality. It traces some of the lineages of anti-colonial resistance through the figure of unhomely women, from Algiers to London, from Nairobi to Bombay. The itinerary sketched out by each of the chapters is intended to provide theoretical footholds towards figuring women as political subjects in the postcolonial city, and by extension, including subjectivity as a key ingredient of any theory and practice of feminist citizenship.

My concluding gesture is an attempt at articulating a feminist ideal of citizenship in the postcolonial city that is irrevocably materialist in its concerns and orientation. My conclusions are influenced by postcolonial feminist evocations of the "cartographies of struggle" (Mohanty), and "scattered hegemonies" (Kaplan and Grewal) that challenge the binary divisions of space; likewise, my critique is embedded in theories that foreground the unevenness of both capitalist development and literary and artistic forms as evidenced in the representational politics of the postcolonial city.

Indeed, feminists have seized upon the city to articulate a theory of difference, or more specifically, to mark the "effects" of difference in urban space.[23] Iris Marion Young's essay "The Ideal of Community and the Politics of Difference" offers a veritable template for a feminist theorization of the city.[24] Below I will sketch not just the salient points of Young's model of an "unoppressive city" but also critique it for the ways in which her universalist project is still one that does not take adequate account of the postcolonial city. Her essay, thus, provides me with an occasion to move my analysis from that of literary and political representations of the city and gender in my previous chapters to building upon, by way of critique, an emancipatory tradition in feminist theory and its imagining of an "un-oppressive city".

Young's essay picks up, significantly for my purposes, on the resilient tension between feminism and community, and between community and the city. The long history of colonialism's exploitative attitude towards native custom and community has justifiably made feminists suspicious of merely reversing the strategy whereby community becomes the ground for resistance. Communities, after all, have been crucial sites of gender violence and discrimination. Similarly, when theorists like Partha Chatterjee and Ashis Nandy posit community as an antidote to the psychic and material devastation caused by urbanizing globalization (see chapter 3), community is rendered antithetical to class and gender solidarities. Young's essay attacks the ideal of community for the ways in which it masks differences and paradoxically generates "borders, dichotomies and exclusions" (301). She suggests that a celebration of community lends itself to a denial of real violence that exists in face-to-face societies and sets up a problematic opposition between authentic and inauthentic societies, "detemporalis(ing)" any understanding of social change (302). Foregrounding the limits of participatory democratic communitarianism in which women are typically constructed as models because they are considered inherently more caring and democratic, Young argues that such a conceptualization of women's political capacities is not only essentialist, but clearly limiting and even oppressive, and places the burden of maintaining community squarely on women.

The multiplicity and complexity of social processes that undergird urban life circumvent the ideal of identification with the other as a condition for progressive politics. On the contrary, Young argues, "politics must be conceived as a relationship of strangers who do not understand one another in a subjective and immediate sense, relating across time and distance" (317). City life, she suggests, is the "being-together' of strangers"—who experience each other as other, different, and unable to understand each other (318). Indeed, Young, like other postmodernists, reminds us that cities are also pleasurable and enjoyable spaces where we are thrown together with strangers. The "aesthetic of inexhaustibility" created by the "juxtaposition of incongruous styles and functions" contributes to "this pleasure in detail and surprise" (318). Within these spaces of entertainment, consumption and politics, people interact with differences, such as consuming ethnic foods, without necessarily adopting them as their own. There is, consequently, the production of a social inexhaustibility—with the ever-present potential for the formation of new social and political groups "around specific interests" (319). On Young's view, city life, then, is to be celebrated, in spite of, and against its modernist characterization as alienating and bureaucratic, for its "energy, cultural diversity, technological complexity, and the multiplicities of its activities" (317).

"The unoppressive city is thus defined as openness to unassimilated otherness", asserts Young (319). She acknowledges that such openness does not exist in our social relations yet: what she is articulating is an ideal that seeks justice and an end to oppression via a resolute commitment to "a politics of difference" (319) such that difference needs to be defined as "the irreducible particularity of entities" (304), where particularity also means their materiality, their contingency, in opposition to an idealistic construction of unity based on unreal essences.

City's Limits

But what if Young's model of the "unoppressive city" was made to confront the particular historical and material coordinates of the postcolonial city, within which theories of difference have to, of necessity, contend with the "effects" of difference? For sure, these effects would have to be located within the political economy of contemporary capitalism, which in the urban context must take into account what David Harvey lists in the context of New York city's Tompkins Square Park riots of the 1980s, as the

> social processes which create homelessness, promote criminal activities of many sorts (from real estate swindles and the crack trade to street muggings), generate hierarchies of power between gentrifiers and the homeless, and facilitate the emergence of deep tensions along the major social fault-lines of class, gender, ethnicity, race and religion, lifestyle and place-bound references.[25]

Harvey's response to Young partakes of a more general skepticism towards postmodernist celebrations of difference in the city from the standpoint of a materialist critique of the city. He points out that "on a good day, we could celebrate the scene within the park as a superb example of urban tolerance for difference, an exemplar of what Iris Marion Young calls 'openness to unassimilated otherness'", but "that difficulty is highlighted on a bad day in the park" when "the potentiality for 'openness to unassimilated otherness' breaks apart" and we find "sociality collapsing into violence" as the "so-called forces of law and order battle to evict the homeless, erect barriers between violently clashing factions".[26] In fact, as my previous chapters point out, the city is increasingly an un-open arena, with extensive privatization, colonization and masculinization of space emerging as key processes of neo-liberal domination.[27]

Although in her rejection of a massive overhaul of mass urban society, Young provides a valuable pointer to the sources of radical political organizing that need to be located within existing structures, she nevertheless relinquishes the task of delineating the "givens" of global capitalism and multi-national patriarchies, for instance, upon which her model of the unoppressive city of necessity relies. More pointedly, her evocation of overhauling urban space as too idealistic skirts the massive restructuring of space undertaken by global capitalist forces, and the possibilities inherent in urban rebellion.

Young treads the slippery slope where difference becomes a commodity in its own right, an aspect of urban style, and ultimately it merely takes the place of community in her analysis. In its emphasis on the pleasures of the city, and its "aesthetic inexhaustibility", Young's essay glosses over the ambiguity and limit of the liberatory potential of capitalist cities. Elizabeth Wilson attributes this process of the aestheticization of even the "unpleasurable" to the postmodern culture of the post-industrial corporate city that "perceives all experience in aesthetic terms".[28] Stephen Haymes refers to other critics such as Cross and Keith who call attention to the manner in which in the postmodern city "ethnicity is celebrated in the collage of the exotic cultural pick-and-mix, while race remains taboo, and is anything but playful".[29]

As more and more Third World women are being pushed into sweatshops and on to the global assembly line this particular articulation of global cultural and economic flows in the global metropolis might allow Colombian rain-forest activists and Indian fishworkers to come together on the streets of Montreal. But one cannot lose sight of the fact that that coming together is preceded and accompanied by a history of brutal colonization and neo-imperialist arrangements. Economic and cultural globalization has rendered resistance highly localized and fragmented, while it makes its own push toward transcending spatial barriers, heralding an "end of geography". The danger in de-territorializing communities involves the erasure of geographic power, of the uneven development of late capitalism that renders sharing of locale, or not having access to one, as providing an urgently needed basis of political and feminist organizing.

Young's argument in its polemicism sets up false oppositions between an unreconstructed communitarianism based on friendship, mutuality and an erasure of hierarchies on the one hand, and difference, with its postmodern evocation of radical openness to strangers, to city life, and to a new politics based on that difference. Here it is important to point out that Young's critique of communitarians reflects back on her own thesis—for there seems to be an assumption of non-hierarchical difference within "difference". By elevating difference into a mode of being in the city, Young's theory runs the risk of precluding attempts to understand the other's standpoint, of the attempt to empathize, to inhabit the place of the other, to engage in a politics of solidarity without affinity.

Whereas postmodern theorists have been quick to point out that ideals of community erase differences between individuals, they have been less forthcoming in theorizing differences between groups, communities and classes. There is instead a flattening of the differences and asymmetries between different groups in the service of an idealized city that will be governed on the principle of difference. In attacking the very notion of community, Young needs to differentiate between an understanding of community that sees it as natural, a given and essential, and one that sees it as always and already negotiated, deconstructive and struggled-for. A materialist-feminist ideal of community suggests that individuals are not in any essential way tied to community, that that consciousness comes out of both experience and analysis and an engagement with political agency.

If the standard urban narratives identified by previous chapters romanticized the figure of the stranger in the city as flaneur, that figure is now transformed into a vivid panorama of multitudes of strangers in the city. Young thus proposes a "politics of difference" in which the model of the unoppressive city "offers an understanding of social relations without domination in which persons live together in relations of mediation among strangers with whom they are not in community" (303). Here the word "strangers" needs to be read more closely—while some strangers can evoke feelings of bonding without necessarily leading to intimate relationships, other strangers can instill fear and rage, especially as public spaces are increasingly privatized, policed, terrorized and rendered precarious. Finally, the embodiment of the strangers as men, women, black, white, rich, poor, old, young needs to be made relevant even as an ideal of postcolonial feminist citizenship strives for justice.

Feminist Citizenship

In this book I have contextualized abstract notions of women's place in theoretical and literary writings on the contemporary city, and presented a theory of the postcolonial city as conjuncture in which unhomely women can be figured as subjects and citizens. The task of describing the contemporary urban conjuncture is of course laden with risks because as Haraway points out "what people are experiencing is not transparently clear, and we lack sufficiently subtle connections for collectively building effective theories of experience" (173). For Haraway, the defining image of our globalizing spatio-temporal world is that of a woman working in the integrated circuit, performing work that redefines and overhauls all older notions of work, spaces and bodies and relationship to both the household and the polis within the global city. For others, the defining image is that of a slum woman, Chamoiseau's squatter-citizen, doggedly picking up the refuse of the world to create home for herself in the global city. This image too forces us to reconsider our sense of home and citizenship, indeed our sense of belonging to a world and survival in it. Neither image is complete or decisive.

Ultimately a critique of the global city cannot eschew a critique of global capitalism, which need not rest on evoking nostalgia for a lost world. For nestled within global cities is the disruptive presence of the postcolonial city that combines, in an uneven way, the archaic and the modern, the rural and the urban, a veritable conjuncture of the present. The figure of unhomely women, located as they might be in the vast terrain of Silicon Valley, or in the prison-factories of the free trade zones, or in the slums of our mega-cities, or as illegal aliens working in prosperous homes, calls for a rethinking of work, feminist solidarity and of citizenship that is resolutely postcolonial. The very dispersion of Third World women throughout the globe is a consequence of colonialism and global capitalism, free markets and unfair trade, and is difficult to read as even a potentially emancipatory massing together of women. Yet building coalitions and alliances is a fact of survival. A feminist project of citizenship in the postcolonial city is thus a project that seeks to insert women's work, solidarity and political subjectivity as a critical confluence of belonging in the postcolonial city.

Coda

Figure 1   This photograph of a wall in Southall is reproduced at The Southall Story exhibition at the Royal Festival Hall, South Bank Centre, London. The multi-media interactive exhibition on view from April 14 to May 11, 2010 in London was created by artistic director Kuljit Bhamra, alongside creative directors Shakila Maan and Ammy Phull (Image taken by Rashmi Varma).

The various fragments of writing on the wall installation here are presented in palimpsestic form. Older writings are erased, new words pile up on each other and are written with uneven intensity and fleeting attachment. Different identities contend for space in this layered urban form that is also a flat surface. But there is plenty of empty space for new words and new histories to be inscribed. I offer this as a final image of the postcolonial city as conjuncture.

Notes

Notes to the Preface

1. The United Nations had estimated that from 2008 more than half of the world's population would live in cities. See UN Population Division, *World Urbanization Prospects: The 2003 Revision*. Mike Davis, in his devastating diagnosis of our contemporary globe as the "planet of slums", calls the outstripping of rural people in the world by an urban populace a "watershed in human history, comparable to the Neolithic or Industrial revolutions". See Mike Davis, *Planet of Slums* (London: Verso, 2006), 1. In these cities, already about one billion people live in slums—their experience of urbanity consists of unrelenting precarity, violence, poverty and continuous struggles to survive.

2. Andreas Huyssen writes that much of "the intense scholarly interest in city cultures" that had been "emerging since the 1970s" in the humanities was typically "energized by a critical nostalgia for a kind of urban formation that really belonged to that earlier stage of a heroic modernity, rather than to our own time: the Paris of Baudelaire and Manet, fin de siècle Vienna, the London of Bloomsbury, Weimar Berlin and the New York of the Harlem Renaissance". For Huyssen, "as valuable memory work, these studies of the classical modernist cities and their culture stand in the shadow of urban transformations of our own age." Therefore, he argues, "it is no coincidence that they often betray a sense of loss, if not a nostalgia for the modernist city, a nostalgia that is no doubt fed by the insight that these prototypical modernist cities, with their sense of vibrant futures, are fast becoming part of history, rather than representing the cutting edge of global developments". See Andreas Huyssen, ed. *Other Cities, Other Worlds: Urban Imaginaries in a Globalizing Age* (Durham, N.C., and London: Duke University Press, 2008), 8–9. While I would be more hesitant than Huyssen in consigning these erstwhile modernist cities into the realm of history, I find theoretical and personal resonance in his pointing out the centrality of these cities in the West in the history of the urban imaginary.

3. Strikingly, this lack of theorization of the postcolonial city has been a feature of postcolonial studies in general. Ashley Dawson and Brent Hayes Edwards lay out the challenge of writing about postcolonial cities thus: "the analysis of global cities of the South would be a fertile area of inquiry in recent postcolonial studies. Oddly, though, postcolonial scholars have been largely silent. This omission is perhaps a product of postcolonial theory's largely retrospective gaze . . . But if postcolonial theory is to retain its relevance by attending to the forces of globalization, it will have to address the evolving social conditions and economic situation of the twenty-first century's megacities."

See "Introduction: Global Cities of the South", *Social Text 81* 22, no. 4 (Winter 2004): 1–8, 3.

4. Redirecting focus from the big Indian cities, one can see in some recent Indian writing in English a belated interest in small towns such as Patna, represented as a locale that produces varieties of vernacular cosmopolitanisms. See Amitava Kumar, *Bombay London New York* (New York: Routledge, 2002) and Siddhartha Chowdhury's novel *Patna Roughcut* (New Delhi: Picador, 2005). While I share with the authors of these books the experience of growing up in Patna in the 1970s and 1980s, I find that their experience has been rendered in distinctively masculine registers.

5. Sunil Khilnani writes: "India's existing cities: places like Murshidabad, Fyzabad or Patna all might have picturesque architectural merits, but otherwise were best avoided" by the British colonialists. See his *The Idea of India* (New Delhi: Penguin Books, 1997), 111. Following Khilnani's account, Patna could not make it into the story of postcolonial urbanism in India.

Notes to the Introduction

1. Henri Lefebvre points out the distinction between the "representation of space" and "representational space". Whereas the former entails an understanding of space as static and ahistorical, the latter, he argues, "is alive. . . . It embraces the loci of passion, of action and of lived situations. . . . It is essentially qualitative, fluid and dynamic". See Henri Lefebvre, *The Production of Space*, trans. Donald Nicholson-Smith (Oxford: Blackwell, 1991), 42.

2. The Merriam-Webster Dictionary defines "conjuncture" as "a combination of circumstances of events usually producing a crisis". See Merriam-Webster Online Dictionary. Typically, conjuncture is seen as a different conceptual category from structure. See Robert Brenner, "Structure versus Conjuncture: The 2006 Elections and the Rightward Shift", *New Left Review* 43 (January–February 2007) pp. 33–59. My analysis aims to emphasize the inextricable relationality of structure and conjuncture. For the idea of crisis as key to the concept of conjuncture, see Walden Bello, "A Global Conjuncture: The Multiple Crises of Global Capitalism", *Frontline* 19, no. 18 (August 31–September 13, 2002). http://

3. I use the term "modernist city" to suggest that twentieth-century cities expressed modernist ideas in all their ambiguity and contradictoriness. The term has as much to do with the process of modernization as with the representation of modern life. In other words, the modernist city can be seen as an extension and reflection of modernist style on the constantly changing contours of modernity. The organization of cities and the spatial distribution of power along racial, class and gender lines was a part of what has been commonly termed "the modernist project". See Paul Rabinow, *French Modern*: *Norms and Forms of the Social Environment* (Cambridge: MIT Press, 1989); Marshall Berman, *All That Is Solid Melts into Air* (New York: Simon and Schuster, 1981).

4. Georg Simmel, "The Metropolis and Mental Life" (1903), reprinted in *The Sociology of Georg Simmel*, trans. and ed. Kurt H. Wolff (New York: Free Press, 1964), 410.

5. Walter Benjamin, *The Arcades Project* (Cambridge: Harvard University Press, Belknap Press, 1999), 872.

6. Charles Baudelaire [*Fleurs du Mal*]; T. S. Eliot [*The Waste Land*]; James Joyce [*Ulysses*]; Andre Breton [*Nadja*]; Virginia Woolf [*Mrs Dalloway*], to name just a few practitioners of modernism, are only some of the writers who dwelled

extensively on the relationship between urban space and the fragmentation of the subject.

7. Simmel, "The Metropolis and Mental Life", 410.
8. Benjamin, *The Arcades Project*, 879.
9. Raymond Williams, *The Country and the City* (New York: Oxford University Press, 1973).
10. See Anthony Vidler, *The Architectural Uncanny: Essays in the Modern Unhomely* (Cambridge: MIT Press, 1992); xi. Mid-twentieth-century inheritors of this conservatism would include the Chicago School of urban sociology that saw the city as a cancer on the body of organic social life and culture. Conservative responses to modern urbanism have also found a surprising resonance in contemporary anti-urban discourses critical of the centralization and monumentalization of spaces in the city, seen as a negative legacy of the grand narratives of progress and development.
11. After all, the major revolutions of the twentieth century, in Russia, China and Cuba, had all been theorized in terms of peasant mobilizations. See Regis Debray, *Revolution in the Revolution? Armed Struggle and Political Struggle in Latin America* (New York: Monthly Review Press, 1967).
12. Mike Davis, "The Urbanization of Empire: Megacities and the Laws of Chaos", *Social Text* 81 22, no. 4 (Winter 2004): 9–16, 9.
13. See Manuel Castells, *The Urban Question: A Marxist Approach*, trans. A. Sheridan (Cambridege: MIT Press, 1977) for his reading of urbanism as less useful as an analytic tool than as an *ideology* signifying the urban as an inherently superior and inevitable aspect of social growth.
14. Gauri Viswanathan, "Raymond Williams and British Colonialism: The Limits of Metropolitan Cultural Theory", in *Views beyond the Border Country: Raymond Williams and Cultural Politics*, ed. Dennis L. Dworkin and Leslie G. Roman, 217–220, 220 (New York: Routledge, 1993). Viswanathan analyses "Wiliams's 'silence' about imperialism" as "less a theoretical oversight or blindness than an internal restraint that has complex methodological and historical origins" (218). Whereas she hails Williams's text as "the exemplary text linking English social formation with the economics of imperialism", one that acknowledges an outside to the formation of English national culture as predicated on an imperial system, she argues that Williams ultimately fails to fully theorize the "relationality of British imperialism and culture" (219–220).
15. See Frederick Cooper, "Introduction", in *Struggle for the City: Migrant Labour, Capital, and the State in Urban Africa*, ed. Frederick Cooper (Beverly Hills/London/New Delhi: Sage Publications, 1983) for pointing to Marxist geographers' (like Castells and Harvey) "underdeveloped remarks" about "dependent urbanism", even as Africanists study Africa as "separate from European capitalist development" (26).
16. See Fredric Jameson, *Postmodernism, or, the Cultural Logic of Late Capitalism* (Durham, N.C.: Duke University Press, 1991); David Harvey, *The Condition of Postmodernity: An Enquiry into the Origins of Cultural Change* (Oxford: Blackwell Publishers, 1990) for analyses of postmodern (late-capitalist) urbanity.
17. Guy Debord, *Society of the Spectacle* (Detroit: Black and Red Books, 1977).
18. For an excellent theorization of neo-liberalism, see Pierre Bourdieu, "The Essence of Neoliberalism", http://www.analitica.com/biblioteca/bourdieu/neoliberalism.asp. Accessed on December 23, 2003. Bourdieu names neoliberalism as the "dominant discourse" of our times, in which the economic world is imagined as "a pure and perfect order", liberated from concerns of social fairness and political collectivities.

19. See Manuel Castells, "European Cities, the Informational Society, and the Global Economy", *New Left Review*, no. 204 (March–April 1994): 18–32. Bourdieu analyzes neo-liberalism as heralding the "absolute reign of flexibility". See his "The Essence of Neoliberalism".

20. Michael Sorkin, *Variations on a Theme Park: The New American City and the End of Public Space* (New York: Hill and Wang, 1992); James Holston and Arjun Appadurai, "Cities and Citizenship", *Public Culture* 8 (1996): 187–204. In fact, Holston and Appadurai make use of cities in various ways—cities inscribe power; cities make manifest as well as generate it; cities are strategic arenas for its exercise as well as operate as stage and site.

21. Manuel Castells, *The City and the Grassroots* (London: Edwin Arnold, 1983), 284.

22. Engen F. Isin, ed., *Democracy, Citizenship, and the Global City* (London: Routledge, 2000), 3.

23. See Saskia Sassen, *The Global City: New York, London, Tokyo*, 2d ed. (Princeton: Princeton University Press, 2001). See also Saskia Sassen, "The Global City: Strategic Site/New Frontier", in *Democracy, Citizenship, and the Global City*, ed. Engin Isin (London: Routledge, 2000).

24. Huyssen points out usefully that "much of the exuberant language of global flows and networks can be traced back to . . . the utopianism of technological communications", in which "real space would yield to virtual space". In Andreas Huyssen, ed., *Other Cities, Other Worlds: Urban Imaginaries in a Globalizing Age* (Durham, N.C., and London: Duke University Press, 2008), 9.

25. Holston and Appadurai,, "Cities and Citizenship".

26. Frantz Fanon, *The Wretched of the Earth*, trans. Constance Farrington (New York: Grove Press, 1963). Page references are in text.

27. See Johannes Fabian, *The Time of the Other: How Anthropology Makes Its Object* (New York: Columbia University Press, 1983).

28. Anthony D. King, "Colonial Cities: Global Pivots of Change", in *Colonial Cities: Essays in a Colonial Context*, ed. Robert Ross and J. Telkamp, 7–32, 23 (Dordrecht, the Netherlands: Martinus Nijhoff, 1985).

29. Anthony King defines the colonial city as one where the dominant minority is culturally European; it is created by the emergence of world capitalism; and eventually becomes part of an independent nation state ("Colonial Cities", 9). Similarly, Balandier sees the colonial city's distinctive features as comprising those of the colonial process itself in which a foreign minority (racially, religiously and ethnically different from the suppressed majority) dominates (economically, militarily, technologically and as a result, socially) the indigenous population. The two communities remain in an "antagonistic relationship" such that the colonized people are subjected "as instruments of colonial power". Further, an industrial society is imposed upon a non-industrial one. See Georges Balandier, "The Colonial Situation: A Theoretical Approach," in *Social Change: The Colonial Situation*, ed Immanuel Wallerstein, 34–61 (New York, John Wiley & Sons, 1966).

30. King, "Colonial Cities"; 8.

31. Thus, Fanon remarks that the capital city of Algiers was "the nervous system of the enemy apparatus" and indeed during World War II served as a major base for the French military. See his "Algeria Unveiled", in *Studies in a Dying Colonialism* (New York: Grove Press, 1967), 53.

32. King, "Colonial Cities", 13.

33. Horne notes how even early-nineteenth-century French travellers to Algeria had remarked upon the presence there of a relatively sophisticated "civilisation" involving cities, institutions of learning and high degrees of general literacy. It is noteworthy, then, that later French writers such as Andre Gide

in works such as *Amyntas* and *L'Immoraliste*, and *pied noir* writers such as Albert Camus in *L'Ete* and *L'Etranger* represented Algeria as lacking in civil society, marked by an oppressive heat and desolate landscape. Camus went to the extent of seeing Algiers as a city "sans passe", without a past. Such representations seemed to accompany the changing political project of the French regarding Algeria, in the face of increasing uneasiness and political turmoil. See Alistair Horne, *A Savage War of Peace: Algeria, 1954–1962* (New York: Penguin Books, 1979); 29.

34. See Rabinow, *French Modern.* .

35. Quoted in Mahmood Mamdani, *Citizen and Subject: Contemporary Africa and the Legacy of Late Colonialism* (Princeton: Princeton University Press, 1996), 149–50.

36. Marshal Bugeaud had declared before the French National Assembly in 1840: "Wherever there is fresh water and fertile land, there one must locate *colons*, without concerning oneself to whom these lands belong". See Horne, *A Savage War of Peace*, 30.

37. The same kind of contrast could be attributed to numerous other twentieth-century colonial cities including Delhi, where colonial New Delhi was marked by open vistas with their broadly laid-out tree-lined streets, while Old Delhi consisted of a dense network of alleys and narrow streets inhabited by natives both rich and poor.

38. See Homi Bhabha, *The Location of Culture* (London: Routledge, 1994), 44.

39. Fanon, *The Wretched of the Earth*, 30.

40. Bhabha, *The Location of Culture*, 44.

41. Bhabha, *The Location of Culture*, 45.

42. Fanon, *The Wretched of the Earth*

43. See Fanon, "Algeria Unveiled".

44. For Ashley Dawson and Brent Edwards, the latter term might "offer a useful intervention, a new cartography (rather than simply a more palatable term for the 'third world')". For them, "the term South must indicate a criticism of the neo-liberal economic elite and its management of the globe according to a developmentalist paradigm". See their "Introduction: Global Cities of the South", *Social Text 81* 22, no. 4 (Winter 2004), 2.

45. It is interesting to see how postcolonial cities are typically also referred to as "Third World" cities. Whereas the term "Third World" foregrounds economic development processes that have been spectacularly uneven and unequal, the term "postcolonial" allows me further scope to understand the multiple layers that constitute these cities as physical, economic and ideological spaces, as well as allows me to turn the focus on the colonial history of these cities.

46. Mike Davis characterizes late capitalist urbanization as a "legacy of a global political conjuncture" emanating out of a worldwide agrarian crisis, and the debt crisis in the 1970s that created the IMF-led restructuring of the Third World in the 1980s. See Mike Davis, *Planet of Slums* (London: Verso, 2006), 14–16. My arguments seek to establish an older genealogy of contemporary urban and capitalist crises, locating them in the history of colonial rule from the nineteenth century onwards (itself inseparable from capitalist developments of that century).

47. The case of Latin America is in this discussion especially interesting and complex. Although this book focuses on the postcolonial city of South Asia and Africa, it is important to note that cities in Latin America experienced postcoloniality prior to those in South Asia and Africa, and hence they "participated fully in the utopian and revolutionary promises of twentieth-century Western modernity", as suggested by Huyssen. See his "Introduction:

World Cultures, World Cities", in his *Other Cities, Other Worlds*, 19. This "full" participation can be read in contrast to the vexed incorporation of African and South Asian cities into the project of modernization.

48. See Sassen, "The Global City: Strategic Site/New Frontier" and *The Global City: New York, London, Tokyo*. See also John Friedman, "The World City Hypothesis", *Development and Change* 17, no 1 (1986): 69–84 for an elaborate hierarchy of "core primary world cities", "semiperipheral primary world cities", "core secondary world cities" and "semi-peripheral secondary world cities".

49. See Rashmi Varma, "Provincializing the Global City: From Bombay to Mumbai", *Social Text 81* 22 (Winter 2004): 65–90.

50. To this end we can refer to Anthony King's argument that in a sense all cities are world cities now, subject to the vagaries of global capitalism, its tense negotiations with nation states and local cultures. See his *Urbanism, Colonialism, and the World Economy* (London: Routledge, 1990), 82.

51. Partha Chatterjee, *The Politics of the Governed* (New Delhi: Permanent Black, 2004), 144.

52. Chatterjee, *The Politics of the Governed*, 143.

53. Doreen Massey writes: "Space is created out of the vast intricacies, the incredible complexities, of the interlocking and the non-interlocking, and the networks of relations at every scale from local to global". See her *Space, Place and Gender* (Minneapolis: University of Minnesota Press, 1994), 155–156.

54. See the work of Fanon, King and Rabinow discussed above.

55. Sunil Khilnani, *The Idea of India* (New Delhi: Penguin Books, 1997), 110.

56. Khilnani, *The Idea of India*, 110.

57. Chatterjee, *The Politics of the Governed*, 134; Nirmal Kumar Bose, "Calcutta: A Premature Metropolis", *Scientific American* 213, no. 3: 91–102.

58. Frederick Cooper, "Introduction" in *Struggle for the City: Migrant Labour, Capital, and the State in Urban Africa*, ed Frederick Cooper (Beverly Hills/London/New Delhi: Sage Publications), 7–8.

59. Simon Gikandi, "Reason, Modernity and the African Crisis", in *African Modernities*, ed. Jan-Georg Deutsch, Peter Probst and Heike Schmidt, 135–157, 143 (London: James Currey, 2002).

60. Chidi Okonkwo, *Decolonization Agnostics in Postcolonial Fiction* (Basiajstoke: Palgrave Macmillan, 1999), xii. See also Neil Lazarus and Rashmi Varma, "Marxism and Postcolonial Studies", in *Critical Companion to Contemporary Marxism* (London: Brill Academic Press, 2008).

61. John Comaroff, "Governmentality, Materiality, Legality, Modernity: On the Colonial State in Africa", in *African Modernities*, ed. Jan-Georg Deutsch, Peter Probst and Heike Schmidt, 105–134, 130 (London: James Currey, 2002).

62. Theorists such as the Mexican intellectual and activist Gustavo Esteva and the Indian scholar Ashis Nandy are only two examples of such critics, who have critiqued the postcolonial state from an anti-modern perspective. Eco-feminism and varieties of Third World and postcolonial feminisms have also emerged out of the project of rejecting western modernity.

63. Bhabha, *The Location of Culture*, 237.

64. See Fredric Jameson, *A Singular Modernity: Essay on the Ontology of the Present* (London: Verso, 2002).

65. See Neera Chandoke, "The Postcolonial City", *Economic and Political Weekly* 26 no. 50 (December 14, 1991): 2868–2873.

66. Davis, *Planet of Slums*, 19.

67. Davis, "The Urbanization of Empire", 11.

68. Davis, "The Urbanization of Empire", 12.

69. Patrick Chamoiseau, *Texaco: A Novel* (New York: Vintage, 1998).

70. Ashley Dawson, "Squatters, Space, and Belonging in the Underdeveloped City". *Social Text 81* no. 4 (Winter 2004): 17–34, 19.
71. Frantz Fanon, "Algeria Unveiled". All subsequent page references will appear in the main body of the chapter.
72. See Patricia Price-Chalita, "Spatial Metaphor and the Politics of Empowerment: Mapping a Place for Feminism and Postmodernism in Geography?" *Antipode* 26, no. 3 (1994): 236–254, 246.
73. Horne, *A Savage War of Peace*, 185.
74. Barbara Harlow, "Introduction" to Malek Alloula, *The Colonial Harem*, trans. Myrna Godzich and Wlad Godzich (Minneapolis: University of Minnesota Press, 1987), xiv.
75. Harlow, "Introduction", xvi.
76. King, "Colonial Cities", 21.
77. Gillian Rose, *Feminism and Geography: The Limits of Geographical Knowledge* (Minneapolis: University of Minnesota Press, 1993), 150.
78. Examples of such a recasting are Inderpal Grewal and Caren Kaplan, who have written about "scattered hegemonies". See their edited volume *Scattered Hegemonies: Postmodernity and Transnational Feminist Practices* (Minneapolis: University of Minnesota Press, 1994). Teresa de Lauretis's delineation of the place of the lesbian consists of "dancing about a region of cognitive gaps and negative semantic spaces". See her "Eccentric Subjects", *Feminist Studies* 16:115–150. Gloria Anzaldua evokes "borderlands" as the locus of a woman of color who "exists in the interstices, the left-over or excess space of the worlds she inhabits". See her *Borderlands/La Frontera: The New Mestiza* (San Francisco: Spinsters/Aunt Lute, 1987), 20. bell hooks refers to the margin as a space of habitation for black women. It is a space that is also "a profound edge". See her *Yearning: Race, Gender and Cultural Politics* (London: Turnaround Press, 1991), 149. Pratibha Parmar argues that the stories of black British women's struggles over issues of class, sexuality, race and gender thwart "that binary hierarchy of centre and margin" such that "the margin refuses its place as the 'Other'". See her "Black Feminism" in *Identity: Community, Culture, Difference*, ed. Jonathan Rutherford (London: Lawrence and Wishart, 1990), 101.
79. Anzaldua, *Borderlands/La Frontera*.
80. Minnie Bruce Pratt, *Rebellion: Essays, 1980–1991* (New York: Firebrand Books, 1991).
81. I only tangentially draw upon Freud's notion of the *unheimlich* (as elaborated in his 1919 essay) and my intention is not to engage with his terms in any direct way. Nor am I entirely aligning my readings with what Anthony Vidler writes of as "the contemporary sensibility that sees the uncanny erupt in empty parking lots around abandoned or run-down shopping malls, in the screened *trompe l'oeil* of simulated space, in, that is, the wasted margins and surface appearances of postindustrial culture, this sensibility has its roots and draws its commonplaces from a long but essentially modern tradition. Its apparently benign and utterly ordinary loci, its domestic and tawdry settings, its ready exploitation as the frisson of an already jaded public, all mark it out clearly as the heir to a feeling of unease." See Vidler, *The Architectural Uncanny: Essays in the Modern Unhomely* (Cambridge: MIT Press, 1992). My commitment to a project of postcolonial feminist citizenship is precisely to unsettle modernity's received and self-describing assertion of a generalized homelessness.
82. Karl Marx, *The Economic and Philosophical Manuscripts*, in *Early Writings* (New York: Vintage, 1975), 351. Translated by Rodney Livingstone & Gregor Benton. Introduction by Lucio Coletti.

83. Chantal Mouffe, "Feminism, Citizenship and Radical Democratic Politics". In *Feminists Theorize the Political*, ed. Judith Butler and Joan Scott, 369–384; 376 (New York: Routledge, 1992).
84. Mouffe, "Feminism, Citizenship and Radical Democratic Politics", 378–379.
85. Iris Marion Young, "The Ideal of Community and the Politics of Difference", in *Feminism/Postmodernism*, ed. Linda Nicholson (New York: Routledge, 1990).
86. See David Harvey, *Consciousness and the Urban Experience* (Baltimore: Johns Hopkins University Press, 1985).
87. Pierre Bourdieu, *In Other Words: Essays toward a Reflexive Sociology*, trans. Mathew Adamson (Cambridge: Polity Press, 1990).
88. Priscilla Connolly, "Mexico City: Our Common Future?" *Environment and Urbanization* 11, no. 1 (April 1999), 56.
89. Andy Merrifield, *Metromarxism: A Marxist Tale of the City* (New York: Routledge, 2002), 23.
90. Pascale Casanova, "Literature as World". *New Left Review* 31 (January–February 2005).
91. Franco Moretti, "Conjectures on World Literature", in *Debating World Literature*, ed. Christopher Prendergast (London and New York: Verso, 2004), 148–162, 149–150.
92. In this my reading also draws upon the critical tradition of theorists such as Adorno who interpreted modernism as a refusal of modernity, in particular the hegemony of capitalist culture. My arguments suggest that radical postcolonial literature could similarly be read as a refusal of colonial capitalist cultural domination.
93. See Franco Moretti, "On the Novel", in *The Novel,* vol. I, *History, Geography, and Culture*, ed. Franco Moretti (Princeton: Princeton University Press, 2006), ix–x.
94. Fredric Jameson, "Modernism and Imperialism", in *Nationalism, Colonialism and Literature*, by Terry Eagleton, Fredric Jameson and Edward Said (Minneapolis: University of Minnesota Press, 1990).
95. Nicholas Brown, *Utopian Generations: The Political Horizon of Twentieth-Century Literature* (Princeton: Princeton University Press, 2005), 2–3.
96. Ngugi wa Thiong'o, *Writers in Politics* (London: Heinemann, 1981), 70.
97. Fredric Jameson, "Third-World Literature in the Era of Multinational Capitalism", *Social Text* 15 (1986): 65–88, 68.

Notes to Chapter 1

1. Virginia Woolf, *Mrs Dalloway* (1925) (New York: Harcourt Brace and Company, 1997), 16.
2. Paul Gilroy, *Postcolonial Melancholia* (New York: Columbia University Press, 2004).
3. I use the term "imperial" as well as the term "colonial" to describe London's global status in the early decades of the twentieth century. While "imperial" suggests London's pre-eminent status in the world capitalist system, "colonial" makes explicit the connection between London's imperial status and its control of territories (economic and political) outside of Britain's national borders.
4. Jacques Derrida, "Spectres of Marx", *New Left Review* I/205 (May–June 1994) 31–58.
5. Derrida writes of how "at bottom, the spectre is the future, it is always to come, it presents itself only as that which could come or come back". He

argues that the very "mode of presence of a spectre" is that it is "not yet there". See "Spectres of Marx".

6. See Johannes Fabian, *The Time of the Other: How Anthropology Makes Its Object* (New York: Columbia University Press, 1983) for an account of the "denial of coevalness" constitutive of colonial anthropology, in which the time of the native is in the past. The particular moment in Woolf's text discussed above suggests the entanglement of modernism and imperialism as projects involving temporal and spatial control.

7. Quoted in Will Self, "The City that Forever Resists the Rational". *New States-man.* July 7, 2003, 32. Peter Ackroyd's best-selling *London: The Biography* (New York: Anchor Books, 2003) is replete with tropes of death and regeneration that dominate London's history.

8. David L. Pike, "Modernist Space and the Transformation of Underground London", in *Imagined Londons*, ed. Pamela Gilbert (Albany: State University of New York Press, 2002), 101–120, 107.

9. Andrea Levy, *Small Island* (London: Review, 2004), 2.

10. See Malcolm Bradbury and James McFarlane, eds, *Modernism, 1890–1930* (New York: Penguin Books, 1976), 179.

11. See the chapter on London from 1890 to 1920 by Bradbury in Bradbury and McFarlane, *Modernism* for a discussion of the shift in London's reputation as a middle-class, primarily commercial city into a center of European literary activity around World War I (172–190).

12. The view of the western metropolis as the universal prototype of all urban centers has been pervasive through much of the twentieth century, including in contemporary understandings of the "global city", in which London, New York, and Tokyo continue to provide prototypes of cities elsewhere. See Saskia Sassen, *The Global City: New York, London, Tokyo*, 2d ed. (Princeton: Princeton University Press, 2001). See also Rashmi Varma, "Provincializing the Global City: From Bombay to Mumbai", *Social Text 81* 22 (Winter 2004), 65–90.

13. Richard Sennett writes that London on the eve of World War I "displayed the spoils of a global reach unknown since the Roman Empire". See *The Flesh and Stone: The Body and the City in Western Civilization* (New York: W. W. Norton, 1994), 317. Edward Said notes that in 1914 Europe held about 85 percent of the earth's surface, and Britain was the most pre-eminent imperial nation among the European powers. See his *Culture and Imperialism* (New York: Vintage Books, 1994); 8. But in the space of about twenty years, by the end of World War II, Britain had begun pulling back from its colonial possessions. The intensity and pace of that withdrawal was bound to have a profound effect on almost every aspect of British life, especially in the world imaginings of its citizens.

14. Pamela Gilbert points out that the differences between Victorian and modernist representations of London were though "apparently contradictory but actually continuous". See Gilbert, *Imagined Londons*, 6. My analysis partakes of this view but is also invested in noting the discontinuities between late-Victorian and modernist culture.

15. While scholars have cogently argued that there was no one modernism, Perry Anderson cautions us that modernism could ultimately end up as an empty signifier if it is divested from its political meaning of revolution. My analysis attempts to apprehend the very material implications of a seemingly elusive *zeitgeist* that converged on urban space and delineated it as the quintessential symbol of modernity. See Perry Anderson, "Modernity and Revolution" in *Marxism and the Interpretation of Culture*, ed. Cary Nelson and Lawrence Grossberg (Urbana: University of Illinois Press, 1988), 317–338. Further, the

fact that virtually all the major European metropoles were involved in large-scale colonial enterprises by the time of World War I does impart a commonality to these spaces (both at home and abroad) of European modernity. To not perceive this commonality would be another manifestation of academic colonialism that makes impossible a discussion of European modernism as a coherent category (when its implications on the colonized were often quite organized and "planned"). See also Fredric Jameson, *A Singular Modernity: Essay on the Ontology of the Present* (London: Verso, 2004).

16. By employing the term "modernist city" I intend to focus on the ways in which the modernist city reflected modernism in all its ambiguity and contradictoriness. In other words, the modernist city can be seen as a complicated reflection and production of the literary and artistic style of modernism that was crucially constituted by the desire of putting order (planning) on the chaotic elements (the modern city) of modernity. The city, in my view then, constitutes a form that coalesces modernity and modernization, as has been elaborated by Marshall Berman in *All That Is Solid Melts into Air* (New York: Simon and Schuster, 1981). Thus, the term "modernist city" comprises another narrative space for modernity and modernism, even as literary and artistic modernisms provide us with a rich repertoire of images and emotions that enable new ways of experiencing and inhabiting the modern city.

17. See John McLeod, *Postcolonial London: Rewriting the Metropolis* (London: Routledge, 2004), 5. See also John Clement Ball, *Imagining London: Postcolonial Fiction and the Transnational Metropolis* (Toronto: University of Toronto Press, 2004).

18. See Daniel Bell, *The Cultural Contradictions of Capitalism* (New York: Basic Books, 1975), 19. Michel de Certeau traces the emergence of the concept of a city as urban fact that could "be dealt with as a unity determined by an urbanistic ratio," to city planning which entailed the thinking of both "the very plurality of the real and to make that way of thinking the plural effective". Thus, rational organization along with its "'speculative' and classificatory operations" that both differentiate and redistribute the parts and the functions of the city would get rid of the waste products of "a functionalist administration"—the waste products being abnormality, deviance, illness, death, etc. . Though de Certeau does not focus on gender and sexuality, nor on race and class, these were undoubtedly instrumental concepts in designating what constituted the detritus of the modern imperial urban complex. See *The Practice of Everyday Life* (Berkeley and Los Angeles: University of California Press, 1988), 94–95.

19. Sennett, *The Flesh and Stone*, 319.

20. Sennett, *The Flesh and Stone*, 322.

21. Sennett, *The Flesh and Stone*, 322. .

22. Sennett, *The Flesh and Stone*, 320– 323. For illustrative examples, see especially Henry Mayhew, *London Labour and the London Poor*, ed. John Rosenberg (New York: Dover, 1968); William Booth, *In Darkest England and the Way Out* (London: International Headquarters of Salvation Army, 1890).

23. Anne McClintock suggests how "Victorian social planners drew deeply on social Darwinism and the idea of degeneration to figure the social crises erupting relentlessly in the cities and colonies". In particular, she argues that cataloguing and measuring social groups fit in with "the inherently imperial project of Victorian empiricism". See *Imperial Leather* (New York: Routledge, 1995), 46.

24. See Gareth Stedman Jones, *Outcast London* (New York: Pantheon, 1971).

25. Ian Baucom, *Out of Place* (Princeton: Princeton University Press, 1999), 57. Baucom writes of Ruskin's view of London that saw the city as a "savage" waste ground, inhabited by "Arabs" and "Gipsys" (in *Seven Lamps of Architecture*), quoted in Baucom, *Out of Place*, 61. Henry Mayhew wrote of the London poor as "the vagabond savage"; T .H. Huxley compared the East London poor with the Polynesian savage; William Booth compared the poor to African pygmies; William Barry in *The New Antigone* (London: Barry, 1887) compared slums to slave ships. The poor were widely regarded as belonging to another country, the "dark continent" (Sims). Engels, too, had referred to the working classes as a "degenerate race". See Friedrich Engels, *The Condition of the Working Class in England* (1844), trans. W. O. Henderson and W. H. Chaloner (Stanford, Calif.: Stanford University Press, 1958); 4. After the abolition of slavery in 1834 even the poor blacks of the Caribbean were supposed to be better than "the wretched half-starved weavers" of England, according to attorney William Shand. He is quoted in Catherine Hall, "What Is a West Indian?" in *West Indian Intellectuals in Britain*, ed. Bill Schwarz (Manchester: Manchester University Press, 2003), 31–50, 39.
26. Baucom, *Out of Place*, 36.
27. McClintock writes how "crises in the cities (were) compounded by crises in the colonies". See *Imperial Leather*, 46. Baucom suggests, along similar lines that "a metropolitan crisis in the imagined community of Englishness is at once imitative and prophetic of an imperial crisis" such that the urban ghetto and the imperial frontier were "troped as descriptively interchangeable". See *Out of Place*, 61. The production of the two sorts of crises was thus deeply integral to the maintenance and consolidation of the colonial project.
28. Raymond Williams, *The Country and the City* (London: the Hogarth Press, 1985; first published 1973), 229.
29. Recent scholarship has sought to rectify this omission. See Peter Fryer, *Staying Power: The History of Black People in Britain* (London: Pluto Press, 1984) and *Black People in the British Empire: An Introduction* (London: Pluto Press, 1988) for a historical account of the presence of black people in Britain since the seventeenth century. Planters had returned to Britain with black servants who worked as pages and laundry maids. By the eighteenth century, about 20,000 black people were present in London, working as pages, cooks, valets, maids, coachmen, beggars and street singers, and roughly comprising about 3 percent of the city's population. See Anna Marie Smith, *New Right Discourse on Race and Sexuality: Britain, 1968–1990* (Cambridge: Cambridge University Press, 1994). See also Shompa Lahiri, *Indians in Britain: Anglo-Indian Encounters, Race and Identity, 1880–1930* (London and Portland, Ore: Frank Cass, 2000);and Rozina Visram, *Ayah, Lascars and Princes: The Stories of Indians in Britain, 1700–1947* (London: Pluto Press, 1986).
30. See McClintock, *Imperial Leather*, 72.
31. Baucom, *Out of Place*, 56.
32. Engels, *The Condition of the Working Class in England*, 148.
33. The twentieth century also saw the introduction of electric trains in the London underground and the introduction of the motorways, paving the way for faster transportation from one part of the city to another.
34. Quoting Gustave Le Bon's assertion that "crowds are everywhere distinguished by feminine characteristics," Huyssen notes what Theodor Adorno also saw in the deployment of mass culture by modernism, the "threat of castration" as one of the constitutive features of male psychology. See Andreas

Huyssen, *After the Great Divide: Modernism, Mass Culture, Postmodernism* (Bloomington: Indiana University Press, 1986), 52.

35. See Walter Benjamin, "Motifs in Baudelaire" in *Illuminations*, trans. Hannah Arendt (New York: Schocken Books, 1967), 155–200. The surrealism of Baudelaire's writing, its ability to evoke the perceived unreality of the modern city, and its disjuncture with all previous notions of urban space has become a central point of reference in twentieth-century theories of modernity.

36. For an analysis of Benjamin's writings on the city in which he expresses sentiments not dissimilar from Baudelaire's, especially in his essays "A Berlin Chronicle" and "Central Park", see Rey Chow, "Walter Benjamin's Love Affair with Death", in *New German Critique* 48 (Fall 1989), 61–86.

37. See Benjamin, "Motifs in Baudelaire ", 169.

38. Chow does not comment on the disappearance of the masses as a political entity, indicating the political loss inherent in modernism's reading of urban space. The deployment of women's bodies as either faceless, deformed or monstrous in the modernist discourse on the city created a powerful analogy between city spaces and spaces of the feminine body and also influenced thinking about gendered political agency in the city. McClintock points this out in accounts of the labyrinthine city that "projected the female body onto the modern city as its first shape" (McClintock, *Imperial Leather*, 82). But there were also the growing multitudes who were racially and culturally Other to the normative female subject of feminist literary criticism.

39. See Anke Gleber, "Female Flanerie and the Symphony of the City", in *Women in the Metropolis: Gender and Modernity in Weimar Culture*, ed. Katharina von Ankum (Berkeley and Los Angeles: University of California Press, 1997): 67–88, 68.

40. Jamie Owen Daniel points out that the *flaneur* "was able to experience modernity from the bifurcated 'subject position' of an acculturated man of letters who could divest himself of his individualized bourgeois identity at will in order to become just another 'man of the crowd'". See "Strategies of Detachment: Modernist Impersonality and Bodily Loss between the Wars," Dissertation: University of Wisconsin-Milwaukee, 1995.

41. See Walter Benjamin, "A Berlin Chronicle", in *Refelctions: Essays Aphorisms, Autobiographical Writings*, trans. Edmund Jephcott. New York: Schocken Books, 1986, 11. The figure of the *flaneur* became the archetypal subject of urban modernity, originally drawn from nineteenth-century French culture and literature. In England as well, the aesthete or the dandy was viewed as a typically urban figure, distilling through his experiences new literary and artistic forms that were organically tied to London's new metropolitan forms. See Bradbury, "London 1890–1920", 81.

42. See Chow, "Walter Benjamin's Love Affair with Death", 85.

43. See Daniel, "Strategies of Detachment".

44. Huyssen points to the "fundamentally differing social and psychological constitution and validation of male and female subjectivity in modern bourgeois society" in which the woman writer does not find the "reification of self in the aesthetic product quite as attractive and compelling an ideal as the male writer" (*After the Great Divide*, 46).

45. Judith Walkowitz, *City of Dreadful Delight: Narratives of Sexual Danger in Late-Victorian London* (Chicago: University of Chicago Press, 1992); 39.

46. See Adrian Rifkin, *Street Noises: Parisian Pleasure–1900–1940* (Manchester: Manchester University Press, 1993); 9. The motorcar enabled people to live at a distance from their work place, cinema turned entertainment into a mass industry, modern weapons and methods of warfare rendered cities vulnerable, and advertisements for products enabled mass consumption and

created new desires and identities. For an analysis of how the rise of the advertising industry took the private realm into the public, and took the public (such as scenes of empire) into every home, see McClintock, *Imperial Leather*, 209, ff. For revisionist and feminist accounts of modernism, with (through a more diverse and inter-disciplinary methodology) a focus on popular culture of the modernist era, see, for instance, Rita Felski, *The Gender of Modernity* (Cambridge: Harvard University Press, 1995); Rachel Bowlby, *Just Looking: Consumer Culture in Dreiser, Gissing and Zola* (London: Methuen, 1985).

47. On this point, see Michelle Sipe, "Romancing the City: Arthur Symons and the Spatial Politics of Aesthetics in 1890s London", in Gilbert *Imagined Londons*, 69–84, 70.

48. Sophie Watson and Katherine Gibson "Postmodern Cities, Spaces and Politics: An Introduction", in *Postmodern Cities and Spaces*, ed. Sophie Watson and Katherine Gibson (Oxford: Blackwell, 1995), 1–12, 4.

49. Walkowitz, *City of Dreadful Delight*. See also Elizabeth Wilson, "The Invisible Flaneur", in Watson and Gibson, *Postmodern Cities and Spaces*, 59–79.

50. Alexandre-Jean-Baptiste Parent-Duchalet, an early-nineteenth-century Parisian public health official saw prostitutes as "a noxious part of the environment, identifiable and controllable, not unlike sewers or decaying meat". See *De la prostitution de la ville de Paris*, 2 vols. (Paris: J.-B. Bailliere, 1836); quoted in Luise White, *The Comforts of Home: Prostitution in Colonial Nairobi* (Chicago: University of Chicago Press, 1990), 2–3.

51. Walter Benjamin, "Central Park", *New German Critique*, no. 34 (Winter 1985), 32–58, 42.

52. See Bowlby, *Just Looking.*

53. Edward Long wrote: "The lower class of women in England are remarkably fond of blacks." See his *Candid Reflections* (London: T. Lowndes, 1772), 48. See McClintock, *Imperial Leather*, 42 ff for an analysis of how women and blacks were analogized.

54. McClintock, *Imperial Leather*, 56.

55. McClintock, *Imperial Leather*, 53.

56. Since at least the mid-nineteenth century in London working-class women, especially seamstresses and domestic servants, were present in overwhelming numbers. For the rising numbers of working-class women working in the city throughout the nineteenth century see McClintock, *Imperial Leather*, 85. See also Eunice Lipton, "The Laundress in Late Nineteenth-Century French Culture: Imagery, Ideology and Edgar Degas", in Frascina and Harrison eds. *Modern Art and Modernism*, 275–283, London: Sage, 1982. Wilson, "Invisible Flaneur". Deborah Epstein Nord, in her book *Walking the Victorian Streets: Women, Representation, and the City* (Ithaca: Cornell University Press, 1995), examines the role of middle-class unmarried women in the 1880s who "for a time lived out the possibility of social and economic independence" (182), as well as the evolution of the role of "the female social investigator" performed by middle-class women at the turn of the century (207–236). Walkowitz in *City of Dreadful Delight* also describes the entry of a whole new range of women—shopping ladies, Salvation Army lasses, charity workers, matchgirls on strike and glorified spinsters—on to the contested terrain of London in the 1880s (41–80). For an overall view, see Janet Wolff, *Feminine Sentences: Essays on Women and Culture* (Berkeley and Los Angeles: University of California Press, 1990).

57. See Kumkum Sangari and Sudesh Vaid, eds. *Recasting Women: Essays in Colonial History* (New Delhi: Kali for Women, 1989) for accounts of how the

western ideology of separate spheres was part of Britain's cultural imperialism in India and its cultural construction of Indian womanhood.

58. See Liz Heron, ed. *City Women: Stories of the World's Great Cities* (Boston: Beacon Press, 1993), 2.

59. Imperialist ideologies of gender still occur only as footnotes, when they do at all, even in more recent studies of gender and modernity. See Felski, *The Gender of Modernity*; Bonnie Kime Scott, ed. *The Gender of Modernism: A Critical Anthology* (Bloomington: Indiana University Press, 1990). Anne McClintock's *Imperial Leather* has enabled important avenues of inquiry in this regard, opening up the archive of imperial metropolitanism to questions of race and colonialism while remaining rigorously loyal to her scholarly commitments to feminist inquiry.

60. See essays in Sangari and Vaid, *Recasting Women.*

61. See Susan Buck-Morss, "The *Flaneur*, the Sandwichman and the Whore: The Politics of Loitering", *New German Critique* 39 (Fall 1986), 99–140, 118.

62. De Certeau, "Walking in the City", in *The Practice of Everyday Life*, 97.

63. De Certeau, "Walking in the City", 103.

64. Rifkin notes in the case of France that the *trajet*, or the trace of the *flaneur*'s wanderings in the city, became "a highly finished genre amongst Parisian intellectuals . . . combining the *recit*, the memoir, the diary and different forms of fiction". See *Street Noises*, 20.

65. As already discussed earlier, planning as a political enterprise had been particularly reactive to the experiences of the French Revolution, the Paris Commune and other mass upheavals.

66. Sennett, *Flesh and Stone*, 323.

67. Sennett, *Flesh and Stone*, 347.

68. Baucom, *Out of Place*, 59.

69. Baucom, *Out of Place*, 57.

70. Victorian England was riven with contradictory attitudes towards the loss of organic or local space in urbanity. While on the one hand, middle-class men of letters often took on the role of being social investigators with the freedom to walk about the city in order to record social conditions, the threat of nomadism to a stable civilization lurked dangerously in the national imagination. Henry Mayhew famously wrote of "two distinct and broadly marked races"—that of "the vagabond" and that of the "citizen". See *London Labour and the London Poor* (London: Charles Griffin and Company, 1851), 1–2, in Baucom, *Out of Place*, 62.

71. De Certeau, *The Practice of Everyday Life*, 101.

72. See Michel Foucault, "Of Other Spaces", *Diacritics* vol. 16 (Spring 1986): 22–27.

73. De Certeau, *The Practice of Everyday Life*, 93.

74. This idea of women walking the streets has also been taken up in Deborah Epstein Nord's book, *Walking the Victorian Streets.*

75. See Benjamin, "Central Park", 41.

76. Erin Carlston, *Thinking Fascism: Sapphic Modernism and Fascist Modernity* (Stanford, Calif.: Stanford University Press, 1994). See also Bonnie Kime Scott, *The Gender of Modernism.*

77. Woolf is the only woman writer, and *Mrs Dalloway* is the only woman-authored text that is mentioned by Malcolm Bradbury in his essay on the place of London in the geography of modernism. The essay is contained in a series of canonical readings of modernism enshrined in Bradbury's 1976 edited anthology of essays entitled *Modernism*. See also Rachel Bowlby for an account of literary modernism's appropriation of Woolf as a modernist writer *par excellence* in *Virginia Woolf: Feminist Destinations* (Oxford: Basil

Blackwell, 1988), 12–13. Woolf's established place within the Bloomsbury Group of course complicates any assessment of her *oeuvre* as counter-modernist. But the emphasis on gender and colonial issues in her writing points us to the critiques of modern imperial and masculinist culture embedded in her work.

78. See Martin Fuchs, "India and Modernity: Towards Decentring Western Perspectives", *Thesis Eleven* 39 (1994): v–xiii, v.

79. See Patrick Williams, "'Simultaneous Uncontemporaneities': Theorising Modernism and Empire", in *Modernism and Empire*, ed. Howard J. Booth and Nigel Rigby (Manchester: Manchester University Press, 2000), 13–38, for an overview of some of these approaches.

80. Jean Rhys, *Voyage in the Dark* (New York: W. W. Norton & Co., 1982). All subsequent page references will be from this edition.

81. The influence of French culture on Dominica, secured by the British in 1805, remained such that the African-Caribbean majority spoke a French patois. Here Rhys was part of a small Protestant elite in a majority Catholic culture. She went to a Catholic school where whites were in a minority.

82. See *Smile Please: An Unfinished Autobiography* (Harmondsworth: Penguin, 1981; first pub. 1979), 135.

83. See Catherine Hall, "What Is a West Indian?" in Schwarz, *West Indian Intellectuals in Britain*, 31–50, 36

84. For her time in France see Jean Rhys, *The Left Bank and Other Stories* (New York: Books for Libraries, 1927) and *Good Morning Midnight* (New York: Penguin, 2000).

85. In Jean Rhys, *The Left Bank and Other Stories*. New York: Books for Libraries; first published 1927, 24. It is not without significance that Rhys's importance as a modernist writer has grown in tandem with the rising influence of feminist and postcolonial literary theory in the 1980s. Even now her novel *Wide Sargasso Sea*, a re-working of Charlotte Bronte's *Jane Eyre* re-set in the Caribbean, remains her best-known work, even as critics like Braithwaite have argued that a celebration of *Wide Sargasso Sea* as a Caribbean novel takes away from a focus on the brutalities of racial exploitation. In fact, *Wide Sargasso Sea* has now become part of the canon of postcolonial texts that are routinely read and taught in the western academy. See Peter Hulme, "The Place of *Wide Sargasso Sea*", *Wasafiri* 20 (1994) and "A Response to Kamau Braithwaite", *Wasafiri* 23 (1996); E. K. Braithwaite, "A Post-cautionary Tale of the Helen of Our Wars", *Wasafiri*, 22 (1995) and in *Roots* (Ann Arbor: University of Michigan Press, 1993); Mervyn Morris, "Oh, Give the Girl a Chance: Jean Rhys and *Voyage in the Dark*", *Journal of West Indian Literature* 3, no.2 (1989): 1–8; Kenneth Ramchand, "Introduction", in Selvon, *Lonely Londoners* (London: Longman Caribbean Series, 1986) [1956], 3–21 for the contentious nature of Rhys's positioning as a Caribbean writer. See also Jean D'Costa, "Jean Rhys, 1890–1979" in *Fifty Caribbean Writers*, ed. Daryl Dance (New York: Greenwood Press, 1986); and Veronica Marie Gregg, "Jean Rhys on Herself as a Writer", in. *Caribbean Women Writers: Essays from the First International Conference, ed.* Selwyn Cudjoe (Wellesley, Mass.: Calaloux Publications, 1990), 109–115 for more detailed explications of Rhys's complex location within literary modernism. See also Bonnie Kime Scott's Introduction to *The Gender of Modernism* for a summary of the canonical controversies surrounding modernism and gender. Canonical modernism also left out writers of the Harlem Renaissance and of the Negritude movement, including an emerging and influential group of West Indian writers in London such as George Lamming and C. L. R. James. See

Veronica Marie Gregg, *Jean Rhys's Historical Imagination: Reading and Writing the Creole* (Chapel Hill: University of North Carolina Press, 1995).

86. See Helen Carr, "Jean Rhys: West Indian Intellectual", in Schwarz, *West Indian Intellectuals in Britain*, 93–113, 96.

87. See Kenneth Ramchand, *The West Indian Novel and Its Background* (London: Faber and Faber, 1970).

88. Judith Kegan Gardiner; *Rhys, Stead, Lessing and the Politics of Empathy* (Bloomington: Indiana University Press, 1989), 22–24.

89. See Sukhdev Sandhu, *London Calling: How Black and Asian Writers Reimagined a City* (London: HarperCollins, 2003).

90. The black majority population of Dominica is "more a part of the place than we were" (*Smile Please*, 50).

91. In many ways, this sense of being outside the dominant culture, as exiles, comprised the predicament of other modernist writers well. In Edward Said's writings Joseph Conrad occupies the space of the quintessential outsider in the modern world. He writes of how Conrad knew that "your self-consciousness as an outsider can allow you actively to comprehend how the machine works, given that you and it are fundamentally not in perfect sympathy or correspondence. Never the wholly incorporated and fully acculturated Englishman, Conrad therefore preserved an ironic distance in each of his works." See *Culture and Imperialism*, 25.

92. Critics Rosalind Miles and Peter Wolfe quoted in Gardiner, *Rhys, Stead, Lessing and the Politics of Empathy*.

93. See Gardiner, *Rhys, Stead, Lessing and the Politics of Empathy*, 6.

94. Gardiner, *Rhys, Stead, Lessing and the Politics of Empathy*, 233.

95. Rhys draws much of the material of the novel from her own life. She came to England in 1907 to study at the Royal Academy of Dramatic Art, only returning once to the Caribbean some thirty years later. In England, she worked as a chorus girl, and during the war, in a soldiers' canteen. In 1919 she traveled to Europe and started writing fiction in Paris in the 1920s. After World War II she disappeared from public life until the publication of her highly acclaimed novel *Wide Sargasso Sea* in 1966.

96. Biographically, we know that Rhys herself was forced to give up acting because she was not able to fully pass as English.

97. As mentioned earlier, Charlotte Bronte's Bertha in *Jane Eyre* is the most canonical instance of such a representation, one that Rhys was to re-write in her novel *Wide Sargasso Sea* published almost thirty years after *Voyage in the Dark*.

98. Huyssen points out that "the theater in bourgeois society was one of the few spaces which allowed women a prime place in the arts, precisely because acting was seen as imitative and reproductive, rather than original and productive" See *After the Great Divide*, 51. The actress in modern literature was read by Baudelaire as "a sort of gipsy wandering on the fringes of a regular society" ("The Salon of 1846: On the Herosim of Modern Life", in *Modern Art and Modernism*, edited by Francis Frascina and Charles Harrison (New York: Harper and Row, 1987), 17–18), and as comprising "a perfect image of the savagery that lurks in the midst of civilization" ("The Painter of Modern Life", in *Modern Art and Modernism: A Critical Anthology*, edited by Francis Frascina and Charles Harrison [New York: Harper and Row, 1987], 25–26). "She is close both to the courtesan and the poet", Baudelaire writes in "The Salon" (25–26). As courtesan, she has affinities with "criminals and kept women—which drift about in the underworld of a great city" (18). Other nineteenth- and early-twentieth-century novels such as Emile Zola's *Nana*,

Flaubert's *Madame Bovary* and Theodore Dreiser's *Sister Carrie* were texts that reflected and produced the dominant trends in the literary representation of women in the city.

99. See Huyssen, *After the Great Divide*, 50.

100. This complex positioning against mass culture while being articulated with it is evidenced in the dandies' fascination with lower-class women in general and in the *flaneur*'s interest in prostitutes in particular. Art historian Eunice Lipton, focusing on the figure of the laundress in the late-nineteenth century, points to the modernist fascination with images of working-class women haunting the outskirts of the city, socially inferior yet sexually titillating. See her "The Laundress," 275–283.

101. When and if the Impressionists showed artistic interest in the working classes, the representations tended to be genre-like depictions of lower-class women working in commercial spaces. See Lipton, "The Laundress", 279.

102. Helen Carr writes about how critics have portrayed Rhys as an unintellectual figure, "working unaware of other writers and in isolation from the intellectual currents of her day". See "Jean Rhys: West Indian Intellectual", 99. Carr points to how Judith Gardiner broke new ground in arguing that Rhys was a literary, self-conscious and modernist writer. See Judith Kegan Gardiner, "Good Morning Midnight; Good Night, Modernism", *Boundary* 2, no 11 (1982–83), 233–251.

103. Charles Baudelaire, "The Painter",23–27.

104. Rey Chow writes of how "for the male fetishist, the female body 'exists' . . . as an image". See "Walter Benjamin's Love Affair with Death", 81.

105. Karl Marx, *The Economic and Philosophical Manuscripts*, in *Early Writings* (New York: Vintage, 1975); 323–324, emphasis in the original.

106. See Surrealist magazines such as *Documents, La revolution Surrealiste* and *Minotaure* for examples of their use of the mannequin.

107. Guy Debord, *The Society of the Spectacle* (Detroit: Black and Red Books, 1977) [1967].

108. Benjamin reads the capitalist city as emerging from "the effects of man being looked rather than man looking . . . a fascination." See Chow, "Walter Benjamin's Love Affair with Death", 80.

109. Helen Carr, *Jean Rhys* (Plymouth: Northcote House, 1996), 29.

110. Siegfried Kracauer, "The Hotel Lobby", in *The Mass Ornament: Weimar Essays*, trans and ed. Thomas Y. Levin (Cambridge: Harvard University Press, 1995), 173–185. See also Fredric Jameson's discussion of Bonaventura Hotel as archetypal postmodern space in his *Postmodernism, or, the Cultural Logic of Late Capitalism* (Durham, N.C.: Duke University Press, 1991).

111. Benjamin, *Illuminations*. Chow notes Benjamin's interest in "images, which, like scenes of crime, have been left empty". See her "Walter Benjamin's Love Affair with Death", 72.

112. See Baudelaire, "The Salon".

113. Novels by Andre Breton (*Nadja*), Max Ernst (*La Femme 100 Testes*), and photographs by Atget, Brassai and Kertesz, all similarly evoke the city of Paris as the site of the uncanny encounter between strangers and between objects and urban space.

114. Walter Benjamin, "Surrealism: The Last Snapshot of the European Intelligentsia", in *One Way Street and Other Writings*, trans. Edmund Jephcott and Kingsley Shorter (London: Verso, 1985).

115. By the 1880s the urban poor had moved out of the center of London to gain more space for living quarters. Working-class districts now became noticeable due to the introduction of row houses, and a more frugal use of space. Sennett notes that from middle-class standards "the architectural quality

seemed appalling; the housing was depressing, badly built, damp, the out-door privies stinking. By working-class standards, however, the housing was an immense achievement. People slept on a different floor than they ate; the smell of urine and faeces no longer pervaded the interior". See *Flesh and Stone*, 334.

116. Sennett points out how the grim outsides of houses were an important aspect of an urban aesthetic deployed to sharpen demarcations between the outside from the inside, public from private. In fact, as far back as in 1774 a city ordinance had banned any outside markers or distinguishing characteristics. See *Flesh and Stone*, 327.

117. Jameson, "Modernism and Imperialism", 50–51.

118. Gautam Premnath, "Lonely Londoner: V. S. Naipaul and 'the God of the City'", in Gilbert, *Imagined Londons*, 177–192, 184.

119. Kumkum Sangari, "The Politics of the Possible", *Cultural Critique* 7 (Fall 1987), 182.

120. Patrick Williams, "Simultaneous Uncontemporaneities".

121. See David Scott, *Conscripts of Modernity:The Tragedy of Colonial Enlightenment* (Durham, N.C.: Duke University Press, 2004).

122. C. L. R. James, *Beyond a Boundary* (New York: Pantheon Books, 1983), 50.

123. See Paul Buhle, *C .L .R. James: The Artist as Revolutionary* (London: Verso, 1988), 32.

124. C. L. R.James, *Minty Alley*, 2d ed. (London and Port of Spain: New Beacon Books, 1971), 244. All subsequent page references appear in the body of the main text.

125. Kenneth Ramchand, "Introduction" to James, *Minty Alley*. 14.

126. C. L. R.James, "The Nucleus of a Great Civilization", in *Letters from London* (Oxford: Signal Books, 2003), 111–125, 111.

127. James, *Letters from London*, 66.

128. Ramchand, "Introduction" to James, *Minty Alley*. 5, 12.

129. Ramchand, "Introduction" to James, *Letters from London*, xvi.

130. James, "Houses", in *Letters from London*, 59–70, 64.

131. James, *Letters from London*, 67.

132. James, *Letters from London*, 94.

133. James, *Letters from London*, 98.

134. James, *Letters from London*, 100.

135. James, *Letters from London*, 102.

136. C. L. R. James, "The Women", in *Letters from London*, 93–107. In this piece James also wrote about the absence of colour prejudice among white English women. In fact, he found possibilities of deep friendship and solidarity among white English women and foreign men of different colours and accents.

137. Doubts about the whiteness of Creoles were persistent but also creoleness itself was subjected to changing meanings. See Hall, "What Is a West Indian?"

138. Sander Gilman, "The Hottentot and the Prostitute: Toward an Iconography of Female Sexuality". In *Difference and Pathology: Stereotypes of Sexuality, Race and Madness* (Ithaca: Cornell University Press, 1985): 176–198. Interestingly, Andrea Levy in *Small Island* instills this abjected body with a proto-African nationalism in the figure of the articulate black man in the Empire Exhibition of 1924.

139. Kenneth Ramchand, Introduction to Sam Selvon's *Lonely Londoners*, 3.

140. Josephine Baker became quite a phenomenon in Europe. Jazz formed an important element in the spread of black culture in fashionable urban locales. See Nancy Nenno "Femininity, the Primitive, and Modern Urban

Space: Josephine Baker in Berlin", in von Ankum, *Women in the Metropolis*, 145–161.
141. See Premnath; "Lonely Londoner", 185.
142. Premnath; "Lonely Londoner", 184.
143. Sue Thomas, *The Worlding of Jean Rhys* (Westport, Conn.: Greenwood Press, 1999), 103.
144. Schwarz's claim that "Samuel Selvon's The *Lonely Londoners* marks the comprehensive inauguration of this sub-genre of the West Indian novel, and in so doing, invented a new diasporic realism" is on this reading historically inaccurate. *Lonely Londoners* was first published in 1956, some twenty years after Rhys's novel. See his "Introduction" to *West Indian Intellectuals in Britain*, 9.

Notes to Chapter 2

1. Bronislaw Malinowski, "Introduction", in *Methods of Study Culture Contact in Africa* (London: Memorandum XV of International Institute of African Languages and Cultures 1938), vii–xxxviii, vii–x. For analyses of the role of anthropology in the colonial enterprise see Talal Asad, ed. *Anthropology and the Colonial Encounter* (Atlantic Heights, N.J.: Humanities Press, 1973); Gaurav Desai, *Subject to Colonialism: African Self-Fashioning and the Colonial Library* (Durham, N.C.: Duke University Press, 2001); and Johannes Fabian, *Time and Its Other: How Anthropology Makes Its Object* (New York: Columbia University Press, 1985).
2. The British government declared East Africa (as Kenya was then known) as a crown protectorate in 1895. At the time, there were no pre-colonial cities in the Kenyan interior as such, although there were "central places" or nodes of exchange around which caravan towns existed since the end of the eighteenth century. The British overlaid the pre-colonial landscape with their own spatialized grids of control. Roger Kurtz refers to this as a "tri-faceted, non-integrated spatiality" that was irrevocably altered by the Ugandan railway. See Kurtz, *Urban Obsessions, Urban Fears: The Postcolonial Kenyan Novel* (Trenton, N.J.: Africa World Press,, 1998), 76.
3. See Jean Hay, "Historical Background", in *Coming to Birth* , by Marjorie Oludhe Macgoye (New York: Feminist Press of the City University of New York, 2000), 194.
4. Nairobi's Maasai name means "place of cold waters", suggesting a place of calm and repose.
5. See Kurtz, *Urban Obsessions*, 6.
6. Kenya has had an extremely high rate of urban growth since independence in 1963. As well, the growth rate in urban areas has been twice that of the nation overall in what is still a largely under-urbanized region. In Nairobi, the capital of Kenya, this growth has been seven-fold since independence.
7. The British colonialists actively encouraged white farmers, from Britain and South Africa, to settle on land in East Africa. In 1914, there were more than five thousand settlers who had been rewarded with the best, most fertile land in central Kenya. By 1950 there were about twenty thousand white settlers. See Hay, "Historical Background".
8. Nairobi replaced and overtook medieval and early modern urban centers such as Mombasa that had pre-existed British colonial rule and had been an important trading node in the Indian Ocean commercial traffic (Arabs, Portuguese). Nairobi was strictly a colonial creation.

9. See Simon Gikandi, "Reason, Modernity and the African Crisis", in *African Modernities*, ed. Jan-Georg Deutsch, Peter Probst and Heike Schmidt (Portsmouth, N.H.: Heinemann and Oxford: James Currey, 2002), 135–157, 136.

10. See AbdouMaliq Simone, *For the City Yet to Come: Changing African Life in Four Cities* (Durham, N.C.: Duke University Press, 2004), 1.

11. Simone, *For the City Yet to Come*, 1.

12. See Mahmood Mamdani, *Citizen and Subject: Contemporary Africa and the Legacy of Late Colonialism* (Princeton: Princeton University Press, 1996).

13. Mamdani, *Citizen and Subject*, 17–18.

14. Mamdani, *Citizen and Subject*, 17–18.

15. Mamdani, *Citizen and Subject*, 19.

16. Mamdani, *Citizen and Subject*, 22. Mamdani in fact argues that "the interethnic divide is" also "an effect of a larger split, also politically enforced, between town and country" (24).

17. David Simon, "Rethinking Cities, Sustainability, and Development in Africa", in *Sacred Spaces and Public Quarrels: African Cultural and Economic Landscapes* , ed. Ezekiel Kalipeni and Paul T. Zeleza (Trenton, N.J.: Africa World Press, 1999), 17–42, 20.

18. Simon, "Rethinking Cities", 23–24.

19. See the discussion in the Introduction.

20. There were three main divisions in the city's plans: white railway officers' quarters, native housing and the Indian bazaar that would serve as a buffer between the white and the black native parts. The Williams Report of 1907, the Simpson Report of 1913, and the Feetham Report of 1926 of the Planning Commission all recommended explicit racial segregation as the basis for city planning. See Andrew Hake, *African Metropolis: Nairobi's Self-Help City* (London: Sussex University Press, 1977).

21. Cited in R. van Zwanenberg, "History and Theory of Urban Poverty in Nairobi: The Problem of Slum Development", *Journal of East African Research and Development* 2 (1972), 167–203.

22. Unlike other capital cities in settler colonies, Nairobi did not require a permanent labor force as the city lacked an industrial base. Most Africans in the city were male migrants or those in the service sector, working as servants and prostitutes. The post-war economic boom led to the proliferation of an informal sector—hawkers, barbers, etc.—the out-of-works and undesirables that the colonial state wanted removed annually.

23. Luise White, *The Comforts of Home: Prostitution in Colonial Nairobi* (Chicago: University of Chicago Press, 1990), ix.

24. White, *The Comforts of Home*.

25. White, *The Comforts of Home*, 20.

26. Frederick Cooper, "Introduction", in *Struggle for the City: Migrant Labour, Capital, and the State in Urban Africa*, ed. Frederick Cooper (Beverly Hills/London/New Delhi: Sage Publications), 8.

27. Immigration restrictions before World War II produced a male-female ratio of 9:1. Even after restrictions were lifted after the war, and around independence, the ratio was 3:1.

28. White, *The Comforts of Home*, ix.

29. See Kenyatta's commentary in *Facing Mount Kenya* (New York: Vintage, 1965) on female circumcision at the center of debates about tradition and modernity. Kenyatta opposed the ban on clitoridectomy, and said it should be left to education and conscience See J. Murray-Brown, *Kenyatta* (Fontane: London, 1974). See Carolyn Martin Shaw for a gendered critique of Kenyatta in *Colonial Inscriptions: Race, Sex and Class in Kenya* (Minneapolis: University of Minneapolis Press, 1995).

30. John Lonsdale, "Jomo Kenyatta, God and the Modern World", in *African Modernities*, ed. Jan-Georg Deutsch, Peter Probst and Heike Schmidt (Portsmouth, N.H.: Heinemann and Oxford: James Currey, 2002), 31–66, 53.

31. Lonsdale, "Jomo Kenyatta", 54.

32. Civil society might be defined, using a broad brush-stroke, as that arena of society that is neither totally private nor within the direct purview of the state. Whereas there is an immense body of writings on the theories and philosophies of civil society, my interest here is to ground a general understanding of civil society in the specific, more national as well as local issues as they pertain to the formation of Nairobi as postcolonial capital.

33. Cooper, "Introduction", in *Struggle for the City*, 8.

34. Mamdani locates four moments in the development of civil society in Africa. Civil society's first moment of historical development consisted of "the colonial state as the protector of the society of the *colons*" (19). The second moment comprised the anti-colonial struggle, "a struggle of embryonic middle and working classes" in the native strata for entry into civil society. This kind of an anti-state struggle was basically a struggle for the creation of an indigenous civil society, based on demands for a deracialized state (20). The third moment is the moment of independence that is marked by the birth of a deracialized state but not of civil society because "historically accumulated privilege, usually racial, was embedded and defended in civil society". The fourth moment is characterized by the collapse of an embryonic indigenous civil society and its absorption into political society. This is when the claims of the socialist-developmentalist state assume "a powerful resonance for the educated classes"—in other words, become hegemonic. In this phase, "civil society movements are demobilized and political movements statized". See Mamdani, *Citizen and Subject*, 21.

35. Mamdani in fact argues that whereas the dismantling of racially inherited privilege to unify the victims of colonial racism was a laudable step in the right direction, redistribution happened along regional, religious and ethnic, and sometimes just familial lines. He writes that patrimonialism as "a form of politics restored an urban-rural link in the context of a bifurcated state, albeit in a top-down fashion that facilitated the quest of bourgeois fractions to strengthen and reproduce their leadership" (20). Through the system of clientelism then urban politicians were able to harness rural constituencies and establish links between the urban and the rural. Another link was the single party that unified urban militants with peasant insurrectionists. Mamdani notes that the single party attempted to contain differences, but solutions were always imposed from above. See *Citizen and Subject*.

36. Mamdani, *Citizen and Subject*, 21.

37. Gikandi, "On Language, Power, and National Identity: The Project of African Literature" (paper presented at the Language and Identity in Africa Symposium, Program of African Studies, Northwestern University, April 29–30, 1989), is quoted in Gaurav Desai, *Subject to Colonialism: African Self-Fashioning and the Colonial Library* (Durham, N.C.: Duke University Press), 109.

38. Lonsdale, "Jomo Kenyatta", 44.

39. Lonsdale, "Jomo Kenyatta", 55–56.

40. Gikandi, "Reason, Modernity and the African Crisis", 142.

41. Peter Probst, Jan-Georg Deutsch and Heike Scmidt, "Introduction: Cherished Visions and Entangled Meanings" in Deutsch et al., *African Modernities*, 9.

42. Jomo Kenyatta, *Suffering without Bitterness* (Nairobi: EAPH, 1968), 212.

43. Simon, "Rethinking Cities", 24.

44. See Ngugi wa Thiong'o, *Writers in Politics* (London: Heinemann, 1981), 87.
45. See David Hecht and Maliqalim Simone, *Invisible Governance: The Art of African Micropolitics* (New York: Autonomedia, 1994), 16–22.
46. See Achille Mbembe, "Provisional Notes on the Postcolony", *Africa* 62, no. 1 (1992), 3–37.
47. Mbembe argues "in the postcolony, the *commandement* seeks to institutionalize itself, in order to achieve legitimation and hegemony in the form of a *fetish*". See Mbembe, "The Banality of Power and the Aesthetics of Vulgarity in the Postcolony", trans. J. Roitman, *Public Culture* 4, no. 2 (1992):1–30, 3.
48. Mbembe, "The Banality of Power", 15.
49. Achille Mbembe and J. Roitman, "Figures of the Subject in Times of Crisis", *Public Culture* 7, no. 2 (1995):323–353, 324.
50. Mbembe, Hecht and Simone, and Jean and John Comaroff are the key post-modernist theorists of African politics and culture.
51. Gikandi, "Reason, Modernity and the African Crisis", 149.
52. Jean Comaroff and John Comaroff mark the eclipse of modernist categories such as class, replaced by irregular, menial, piecemeal work, by transient, gain-less occupation, by the experiential contradictions of neo-liberal capitalism, by "uneasy fusions" and the loss of the Utopia of freedom movements. See their "Millennial Capitalism: First Thoughts on a Second Coming", *Public Culture* 12, no. 2 (2000), 291–343. 326. Achille Mbembe and Sarah Nuttall situate their work on Johannesburg against readings that are "nothing but the spatial embodiment of unequal economic relations and coercive segregationist policies." See their "Writing the World from an African Metropolis", *Public Culture* 16, no. 3 (Fall 2004), 347–372, 353.
53. Simon, "Rethinking Cities", 25; Mbembe and Nuttall, "Writing the World", 354.
54. Simon, "Rethinking Cities", 24.
55. Jean Comaroff and John L. Comaroff point out that the "assertion of civil society against the state" is a "burgeoning global phenomenon". See "Millennial Capitalism".
56. See Hecht and Simone, *Invisible Governance*.
57. See Jean-Francois Bayart, *The State in Africa: The Politics of the Belly* (New York: Longman, 1993).
58. Cooper, "Introduction", in *Struggle for the City*, 18.
59. See Comaroff and Comaroff, "Millennial Capitalism", 307.
60. Hecht and Simone, *Invisible Governance*, 15.
61. See Alessandro Triulzi, "African Cities, Historical Memory and Street Buzz", in *The Post-Colonial Question: Common Skies, Divided Horizons*, ed. Iain Chambers and Lidia Curti (London: Routledge, 1996), 78.
62. See Mamdani, *Citizen and Subject*, 3.
63. African socialists like Julius Nyerere argued that rural Africa was pre-capitalist, and had nothing to do with markets, an idea resurrected, Mamdani argues, by Goran Hyden, who writes of a "premarket 'economy of affection'". Hyden argued that the "intrinsic realities" of "Africa" (based on research in Tanzania) have nothing to do with market relationships. See Goran Hyden, *Beyond Ujamaa in Tanzania* (London: Heinemann, 1980) and *No Shortcuts to Progress* (London: Heinemann, 1983), quoted in Mamdani, *Citizen and Subject*, 12–13.
64. See Kurtz, *Urban Obsessionss*, 155, 4.
65. See essays by writers like Soyinka (in the case of Lagos, Nigeria) and Ngugi for an elaboration of their political work in their fiction. See especially Wole Soyinka, "The Writer in a Modern African State", *Transition* 6, no. 3 (1967),

11–13; and Ngugi wa Thiong'o, "The Writer in African Society/Politics", in *Writers in Politics.*

66. See Fredric Jameson, "Third World Literature in the Era of Multinational Capitalism", *Social Text* 15 (1986), 65–88. See also the response of Aijaz Ahmad in *In Theory* (London: Verso, 1992). For a critique of Jameson's theory specifically in relation to Marjorie Macgoye's novel, *Coming to Birth*, see the last part of this chapter. See also Joseph R. Slaughter, "Master Plans: Designing (National) Allegories of Urban Space and Metropolitan Subjects for Postcolonial Kenya", *Research in African Literature* 35, no. 1 (Spring 2004), 30–42.

67. Kurtz points out that many writers, throughout the 1960s and into the early 1970s, identified themselves as East African rather than Kenyan or Tanzanian or Ugandan. This was both the product of British rule in East Africa (which they had attempted to unify as a political entity for rule, but not for resistance), and the postcolonial cultural and economic ties that were forged and elaborated, at least until the break-up of the East African Community in 1977. One feature of the complicated British attitude was that the encouragement accorded the publishing in indigenous tribal languages, for which the East African Literature Bureau was formed in 1948. As a result, Anglophone writing was neglected, and did not see any substantial publication until after independence in 1963. See *Urban Obessions,* 2. Kurtz's argument runs counter to Ngugi wa Thiong'o's analysis of the use of fiction writing in English as a resolutely colonial legacy. Ngugi writes: "Kenyan national literature should mostly be produced in the languages of the various nationalities that make up modern Kenya . . . Kenyan national literature can only grow and thrive if it reaches for its roots in the rich languages, cultures and history of the Kenyan peasant masses who are the majority class in each of Kenya's several nationalities". See *Writers in Politics*, 59.

68. See especially Meja Mwangi's urban trilogy and Marjorie Oludhe Macgoye's novels.

69. M. G. Vassanji, *The In-Between World of Vikram Lall* (Edinburgh: Canongate, 2003). Page references appear in text.

70. Kurtz suggests that the boom in the Nairobi novel began in 1970 with the publication of Leonard Kibera's *Voices in the Dark*, "the first novel to be set entirely in the city and the first to treat the city as a complete microcosm, a world unto itself that stands for what Kenya is rather than merely an aspect of Kenyan society" (*Urban Obsessions*, 71). Kurtz argues that before 1970 the city was either wholly overlooked or treated as a "foil" for "wholesome rural values" (74). After 1970, Nairobi begins to face major crises, and more and more writers turn to the city for subject matter. See *Urban Obsessions.*

71. See Kurtz, *Urban Obsessions*, 91–109. See also Luise White for a history of prostitution in Nairobi, *Comforts of Home.* For a book that occupies a tenuous position between being a sensationalist and a "realistic" account of a city prostitute, see Jasinta Mote's *The Flesh* (Nairobi: Comb Books, 1975), a "first person account" of a real-life Nairobi prostitute.

72. See David Maillu, *The Ayah* (Nairobi: Heinemann Kenya, 1986).

73. See Carole Boyce Davies, "Introduction", in *Ngambika: Studies of Women in African Literature*, ed. Carole Boyce Davies and Anne Adams Graves (Trenton, N.J.: Africa World Press, 1986), 1–23, 3. See G. C. M. Mutiso, "Women in African Literature", *East Africa Journal* 3, no. 3 (March 1971), 4–14; and Kenneth Little, *The Sociology of Urban Women's Image in African Literature* (Totowa, New Jersey: Rowman and Littlefield, 1980).

74. I am grateful to Nilanjana Dutta's seminar paper "The Nation and the Other Woman: A Commentary on Wanja and Douloti" for my course "The Postcolonial

Novel" (Spring 2002) at the University of North Carolina at Chapel Hill for clarifying many related issues for me.

75. Marjorie Oludhe Macgoye, *Coming to Birth* (Nairobi: Heinemann, 1988). All subsequent page numbers will be drawn from this edition and appear in text. *Coming to Birth* also appeared in Britain published by Virago, as part of its New Fiction series.

76. Ngugi wa Thiong'o, *Petals of Blood* (New York: Penguin, 1991). Page references appear in text. David Maugham-Brown argues that "a novel like *Petals of Blood* both draws attention to certain modes in which the effects of neo-colonialism may be 'lived', *and* gives us elements of a theoretical understanding of it." See his *Land, Freedom and Fiction: History and Ideology in Kenya* (London: Zed Books, 1985), 15.

77. Simon Gikandi, *Ngugi wa Thiong'o* (Cambridge: Cambridge University Press, 2000), x.

78. Gikandi, *Ngugi*, 2.

79. Ngugi, *Writers in Politics*, 5–6.

80. See Ngugi, *Writers in Politics*, 87.

81. Ngugi, *Writers in Politics*, 89. Ngugi draws upon dependency theory to argue that underdevelopment is historically produced under modern imperialism, and is as modern as industrial capitalism. Both industrial capitalism and underdevelopment are outcomes of a process of, in Samir Amin's formulation, "accumulation on a world scale". See Sanir Amin, *A Critique of the Theory of Underdevelopment* (2 Volumes) (New York: Monthly Review Press, 1974). Critics of dependency theory point out that it is historically specific but has lapsed into yet another form of ahistorical structuralism, seeing social reality through the binary opposites of development and underdevelopment. Mamdani has stressed the need for history to be read as process. See his *Citizen and Subject*.

82. Drawing on Balandier, Gikandi argues that Ngugi's view of history and cultural formation can be traced to Gikuyu nationalism that emerged out of the contradictions of colonialism and resistance to it. Gikandi, *Ngugi*, 15.

83. Ngugi, *Writers in Politics*, 87.

84. Mamdani writes: "Notwithstanding the colonial claim that traditional Africa was a tribal checkerboard, with each tribe in its own place, we have seen that tribal culture was highly textured and elastic, with the stranger often present on rural ground. For no reason other than to expand their following, the tendency of chiefs was to encourage strangers to settle in their domain. With a state-enforced and tribally circumscribed notion of custom, two related changes occurred. First, the tendency was to homogenize and flatten cultural diversity within the tribe in favor of an official tribal version. Second, the imposition of a tribal law as customary, to be defined and dispensed by a tribal authority, necessarily turned the simple fact of ethnic heterogeneity into a source of tension". See Mamdani, *Citizen and Subject*, 292.

85. Jane Bryce, "Profile: Ngugi: My Novel of Blood, Sweat and Tears". *New African* (August 1982), 36.

86. Davies, "Introduction", 11.

87. Bryce, "Profile", 36.

88. In *Devil on the Cross* (London: Heinemann, 1987), Ngugi similarly presents its heroine Wariinga, a secretary in Nairobi who returns to Ilmorog. Her coming to political consciousness also happens in the countryside that she sees exploited by the city.

89. Charles A. Nama, "Daughters of Moombi: Ngugi's Heroines and Traditional Gikuyu Aesthetics", in *Ngambika: Studies of Women in African Literature*, ed. Carole Boyce Davies and Anne Adams Graves (Trenton, N.J.: Africa World

Press, 1986), 139–149, 139. Nama in fact reads Kenyatta's *Facing Mount Kenya* as an authoritative source of Gikuyu mythology, recalling the legendary period in Gikuyu history when women ruled the land.

90. Ngugi, *Writers in Politics*, 93.
91. The 1950s was the decade of heightened peasant resistance, known as the Mau Mau insurgency, against British colonial rule. The movement, concentrated in the largely Kikuyu dominated central highlands of Kenya, had begun to spread to cities, especially Nairobi. The British dealt with the insurgency with a heavy hand, and introduced repressive measures such as the Emergency in 1952 in order to contain more widespread revolt against colonial power.
92. See Jameson, "Third World Literature", 69.
93. Joseph R. Slaughter, "Master Plans: Designing (National) Allegories of Urban Space and Metropolitan Subjects for Postcolonial Kenya", *Research in African Literatures* 35, no. 1 (Spring 2004): 30–42, 46.
94. Slaughter, "Master Plans", 47.
95. This scene is in marked contrast to the scene of Wanja's arrival in the countryside on a Peugeot matatu, loaded with signs of modernity that she is symbolically bringing with her to the village.
96. When rumors of Paulina's affair in Kisumu reach Nairobi and Martin, he beats her heavily, even as he maintained a wife in Nairobi in Paulina's absence. Gender relations in the countryside created a society in which rural homesteads were mostly inhabited by women and children, with the men away at work on plantations or in cities. Paulina's mother for instance is the head of household in the homestead in the countryside.
97. Working through the gaps between these new and contradictory cultures of modern urban conjugality, Paulina continues to support her family, and to meet people who would be bringing maize, bags of beans or flour or messages from the country.
98. Quoted in John Comaroff, "Governmentality, Materiality, Legality, Modernity: On the Colonial State in Africa" in *African Modernities*, ed. Jan-Georg Deutsch, Peter Probst and Heike Schmidt (London: James Currey, 2002), 107–134, 116. See also Council of World Mission, LMS South Africa Reports, 2–4, housed at SOAS, London.
99. Comaroff "Governmentality", 116.
100. Comaroff, "Governmentality".
101. Pumwani in particular, because of its high density of Kikuyu residents, was subjected to a great deal of surveillance. Kikuyus were often evicted, clearing space for ethnic groups such as Luos to move in.
102. Over 200 Kikuyus were arrested during this Emergency, including Jomo Kenyatta. Operation Anvil introduced the forced repatriation of KEM—Kikuyus, Embus and Merus—to rural stockades or to prisons. About 100,000 men and women were arrested in all. Kikuyus were seen to be the main force in the Mau Mau insurgency. By the time the Emergency was lifted in 1960, three years before independence, about 15,000 Africans and 100 Europeans had been killed.
103. This incident is based on the 1975 disappearance of Kikuyu politician and businessman Josiah Kariuki or J. M, best known for his 1963 account of imprisonment under British rule called *Mau Mau Detainee*. Only his mutilated body showed up. This incident was indicative of the cracks within KANU after the general elections of 1974.
104. It is worth noting that Paulina's entry into the world of politics is presented in sharp contrast to Martin's decline in his dead-end job of selling envelopes.

Notes to Chapter 3

1. "Civil Lines" was the name given by British colonial authorities to areas of a particular town or city in which British civilians and later privileged natives resided. It marked, along with other Western institutions, what Sanjay Srivastava refers to as the "sign of a 'rational' Occident in the 'irrational' Orient". See Sanjay Srivastava "Modernity and Post-coloniality: The Metropolis as Metaphor", *Economic and Political Weekly* (February 17, 1996), 403–412; 403.

2. Sunil Khilnani, *The Idea of India* (New Delhi: Penguin Books, 1997), 109.

3. Until well into the 1970s, the Indian economy was committed to a combination of socialist and capitalist economic systems. However, since the 1980s, under Prime Minister Rajiv Gandhi, the prevailing consensus on the economy began to erode, and the beginning of the 1990s witnessed a radical opening up of the Indian economy to direct foreign investment, partly dictated by the International Monetary Fund's structural adjustment requirements.

4. See Norma Evenson, *The Indian Metropolis: A View towards the West* (New Haven: Yale University Press, 1989), vii. Sunil Khilnani also uses the idea of the city as "the theatre where India's subjection to the British colonists was most graphically and regularly enacted". See *The Idea of India*. 108.

5. David Harvey, *The Condition of Postmodernity: An Enquiry into the Origins of Cultural Change* (Oxford and Cambridge, Mass.: Basil Blackwell, 1989), 261.

6. Srivastava, "Modernity and Post-coloniality", 404.

7. See Dipesh Chakrabarty, "Remembered Villages: Representations of Hindu-Bengali Memories in the Aftermath of Partition", *Economic and Political Weekly* (August 10, 1996): 2143–2151, 2148.

8. This is not to suggest at that villagers in postcolonial India are not marginal, but to point out the a-historical and sentimentalized representations that do not do justice to their agency, nor to the historical and economic processes through which the rural and urban sectors are constituted and immiseration produced.

9. Chakrabarty makes this point in his analysis of the literature of the Partition of India in which displaced urban citizens often expressed their nationalism by evoking ties to an idyllic village of their past childhood, and a return to which symbolized a return to their true home, snatched away by hateful Muslims. See his "Remembered Villages".

10. Partha Chatterjee, *The Politics of the Governed* (New Delhi: Permanent Black, 2004), 140.

11. Khilnani, *The Idea of India,* 109.

12. Chakrabarty, "Remembered Villages", 2145.

13. See Roshan G. Shahani, "Polyphonous Voices in the City: Bombay's Indian-English Fiction", *Economic and Political Weekly* (May 27, 1995): 1250–1254.

14. See Rashmi Varma, "Provincializing the Global City: from Bombay to Mumbai", *Social Text 81* 22 (Winter 2004), 65–90.

15. Chakrabarty, "Remembered Villages", 2145.

16. Ashis Nandy, "The Sociology of Sati," *Indian Express* (October 8, 1987). Reactionary organizations such as the RSS and Shiv Sena have justified their presence in urban neighborhoods by claiming to provide people with a sense of community in alienated situations. The RSS conducts highly militant and masculinized physical exercises for its young male recruits in many urban colonies in India.

17. Chatterjee, *The Politics of the Governed*, 141.

18. Gyan Prakash, "The Urban Turn", *Sarai Reader 02: The Critics of Everyday Life*. 2–7. For a critique of radical social theory's elision of the city in its thinking

about an alternative modernity and consciousness, see Rashmi Varma, "Bad Copy: The Indian City in Postcolonial Theory", paper presented to the "Workshop on India's Global Cities," University of Warwick, May 2007.

19. Chatterjee, *The Politics of the Governed*, 134.
20. Here I am alluding to a wide range of ideological positions within this larger one. A host of very different writers such as Salman Rushdie and Rohinton Mistry and theorists writing in English such as Homi Bhabha have written on the city as the site where "differences" get articulated.
21. See Neera Chandoke, "The Postcolonial City", *Economic and Political Weekly* 26 no. 50 (December 14, 1991): 2868–2873.
22. Edward Soja, *Postmodern Geographies: The Reassertion of Space and Critical Social Theory* (London: Verso, 1988), 3.
23. Khilnani, *The Idea of India*, 109.
24. Chatterjee, *The Politics of the Governed*, 136.
25. Chatterjee, *The Politics of the Governed*; 138. He writes: "Populations are empirical categories of people with specific social or economic attributes that are relevant for the administration of developmental or welfare policies . . . produced by the classificatory schemes of governmental knowledge" (136).
26. Chatterjee, *The Politics of the Governed*, 138.
27. Chatterjee, *The Politics of the Governed*, 147.
28. See Partha Chatterjee, *The Nation and Its Fragments: Colonial and Postcolonial Histories* (Princeton: Princeton University Press, 1993), 135.
29. Prabhat Kumar Mukhopadhyay's *Devi* and Sarat Chandra Chattopadhyay's 1917 novella *Devdas*, both turned into brilliant cinematic depictions of such a modernity by Satyajit Ray in 1960 and Bimal Roy in 1956 respectively, are evocative renderings of the negotiations around literacy, sexuality, marriage, modernity and urbanism. In *Devdas*, the city woman is embodied in the figure of Chandramukhi, a courtesan.
30. Rey Chow, writing in the context of Chinese modernity, identifies this tendency in these words: "Chinese women–. . . the more remote they are from Western urban civilization, the better—for the production of the types of explanation that are intelligible (valuable) to feminism in the West. See Rey Chow, "Violence in the Other Country: China as Crisis, Spectacle, and Woman", in *Third World Women and the Politics of Feminism*, ed. Chandra Mohanty, Ann Russo and Lourdes Torres (Bloomington: Indiana University Press, 1991), 81–100, 93. Chow advocates the incorporation of "the materiality of Westernization as an irreducible part of Asian modern self-consciousness" in which Taiwanese and Hong Kong Chinese will be considered no more or less "authentic" than those from Mainland China (94).
31. One of the most celebrated examples of the urban woman as the site of masculinist debates on tradition and modernity is to be found in Rabindranath Tagore's novel *The Home and the World* (London: Penguin, 2005)
32. Srivastava, "Modernity and Postcoloniality", 411, 408.
33. See Evenson, *The Indian Metropolis*; Jan Morris, Charles Allen, Gillian Tindall, Colin Amery and Gavin Stamp, *Architecture of the British Empire* (London: Weidenfeld and Nicolson, 1986).
34. Sujata Patel, "Bombay's Urban Predicament". In *Bombay: Metaphor for Modern India*, ed. Sujata Patel and Alice Thorner (Bombay: Oxford University Press, 1995), xxiii.
35. Patel, "Bombay's Urban Predicament", xxii.
36. See Anthony King, "Writing Colonial Space: A Review Article", *Society for Comparative Study of Society and History* 37 no. 3 (1995): 541–554, 549. The idea that the colonized city is a reflection, or bad copy, of the metropolitan

city is echoed by writer Nirad C. Chaudhuri ,who saw Calcutta as the illegitimate child of London and Manchester (in Morris, et al., *Architecture of the British Empire*, 74).

37. See Morris et al., *Architecture of the British Empire*, 74, 19. See also Evenson, *The Indian Metropolis*, for a similar analysis of Bombay's special position in the mind of British administrators.

38. Between 1941 and 1951, Bombay's population increased by 76 percent, and rose by 40, 44, and 38 percent in the next three decades. By 1971, two-thirds of the city's population had been born outside it. This pace of growth has slowed down in the 1990s. See Patel, "Bombay's Urban Predicament", xiv.

39. R. Raj Rao, "The Poetry of Bombay City," *The Journal of Commonwealth Literature* 31, no. 1 (1996): 63–70, 63.

40. Rao, "The Poetry of Bombay City", 66.

41. Salman Rushdie, *Imaginary Homelands* (New York: Viking, 1990), 16. Bombay's complex demography consisting of nine million Hindus, two million Muslims, and two million Parsis, Sikhs, Jains, Christians, and Buddhists lends credence to Rushdie's assertion. As will be discussed in later sections, this consensus on Bombay as quintessentially secular is reflected in the way in which the 1993 riots were represented as an aberration from its history of tolerance and diversity.

42. Arjun Appadurai, "Disjuncture and Difference in the Global Cultural Economy", in *Colonial Discourse and Postcolonial Theory: A Reader*, ed. Patrick Williams and Laura Chrisman (New York: Columbia University Press, 1994), 324–339.

43. See Mira Nair, director of Salaam Bombay, quoted in John McCarry, "Bombay: India's Capital of Hope." *National Geographic*. 187, no. 3 (March 1995), 42–67.

44. Indian films of the 1950s and 1960s documented the transformation of Indian values in the postcolonial city, with its inhabitants' struggles with poverty and loss of community, and the effects of materialism and greed, in such films as *Bombay ka Babu, Jaagte Raho* and *Shri 420*. Recent cinema, through such diverse films as *Salaam Bombay* and Mani Ratnam's *Bombay* has continued this tradition, albeit in a different register. These films have had an immense and incalculable influence in shaping the Indian imagination about the metropolitan idea. Through the medium of these films, the bulk of India's population, rural and mostly illiterate, gains access to a globalized metropolitan culture. Bombay itself is also the home of the film industry, popularly known as Bollywood, where dreams of success and fame come true, irrespective of one's religion, caste or class. See also Ranjani Majumdar, *Bombay Cinema: An Archive of a City* (Minneapolis: University of Minnesota Press, 2007).

45. See Sara Mitter, *Dharma's Daughters* (New Brunswick, N.J.: Rutgers University Press, 1991), x.

46. McCarry, "Bombay", 47.

47. Mitter, *Dharma's Daughters,* 7.

48. Suketu Mehta, *Maximum City: Bombay Lost and Found* (New York: Alfred A. Knopf, 2004).

49. Bombay, the financial capital of India, has more than half of the city's population of ten to twelve million people live in slums or are homeless. See Patel, "Bombay's Urban Predicament", xi. In Dharavi, Bombay's largest slum district and possibly the largest slum concentration in Asia, about 600,000 people live in about one square mile area.

50. Khilnani, *The Idea of India,* 138.

51. For a detailed account of the power of this image of Bombay in the Indian imagination, see Jim Masselos's article "Postmodern Bombay: Fractured Discourses", in *Postmodern Cities and Spaces*, ed. Sophie Watson and Katherine Gibson (Oxford: Blackwell, 1995), 199–215.

52. See McCarry, "Bombay".

53. According to Khilnani, "the political imagination of a movement like Shiv Sena shares with the nationalist one the ambition to have a modern, rational, clean and functional city". See Khilnani, *The Idea of India*, 144. I would argue that the Shiv Sena can be credited with turning this urban imaginary into a real contestation for political power.

54. See Dileep Padgaonkar, ed. *When Bombay Burned: Reportage and Comments on the Riots and Blasts from "The Times of India"* (New Delhi: UBS Publishers' Distributors, 1993).

55. See Arjun Appadurai, "Spectral Housing and Urban Cleansing: Notes on Millennial Mumbai", in *Cosmopolitanism*, ed. Carol A. Breckenridge, Sheldon Pollock, Homi K. Bhabha and Dipesh Chakrabarty (Durham, N.C.: Duke University Press, 2002), 54. "'Decosmopolitanization'" erases, to an extent, the agents of change in contemporary Bombay. I use "provincialization" to emphasize the point that the shifts in Bombay's culture are the product of an organized Right-wing project to reclaim Bombay as Maharashtrian and Hindu that is also articulated with its economic realities.

56. See Jayant Lele, "Saffronization of the Shiv Sena: The Political Economy of City, State and Nation" in *Bombay: Metaphor for Modern India*, ed. Sujata Patel and Alice Thorner (Bombay: Oxford University Press, 1995); and Thomas Blom-Hansen, *Wages of Violence: Naming and Identity in Postcolonial Bombay* (Princeton: Princeton University Press, 2001) for the complex history of the rise of the Shiv Sena.

57. One of the first tasks that the Shiv Sena accomplished after forming the state government in 1995 was to rename Bombay as "Mumbai". Although this move can be a populist one, in view of Shiv Sena's ethnic cleansing policies such a move can only be judged as retrograde and fascist.

58. Whereas the terrorist attacks in the city on November 26, 2008 were not followed by riots as some had feared, a glamorous ex-Bollywood actress and TV presenter Simi Garewal went on national television (aired on the private NDTV 24x7 News channel) to say that those people in Bombay who supported Pakistan (she mistook Muslim flags for Pakistani ones) should be "carpet bombed" and eliminated.

59. See for example Jyoti Punwani, "India: Searching for Answers in the Wake of Religious Violence", Seminar, 16–18.

60. See Madhu Kishwar, "Warning from the Bombay Riots", *Committee on South Asian Women Bulletin* 8, nos. 3–4 (n.d.): 21–29, 23–24. The essay appears in the journal's special issue "Women and the Hindu Right."

61. Tanika Sarkar, "Women of the Hindutva Brigade." *Bulletin of Concerned Asian Scholars* 25. no. 4 (1993): 16–24, 17.

62. Sarkar, "Women of the Hindutva Brigade", 17.

63. See Sujata Patel, "The Urban Factor", *Seminar* 411 (November 1993): 27–30.

64. See Tapan Basu, Pradip Datta, Sumit Sarkar, Tanika Sarkar and Sambuddha Sen, eds., *Khaki Shorts and Saffron Flags: A Critique of the Hindu Right*, (Delhi: Orient Longman, 1993), 78–88. for an astute account of the Hindu Right and its attitudes towards women.

65. Sarkar, "Women of the Hindutva Brigade", 21.

66. Gita Sahgal and Nira Yuval-Davis, *Refusing Holy Orders: Women and Fundamentalism in Britain* (London: Virago Press, 1992), 8.

67. Sucheta Mazumdar, "Moving Away from a Secular Vision? Women, Nation, and the Cultural Construction of Hindu India," in *Identity Politics and Women*, ed. Valentine Moghadam (Boulder, Colo.: Westview Press, 1994), 243–273, 246.
68. Radha Kumar, "Identity Politics and the Contemporary Indian Feminist Movement", in *Identity Politics and Women,* ed. Valentine Moghadam (Boulder, Colo.: Westview Press, 1994): 274–292.
69. See Sarkar, "Women of the Hindutva Brigade".
70. Instances of such appropriation are the large-scale "disco garba" dances organized by communal groups on the occasion of Hindu festivals, the adaptation of Hindu epics into television serials, and the use of video cassettes and audio tapes by Right-wing politicians to mobilize "community" women.
71. Arjun Appadurai, "Disjuncture and Difference in the Global Cultural Economy", in *Colonial Discourse and Post-colonial Theory: A Reader*, ed. Patrick Williams and Laura Chrisman (New York: Columbia University Press, 1994), 324–339, 336.
72. Sahgal and Yuval-Davis, *Refusing Holy Orders*, 1.
73. Shashi Deshpande, *That Long Silence* (New Delhi: Penguin Books, 1989), first published by Virago Press in 1988; Vikram Chandra, *Love and Longing in Bombay* (New Delhi: Penguin Books, 1997); Thrity Umrigar, *The Space between Us* (London: Fourth Estate, 2006). All subsequent references from each of these three texts will be provided in the body of the main text.
74. For an extended discussion of Deshpande's marginality with the canon of Indian writers read and studied globally, see Arnab Chakladar, "Of Houses and Canons: Reading the Novels of Shashi Deshpande", *Ariel: A Review of International English Literature* 37, no. 1 (2006): 81–97.
75. Rao, "The Poetry of Bombay City", 65.
76. That she takes on another name in her column called "Seeta" to present her writings to the public, seems to be a compromising gesture between the public and the private. The narrative of a traditional Seeta who was tested for her loyalty and chastity, and who ultimately sacrificed her life for her husband Lord Rama in the Indian epic *Ramayana*, and that of a modern Seeta, one who is able to question her given position in society are shown to be in productive conflict.
77. Deshpande populates the novel with silent and silenced female figures in modern India. The image of Mohan's mother "sitting silently in front of the fire" is for Jaya an image of despair "so great that it would not voice itself . . . a struggle so bitter that silence was the only weapon" (32). His sister Vimala too dies a silent death. Jeeja, the servant's silence, is the result of her being a "realist", beaten as she is daily by her husband, her body more vocal through its bruises and black-eyes than in her silent screams. Jaya herself experiences a writer's block that must confront the slow and dull unfolding of a socially pre-written script for her, such that her own writing can merely be a supplement, or a footnote to that hegemonic account.
78. See Rajeswari Sundar Rajan, "The Feminist Plot and the Nationalist Allegory: Home and World in Two Indian Women's Novels in English", *Modern Fiction Studies* 39, no. 1 (Winter 1993), 71–92. Sundar Rajan's critique also draws upon the novel's publishing history—first published by the feminist press Virago in England, Sundar Rajan questions the implicit claims that she sees the novel makes about representing Third World women.
79. Tharu and Lalita suggest that there seems to have been almost a kind of retreat into the personal realm after independence, a noticeable departure from nineteenth century narratives read by Partha Chatterjee, for instance, that were largely in the form of diaries presenting social commentary. See

Susie Tharu and K. Lalita, eds. *Women Writing in India,* Vol. II: *The Twentieth Century* (New York: The Feminist Press, 1993).

80. Veena Das, "Modernity and Biography: Women's Lives in contemporary India". *Thesis Eleven,* August 1994, 39: 52–62.
81. Khilnani, *The Idea of India,* 136.
82. Deshpande draws upon actual events that took place in Parel, especially from 1982 onwards, when a massive textile strike was organized in Bombay under the leadership of Dr. Datta Samant, and that paralyzed Bombay for some time. Parel has been traditionally a heavily labor dominated area.
83. Achin Vanaik, "Rendezvous at Mumbai", *New Left Review* 26 (March–April 2004): 53–65, 58.
84. See Amrit Gangar, "Tinseltown: From Studios to Industry" in *Bombay and Mumbai: The City in Transition,* ed. Sujata Patel and Jim Masselos (New Delhi: Oxford University Press, 2003), 289.
85. See Praveen Swami, "Mumbai's Mafia Wars", *Frontline,* March 27–April 6, 1999.
86. See "Mafia Gangs Spreading Tentacles around World", *The Navhind Times,* February 8, 2002.
87. "Mafia Gangs".
88. See R. Padmanabhan, "Movie Mafia: The Underworld and 'Bollywood'", *Frontline,* May 21, 1993. See also Albert Clack, "The Wild West Comes to Bollywood", *foreignwire.com,* April 5, 1998.
89. D. S. Soman, "Tightening Mafia Grip—Choking Both Tinsel and Real Worlds", *Business Line,* February 1, 2001. Soman writes: "According to the data compiled and published by the film industry, 90 percent of the films produced are flops, many of them collapsing in the first week".
90. See "Mafia Financing 60 Percent Bollywood Movies", *The Indian Express,* January 8, 2001.
91. Gangar, "Tinseltown", 286.
92. Gangar, "Tinseltown", 281.
93. Except, of course, when it comes to making money through "culture", even though it might be as foreign as Michael Jackson. The Shiv Sena chief Bal Thackeray used mafia money to sponsor a show by Jackson in Mumbai in 1999.
94. Gyan Prakash has pointedly argued that "Bombay has experienced far-reaching transformations, an important aspect of which has been the erosion of the ideal of the modern city as a unity—a unity that was secured through elite domination and was met with confrontation and resistance. The ruins of the elite imaginary bring Bombay face to face with its divided history of urban modernity". See his "Mumbai: the Modern City in Ruins", in *Other Cities, Other Worlds: Urban Imaginaries in a Globalizing Age,* ed. Andreas Huyssen (Durham, N.C.: Duke University Press, 2008), 181–203; 202.
95. Sasskia Sassen, one of the most influential theorists of the global city, writes: "The most powerful of (these) new geographies of centrality at the inter-urban level bind the major international financial and business centers: New York, London, Tokyo, Paris, Frankfurt, Zurich, Amsterdam, Los Angeles, Sydney, Hong Kong, among others. But this geography now also includes cities such as Sao Paulo, Beunos Aires, Bombay, Bangkok, Taipei and Mexico City." See Saskia Sassen, "The Global City: Strategic Site/New Frontier", in *Democracy, Citizenship and the Global City,* ed. Engin F. Isin (London: Routledge, 2000), 51.
96. Vanaik, "Rendezvous at Mumbai", 53.
97. Holston and Appadurai reinforce the oppositionality of city and nation by arguing that "for most of the modern era, the nation and not the city has

been the principal domain of citizenship", and that in fact the triumph of the nation-state over the city had been fundamental to the project of nation building "Preface" in James Holston and Arjun Appadurai, eds. *Cities and Citzenship* (Durham, NC: Duke University Press, 1999) (vii).
98. P. Sainath, "Mumbai: The Glory Days of the Raj?" *The Hindu*, February 13, 2008.

Notes to the Conclusion

1. Monica Ali, "After Woolf", *The Guardian Weekend* (May 27 2006), 22–28.
2. Frears was talking about his film *Dirty Pretty Things* on the lives of illegal immigrants—Nigerians, Eastern Europeans, South Asians—in London's underbelly, in an interview with National Public Radio (US), in July 2003.
3. Melanie Phillips, *Londonistan: How Britain Is Creating a Terror State Within* (London: Gibson Square Books, 2006).
4. Sandra Laville and Vikram Dodd, "One Year on, a London Bomber Issues a Threat from the Dead", *TheGuardian* (July 7, 2006), 1–2.
5. See Niall Ferguson, "Eurabia?" *The New York Times* (April 4, 2004).
6. Thus designs for the Olympic village for 2012 are paying special attention to religious difference in order to create a perfect miniature world in the city. So for instance, planners are ensuring that no toilets in the Olympic village in London will face in the direction of Mecca!
7. Monica Ali, *Brick Lane: A Novel* (New York: Scribner, 2003). Page references appear in text.
8. Hywel Williams, "Britain's Ruling Elites Now Exercise Power with a Shameless Rapacity", *The Guardian* (April 11, 2006), 25.
9. David Harvey, *New Imperialism* (Oxford: Oxford University Press, 2003).
10. Hywel, "Britain's Ruling Elites".
11. See Jane M. Jacobs, *Edge of Empire: Postcolonialism and the City* (London: Routledge, 1996), 72. See especially her chapter "Eastern Trading: Diasporas, Dwelling and Place" (70–102) for a fascinating account of the contestations that took place between conservationists, developers and the "community" of Bengalis in the Spitalfields area, a ward in the Tower Hamlets borough, through the 1980s and early 1990s.
12. K. Robins, "Tradition and Translation: National Culture in its Global Context", in *Enterprise and Heritage: Cross-currents in National Culture*, ed. J. Corner and S. Harvey (New York: Routledge, 1991): 21–44.
13. See works by Manzurul Islam (*The Mapmakers of Spitalfields* [Leeds: Peepal Tree Press, 1998]) and Salman Rushdie (*The Satanic Verses* [London: Penguin, 1989]), among others, for recent fictional accounts of life in a South Asian-ized Brick Lane.
14. Chetan Bhatt, "The Fetish of the Margin: Religious Absolutism, Anti-racism and Postcolonial Silence", *New Formations* 59 (2006), 12.
15. Sukhwant Dhaliwal, "Orange Is Not the Only Colour: Young Women, Religious Identity and the Southall Community", in. *From Homebreakers to Jailbreakers: Southall Black Sisters*, ed. Rahila Gupta (London: Zed Books, 2003), 261–278.
16. Dhaliwal, "Orange Is Not the Only Colour".
17. See Amrit Wilson, *Finding a Voice—Asian Women in Britain* (Virago Press: London, 1978).
18. Bhatt, "The Fetish of the Margin".

19. Ultimately, the challenge of local multiculturalisms proved too threatening and Thatcher abolished the progressive Greater London Council in 1986.
20. From September 2004, the French government has banned the wearing of all visible religious symbols in public schools in France. Whereas this technically applies to all religious markers of faith, the controversy has centered overwhelmingly on the figure of the young Muslim schoolgirl wearing a headscarf. For an analytical history of the issue, see Norma Moruzzi, "A Problem with Headscarves: Contemporary Complexities of Politics and Social Identity", *Political Theory* vol. 22, no. 4 (November 1994) 653–672.
21. Gita Sahgal, "Secular Spaces" in *Refusing Holy Orders: Women and Fundamentalism in Britain*, ed. GitaSahgal and Nira Yuval-Davis (London: Virago Press, 1992), 176.
22. See Valerie Amos and Pratibha Parmar, "Challenging Imperial Feminism", *Feminist Review*, Special Issue, "Many Voices, One Chant", vol. 17 (July 1984), 3–19.
23. Donna Haraway writes of such new feminist cartographic projects as constituting "a mapping of interference", marking not "where differences appear", but "where the effects of difference appear". See her. "The Promises of Monsters" in *Cultural Studies*, ed. Lawrence Grossberg, Cary Nelson and Paula Treichler (New York: Routledge, 1992), 300.
24. Iris Marion Young, "The Ideal of Community and the Politics of Difference" in *Feminism/Postmodernism*, ed. Linda Nicholson (New York: Routledge, 1990). Page references appear in text.
25. David Harvey, "Social Justice, Postmodernism and the City", *International Journal of Urban and Regional Research* 16, no. 4 (December 1992): 588–601, 591.
26. Harvey, "Social Justice", 589–590.
27. See Michael Sorkin, ed. *Variations on a Theme Park: Scenes from the New American City* (New York: Hill and Wang, 1992).
28. Elizabeth Wilson."The Invisible *Flaneur*" in *Postmodern Cities and Spaces*, ed. Sophie Watson and Katherine Gibson (Oxford: Blackwell, 1995), 59–79.
29. Malcolm Cross and Michael Keith, edited *Racism, the City and the State* (London: Routledge, 1993), 8; quoted in Stephen Haymes, *Race, Culture, and the City* (Albany: State University of New York Press, 1995), 111. Haymes himself writes of the process by which black urban culture is exoticized, and blackness made a motif for urban pleasure by evoking a sense of foreignness and danger.

Bibliography

Ackroyd, Peter. *London: The Biography*. New York: Anchor Books, 2003.

Ahmad, Aijaz. *In Theory*. London: Verso, 1992.

Ali, Monica. *Brick Lane: A Novel*. New York: Scribner, 2003.

———. "After Woolf". *The Guardian Weekend* (May 27 2006): 22–28.

Amia, Samir. *A Critique of the Theory of Underdevelopment* (2 Volumes). New York: Monthly Reviw Press, 1974.

Amos, Valerie, and Pratibha Parmar. "Challenging Imperial Feminism". *Feminist Review* 17 (July 1984): 3–19.

Anderson, Perry. "Modernity and Revolution". In *Marxism and the Interpretation of Culture*, edited by Cary Nelson and Lawrence Grossberg, 317–338. Urbana: University of Illinois Press, 1988.

Anzaldua, Gloria. *Borderlands/La Frontera: The New Mestiza*. San Francisco: Spinsters/Aunt Lute, 1987.

Appadurai, Arjun. "Disjuncture and Difference in the Global Cultural Economy". In *Colonial Discourse and Postcolonial Theory: A Reader*, edited by Patrick Williams and Laura Chrisman, 324–339. New York: Columbia University Press, 1994.

———. "Spectral Housing and Urban Cleansing: Notes on Millennial Mumbai". In *Cosmopolitanism*, edited by Carol A. Breckenridge, Sheldon Pollock, Homi K. Bhabha and Dipesh Chakrabarty, 54–81. Durham, N.C.: Duke University Press, 2002.

Balandier, Georges. "The Colonial Situation: A Theoretical Approach". In *Social Change: The Colonial Situation*, edited by Immanuel Wallerstein, 34–61. New York: John Wiley & Sons, 1966.

Ball, John Clement. *Imagining London: Postcolonial Fiction and the Transnational Metropolis*. Toronto: University of Toronto Press, 2004.

Barry, William. *The New Antigone*. London: Barry, 1887.

Basu, Tapan, Pradip Datta, Sumit Sarkar, Tanika Sarkar and Sambuddha Sen. *Khaki Shorts and Saffron Flags: A Critique of the Hindu Right*. Delhi: Orient Longman, 1993.

Baucom, Ian. *Out of Place*. Princeton: Princeton University Press, 1999.

Baudelaire, Charles. "The Painter of Modern Life". In *Modern Art and Modernism: A Critical Anthology*, edited by Francis Frascina and Charles Harrison, 23–27. New York: Harper and Row, 1987.

———. "The Salon of 1846: On the Herosim of Modern Life". In *Modern Art and Modernism*, edited by Francis Frascina and Charles Harrison, 17–18. New York: Harper and Row, 1987.

Bayart, Jean-Francois. *The State in Africa: The Politics of the Belly*. New York: Longman, 1993.

Bhatt, Chetan. "The Fetish of the Margin: Religious Absolutism, Anti-racism and Postcolonial Silence". *New Formations* 59 (2006): 98–115.

Bell, Daniel. *The Cultural Contradictions of Capitalism.* New York: Basic Books, 1975.

Bello, Walden. "A Global Conjuncture: The Multiple Crises of Global Capitalism". *Frontline* 19, no. 18 (August 31–September 13, 2002). http://hinduonnet.com/fline/fl1918/19180620.htm.

Benjamin, Walter. "Motifs in Baudelaire". In *Illuminations*, translated by Hannah Arendt, 155–200. New York: Schocken Books, 1967.

———. "A Berlin Chronicle". in *Reflections: Essays, Aphorisms, Autobiographical Writings*, trans. Edmund Jephcott. New York: Schocken Books, 1986.

———. "Central Park". *New German Critique*, no. 34 (Winter 1985): 32–58.

———. "Surrealism: The Last Snapshot of the European Intelligentsia". In *One Way Street and Other Writings*, translated by Edmund Jephcott and Kingsley Shorter. London: Verso, 1985.

———. The Arcades Project. Cambridge.: Harvard University Press, Belknap Press, 1999.

Berman, Marshall. *All That Is Solid Melts into Air.* New York: Simon and Schuster, 1981.

Bhabha, Homi. *The Location of Culture.* London: Routledge, 1994.

Blom-Hansen, Thomas. *Wages of Violence: Naming and Identity in Postcolonial Bombay.* Princeton: Princeton University Press, 2001.

Booth, William. *In Darkest England and the Way Out.* London: International Headquarters of Salvation Army, 1890.

Bose, Nirmal Kumar. "Calcutta: A Premature Metropolis". *Scientific American* 213, no. 3: 91–102.

Bourdieu, Pierre. *In Other Words: Essays toward a Reflexive Sociology.* Translated by Mathew Adamson. Cambridge: Polity Press, 1990.

———. "The Essence of Neoliberalism". http://www.analitica.com/biblioteca/bourdieu/neoliberalism.asp. Accessed on December 23, 2003.

Bowlby, Rachel. *Just Looking: Consumer Culture in Dreiser, Gissing and Zola.* London: Methuen, 1985.

———. *Virginia Woolf: Feminist Destinations.* Oxford: Basil Blackwell, 1988.

Bradbury, Malcolm, and James McFarlane, eds. *Modernism, 1890–1930.* New York: Penguin Books, 1976.

Braithwaite, E. K. *Roots.* Ann Arbor: University of Michigan Press, 1993.

———. "A Post-cautionary Tale of the Helen of Our Wars". *Wasafiri* 22 (1995) 69–78.

Brenner, Robert. "Structure versus Conjuncture: The 2006 Elections and the Rightward Shift". *New Left Review* 43 (January–February 2007) 33–59.

Brown, Nicholas. *Utopian Generations: The Political Horizon of Twentieth-Century Literature.* Princeton: Princeton University Press, 2005.

Bryce, Jane. "Profile: Ngugi: My Novel of Blood, Sweat and Tears". *New African* (August 1982).

Buck-Morss, Susan. "The Flaneur, the Sandwichman and the Whore: The Politics of Loitering". *New German Critique* 39 (Fall 1986): 99–140.

Buhle, Paul. *C. L. R. James: The Artist as Revolutionary.* London: Verso, 1988.

Carlston, Erin. *Thinking Fascism: Sapphic Modernism and Fascist Modernity.* Stanford, Calif.: Stanford University Press, 1994.

Carr, Helen. *Jean Rhys.* Plymouth: Northcote House, 1996.

———. "Jean Rhys: West Indian Intellectual". In *West Indian Intellectuals in Britain*, edited by Bill Schwarz, 93–113. Manchester: Manchester University Press, 2003.

Casanova, Pascale. "Literature as World". *New Left Review* 31 (January–February 2005) 71–90.

Castells, Manuel. *The Urban Question: A Marxist Approach.* Translated by A. Sheridan. Cambridge: MIT Press, 1977.

———. *The City and the Grassroots.* London: Edwin Arnold, 1983.

———. "European Cities, the Informational Society, and the Global Economy". *New Left Review*, 204 (March–April 1994): 18–32.

Chakladar, Arnab. "Of Houses and Canons: Reading the Novels of Shashi Deshpande". *Ariel: A Review of International English Literature* 37, no. 1 (2006): 81–97.

Chakrabarty, Dipesh. "Remembered Villages: Representations of Hindu-Bengali Memories in the Aftermath of Partition". *Economic and Political Weekly* (August 10, 1996): 2143–2151.

Patrick Chamoiseau, *Texaco: A Novel.* New York: Vintage, 1998.

Chandoke, Neera. "The Postcolonial City". *Economic and Political Weekly* 26, no. 50 (December 14, 1991): 2868–2873.

Chandra, Vikram. *Love and Longing in Bombay.* New Delhi: Penguin Books, 1997.

Chatterjee, Partha. *The Nation and Its Fragments: Colonial and Postcolonial Histories.* Princeton: Princeton University Press, 1993.

———. *The Politics of the Governed.* New Delhi: Permanent Black, 2004.

Chow, Rey. "Walter Benjamin's Love Affair with Death". *New German Critique* 48 (Fall 1989): 61–86.

———. "Violence in the Other Country: China as Crisis, Spectacle, and Woman". In *Third World Women and the Politics of Feminism*, edited by Chandra Mohanty, Ann Russo and Lourdes Torres, 81–100. Bloomington: Indiana University Press, 1991.

Chowdhury, Siddhartha. *Patna Roughcut.* New Delhi: Picador, 2005.

Clack, Albert. "The Wild West Comes to Bollywood". foreignwire.com (April 5, 1998) accessed 4 March 2004.

Comaroff, Jean, and John Comaroff . "Millennial Capitalism: First Thoughts on a Second Coming". *Public Culture* 12, no. 2 (2000): 291–343.

Comaroff, John. "Governmentality, Materiality, Legality, Modernity: On the Colonial State in Africa". In *African Modernities*, edited by Jan-Georg, Peter Probst and Heike Schmidt. Portsmouth, NH: Heinemann, 2002. Deutsch, 107–134.

Connolly, Priscilla. "Mexico City: Our Common Future?" *Environment and Urbanization* 11, no 1 (April 1999) 53–78.

Cooper, Frederick. "Introduction". In *Struggle for the City: Migrant Labour, Capital, and the State in Urban Africa*, edited by Frederick Cooper. Beverly Hills/London/New Delhi: Sage Publications, 1983.

Cross, Malcolm and Michael Keith. edited *Racism and the City and the State* (London: Routledge, 1993).

Daniel, Jamie Owen. "Strategies of Detachment: Modernist Impersonality and Bodily Loss between the Wars". Dissertation, University of Wisconsin-Milwaukee, 1995.

Das, Veena. "Modernity and Biography: Women's Lives in Contemporary India. *Thesis Eleven* August 1994, 39: 52–62.

Davies, Carole Boyce "Introduction". In *Ngambika: Studies of Women in African Literature*, ed. Carole Boyce Davies and Anne Adams Graves 1–23. Trenton, N.J.: Africa World Press, 1986.

Davis, Mike. "The Urbanization of Empire: Megacities and the Laws of Chaos". *Social Text 81* 22, no. 4 (Winter 2004): 9–16.

———. *Planet of Slums.* London: Verso, 2006.

Dawson, Ashley. "Squatters, Space, and Belonging in the Underdeveloped City". *Social Text 81* vol. 22, no. 4 (Winter 2004): 17–34.

Dawson, Ashley, and Brent Edwards. "Introduction: Global Cities of the South". *Social Text 81* 22, no. 4 (Winter 2004): 1–8.

D'Costa, Jean. "Jean Rhys, 1890–1979". In *Fifty Caribbean Writers*, edited by Daryl Dance. New York: Greenwood Press, 1986.

Debord, Guy. *Society of the Spectacle*. Detroit: Black and Red Books, 1977 [1967].

Debray, Regis. *Revolution in the Revolution? Armed Struggle and Political Struggle in Latin America*. New York: Monthly Review Press, 1967.

de Certeau, Michel. *The Practice of Everyday Life*. Berkeley and Los Angeles: University of California Press, 1988.

de Lauretis, Teresa. "Eccentric Subjects". *Feminist Studies* 16: 115–150, Spring 1990.

Derrida, Jacques. "Spectres of Marx". *New Left Review* I/205 (May–June 1994) 31–58.

Desai, Gaurav. *Subject to Colonialism: African Self-Fashioning and the Colonial Library* . Durham, N.C.: Duke University Press, 2001.

Deshpande, Shashi. *That Long Silence*. New Delhi: Penguin Books, 1989.

Dhaliwal, Sukhwant. "'Orange Is Not the Only Colour': Young Women, Religious Identity and the Southall Community". In *From Homebreakers to Jailbreakers: Southall Black Sisters*, edited by Rahila Gupta. London: Zed Books, 2003.

Dutta, Nilanjana. "The Nation and the Other Woman: A Commentary on Wanja and Douloti". Unpublished Paper, 2002.

Engels, Friedrich. *The Condition of the Working Class in England.*(1844). Translated by W. O. Henderson and W. H. Chaloner. Stanford, Calif.: Stanford University Press, 1958; London: Penguin, 1984.

Evenson, Norma. *The Indian Metropolis: A View towards the West*. New Haven: Yale University Press, 1989.

Fabian, Johannes. *The Time of the Other: How Anthropology Makes Its Object*. New York: Columbia University Press, 1983.

Fanon, Frantz. *The Wretched of the Earth*. Translated by Constance Farrington. New York: Grove Press, 1963.

———. "Algeria Unveiled". In *Studies in a Dying Colonialism*. New York: Grove Press, 1967.

Felski, Rita. *The Gender of Modernity*. Cambridge: Harvard University Press, 1995.

Ferguson, Niall. "Eurabia?" *TheNew York Times,* April 4, 2004.

Foucault, Michel. "Of Other Spaces". *Diacritics* vol. 16 (Spring 1986): 22–27.

Friedman, John. "The World City Hypothesis". *Development and Change* 17, no. 1 (1986): 69–84.

Fryer, Peter. *Staying Power: The History of Black People in Britain*. London: Pluto Press, 1984.

———. *Black People in the British Empire: An Introduction*. London: Pluto Press, 1988.

Fuchs, Martin. "India and Modernity: Towards Decentring Western Perspectives". *Thesis Eleven* 39 (1994): v–xiii.

Gangar, Amrit. "Tinseltown: From Studios to Industry". In *Bombay and Mumbai: The City in Transition*, edited by Sujata Patel and Jim Masselos. New Delhi: Oxford University Press, 2003.

Gardiner, Judith Kegan. "Good Morning Midnight; Good Night, Modernism". *Boundary* 2, no. 11 (1982–1983) 233–257.

———. *Rhys, Stead, Lessing and the Politics of Empathy*. Bloomington: Indiana University Press, 1989.

Gikandi, Simon. *Ngugi wa Thiong'o*. Cambridge: Cambridge University Press, 2000.

————. "Reason, Modernity and the African Crisis". In *African Modernities*, edited by Jan-Georg Deutsch, Peter Probst and Heike Schmidt, 135–157. Portsmouth, NH: Heinemann and London: James Currey, 2002.

Gilbert, Pamela, ed. *Imagined Londons*. Albany: State University of New York Press, 2002.

Gilman, Sander. "The Hottentot and the Prostitute: Toward an Iconography of Female Sexuality". In *Difference and Pathology: Stereotypes of Sexuality, Race and Madness*, 176–198. Ithaca: Cornell University Press, 1985.

Gilroy, Paul. *Postcolonial Melancholia*. New York: Columbia University Press, 2004.

Gleber, Anke. "Female Flanerie and the Symphony of the City". In *Women in the Metropolis: Gender and Modernity in Weimar Culture*, edited by Katharina von Ankum, 67–88. Berkeley and Los Angeles: University of California Press, 1997.

Gregg, Veronica Marie. "Jean Rhys on Herself as a Writer". In *Caribbean Women Writers: Essays from the First International Conference*, edited by Selwyn Cudjoe, 109–115. Wellesley, Mass.: Calaloux Publications, 1990.

————. *Jean Rhys's Historical Imagination: Reading and Writing the Creole*. Chapel Hill: University of North Carolina Press, 1995.

Grewal, Inderpal, and Caren Kaplan, eds. *Scattered Hegemonies: Postmodernity and Transnational Feminist Practices*. Minneapolis: University of Minnesota Press, 1994.

Hake, Andrew. *African Metropolis: Nairobi's Self-Help City*. London: Sussex University Press, 1977.

Hall, Catherine. "What Is a West Indian?" In *West Indian Intellectuals in Britain*, edited by Bill Schwarz, 31–50. Manchester: Manchester University Press, 2003.

Haraway, Donna. "The Promises of Monsters". In *Cultural Studies*, edited by Lawrence Grossberg, Cary Nelson and Paula Treichler. New York: Routledge, 1992.

Harlow, Barbara. "Introduction". In Malek Alloula*, the Colonial Harem*, translated by Myrna Godzich and Wlad Godzich. Minneapolis: University of Minnesota Press, 1987.

Harvey, David. *Consciousness and the Urban Experience*. Baltimore: Johns Hopkins University Press, 1985.

————. *The Condition of Postmodernity: An Enquiry into the Origins of Cultural Change*. Oxford and Cambridge, Mass.: Blackwell Publishers, 1989.

————. "Social Justice, Postmodernism and the City". *International Journal of Urban and Regional Research* 16, no. 4 (December 1992): 588–601.

————. *New Imperialism*. Oxford: Oxford University Press, 2003.

Hay, Jean. "Historical Background". In *Coming to Birth*, by Marjorie Oludhe Macgoye. New York: Feminist Press of the City University of New York, 2000.

Haymes, Stephen. *Race, Culture, and the City*. Albany: State University of New York Press, 1995.

Hecht, David, and Maliqalim Simone. *Invisible Governance: The Art of African Micropolitics*. New York: Autonomedia, 1994.

Heron, Liz, ed. *City Women: Stories of the World's Great Cities*. Boston: Beacon Press, 1993.

Holston, James, and Arjun Appadurai. "Preface". In *Cities and Citizenship*, edited by Holston and Appadurai. Durham, NC: Duke University Press, 1999.

hooks, bell. *Yearning: Race, Gender and Cultural Politics*. London: Turnaround Press, 1991.

Horne, Alistair. *A Savage War of Peace: Algeria, 1954–1962*. New York: Penguin Books, 1979.

Hulme, Peter. "The Place of *Wide Sargasso Sea*". *Wasafiri* 20 (1994) 5–11.

————. "A Response to Kamau Braithwaite". *Wasafiri* 23 (1996).

Huyssen, Andreas. *After the Great Divide: Modernism, Mass Culture, Postmodernism.* Bloomington: Indiana University Press, 1986.

———. "Introduction: World Cultures, World Cities". In *Other Cities, Other Worlds: Urban Imaginaries in a Globalizing Age.* edited by Andreas Huyssen. Durham, N.C., and London: Duke University Press, 2008.

———, ed. *Other Cities, Other Worlds: Urban Imaginaries in a Globalizing Age.* Durham, N.C., and London: Duke University Press, 2008.

Isin, Engin F., ed. *Democracy, Citizenship, and the Global City.* London: Routledge, 2000.

Islam, Manzurul. Leeds: Peepal Tree Press, 1998.

Jacobs, Jane M. *Edge of Empire: Postcolonialism and the City.* London: Routledge, 1996.

James, C. L. R. *Minty Alley.* 2d ed. London and Port of Spain: New Beacon Books, 1971.

———. *Beyond a Boundary.* New York: Pantheon Books, 1983.

———. *Letters from London.* Oxford: Signal Books, 2003.

Jameson, Fredric. "Third-World Literature in the Era of Multinational Capitalism". *Social Text* 15 (1986): 65–88.

———. "Modernism and Imperialism". In *Nationalism, Colonialism and Literature,* by Terry Eagleton, Fredric Jameson and Edward Said. Minneapolis: University of Minnesota Press, 1990.

———. Postmodernism, or, the Cultural Logic of Late Capitalism. Durham, N.C.: Duke University Press, 1991.

———. *A Singular Modernity: Essay on the Ontology of the Present.* London: Verso, 2002.

Jones, Gareth Stedman. *Outcast London.* New York: Pantheon, 1971.

Kenyatta, Jomo. *Facing Mount Kenya.* New York: Vintage, 1965.

———. *Suffering without Bitterness.* Nairobi: EAPH, 1968.

Khilnani, Sunil. *The Idea of India.* New Delhi: Penguin Books, 1997.

King, Anthony D. "Colonial Cities: Global Pivots of Change". In *Colonial Cities: Essays in a Colonial Context,* edited by Robert Ross and J. Telkamp, 7–32. Dordrecht, the Netherlands: Martinus Nijhoff, 1985.

———. *Urbanism, Colonialism, and the World Economy.* London: Routledge, 1990.

———. "Writing Colonial Space: A Review Article". *Society for Comparative Study of Society and History* 37, no. 3 (1995): 541–554.

Kishwar, Madhu. "Warning from the Bombay Riots". *Committee on South Asian Women Bulletin* 8, nos. 3–4 (n.d.): 21–29.

Kracauer, Siegfried. "The Hotel Lobby". In *The Mass Ornament: Weimar Essays,* translated and edited by Thomas Y. Levin, 173–185. Cambridge: Harvard University Press, 1995.

Kumar, Amitava. *Bombay London New York.* New York: Routledge, 2002.

Kumar, Radha. "Identity Politics and the Contemporary Indian Feminist Movement". In *Identity Politics and Women,* edited by V. Moghadam, 274–292. Boulder, Colo.: Westview Press, 1994.

Kurtz, Roger. *Urban Obsessions, Urban Fears: The Postcolonial Kenyan Novel.* Trenton, N.J.: Africa World Press, 1998.

Lahiri, Shompa. *Indians in Britain: Anglo-Indian Encounters, Race and Identity, 1880–1930.* London and Portland, Ore.: Frank Cass, 2000.

Laville, Sandra, and Vikram Dodd. "One Year On, a London Bomber Issues a Threat from the Dead". *The Guardian* July 7, 2006: 1–2.

Lazarus, Neil, and Rashmi Varma. "Marxism and Postcolonial Studies". In *Critical Companion to Contemporary Marxism.* Edited by Jacques Bidet and Stathis Kouvelakis. London: Brill Academic Press, 2008.

Lefebvre, Henri. *The Production of Space*. Translated by Donald Nicholson-Smith. Oxford: Blackwell, 1991.

Lele, Jayant. "Saffronization of the Shiv Sena: The Political Economy of City, State and Nation". In *Bombay: Metaphor for Modern India*, edited by Sujata Patel and Alice Thorner. Bombay: Oxford University Press, 1995.

Levy, Andrea. *Small Island*. London: Review, 2004.

Lipton, Eunice. "The Laundress in Late Nineteenth-Century French Culture: Imagery, Ideology and Edgar Degas". In *Modern Art and Modernism*, edited by Francis Frascina and Charles Harrison, London: Sage, 1982. 275–283.

Little, Kenneth.*The Sociology of Urban Women's Image in African Literature*. Totowa, New Jersey: Rowman and Littlefield, 1980.

Long, Edward. *Candid Reflections*. London: T. Lowndes, 1772.

Lonsdale, John. "Jomo Kenyatta, God and the Modern World". In *African Modernities*, edited by Jan-Georg et al., 31–66.

Macgoye, Marjorie Oludhe. *Coming to Birth*. 1986; reprint, Nairobi: Heinemann,1988.

"Mafia Financing 60 Percent Bollywood Movies". *The Indian Express*, January 8, 2001.

"Mafia Gangs Spreading Tentacles around World". *TheNavhind Times*, February 8, 2002.

Maillu, David. *The Ayah*. Nairobi: Heinemann Kenya, 1986.

Majumdar, Ranjani. *Bombay Cinema: An Archive of the City*. Minneapolis: University of Minnesota Press, 2007.

Malinowski, Bronislaw. "Introduction". In *Methods of Study Culture Contact in Africa* vii–xxxviii. London: Memorandum XV of International Institute of African Languages and Cultures 1938.

Mamdani, Mahmood. *Citizen and Subject: Contemporary Africa and the Legacy of Late Colonialism*. Princeton: Princeton University Press, 1996.

Marx, Karl. *The Economic and Philosophical Manuscripts*. In *Early Writings*. New York: Vintage, 1975. Translated by Rodney Livingstone and Gregor Benton. Introduction by Lucio Coletti.

Masselos, Jim. "Postmodern Bombay: Fractured Discourses". In *Postmodern Cities and Spaces*, edited by in Sophie Watson and Katherine Gibson, 199–215. Oxford: Blackwell, 1995.

Massey, Doreen. *Space, Place and Gender*. Minneapolis: University of Minnesota Press, 1994.

Maugham-Brown, David. *Land, Freedom and Fiction: History and Ideology in Kenya*. London: Zed Books, 1985.

Mayhew, Henry. *London Labour and the London Poor*. London: Charles Griffin and Company, 1851.

Mazumdar, Sucheta. "Moving Away from a Secular Vision? Women, Nation, and the Cultural Construction of Hindu India". In *Identity Politics and Women*, edited by Valentine Moghadam, Boulder, Colorado: Westview Press, 1994. 3–37, 243–273.

Mbembe, Achille. "Provisional Notes on the Postcolony". *Africa* 62, no1 (1992).

———. "The Banality of Power and the Aesthetics of Vulgarity in the Postcolony." Translated by J. Roitman. *Public Culture* 4, no. 2 (1992): 1–30.

Mbembe, Achille, and Sarah Nuttall. "Writing the World from an African Metropolis". *Public Culture* 16, no. 3 (Fall 2004): 347–372.

Mbembe, Achille, and J. Roitman. "Figures of the Subject in Times of Crisis". *Public Culture* 7, no.2 (1995): 323–353.

McCarry, John. "Bombay: India's Capital of Hope." National Geographic 187, no. 3 (March 1995): 42–67.

McClintock, Anne. *Imperial Leather*. New York: Routledge, 1995.

McLeod, John. *Postcolonial London: Rewriting the Metropolis*. London: Routledge, 2004.

Mehta, Suketu. *Maximum City: Bombay Lost and Found*. New York: Alfred A. Knopf, 2004.

Merrifield, Andy. *Metromarxism: A Marxist Tale of the City*. New York: Routledge, 2002.

Mitter, Partha. *Dharma's Daughters*. New Brunswick, N.J.: Rutgers University Press, 1991.

Moretti, Franco. "Conjectures on World Literature". In *Debating World Literature*, edited by Christopher Prendergast, 149–162. London and New York: Verso, 2004.

———. "On the Novel". In *The Novel*, vol. I: *History, Geography, and Culture*, edited by Franco Moretti. Princeton: Princeton University Press, 2006.

Morris, Jan, Charles Allen, Gillian Tindall, Colin Amery and Gavin Stamp. *Architecture of the British Empire*. London: Weidenfeld and Nicolson, 1986.

Morris, Mervyn. "Oh, Give the Girl a Chance: Jean Rhys and *Voyage in the Dark*". *Journal of West Indian Literature* 3, no.2 (1989): 1–8.

Moruzzi, Norma. "A Problem with Headscarves: Contemporary Complexities of Politics and Social Identity". *Political Theory* vol. 22, no. 4 (November 1994) 653–672.

Mote, Jasinta. *The Flesh*. Nairobi: Comb Books, 1975.

Mouffe, Chantal. "Feminism, Citizenship and Radical Democratic Politics". In *Feminists Theorize the Political*, edited by Judith Butler and Joan Scott, 369–384. New York: Routledge, 1992.

Murry-Brown, J. *Kenyatta* (London: Fontara, 1974).

Mutiso, G. C. M. "Women in African Literature". *East Africa Journal* 3, no. 3 (March 1971): 4–14.

Nama, Charles A. "Daughters of Moombi: Ngugi's Heroines and Traditional Gikuyu Aesthetics". In *Ngambika*, edited by in Carole Boyce Davies and Anne Adams Graves, Trenton, NJ: Africa World Press, 1986. 139–149.

Nandy, Ashis. "The Sociology of Sati". *Indian Express*, October 8, 1987.

Nenno, Nancy. "Femininity, the Primitive, and Modern Urban Space: Josephine Baker in Berlin". In *Women in the Metropolis*, edited by Katharina von Ankum, Berkeley, CA: University of California Press, 1997. 145–161.

Nord, Deborah Epstein. *Walking the Victorian Streets: Women, Representation, and the City*. Ithaca: Cornell University Press, 1995.

Okonkwo, Chidi. *Decolonization Agnostics in Postcolonial Fiction*. Basingstoke: Palgrave Macmillan, 1999.

Padgaonkar, Dileep, ed. *When Bombay Burned: Reportage and Comments on the Riots and Blasts from "The Times of India"*. New Delhi: UBS Publishers' Distributors, 1993.

Padmanabhan, R. "Movie Mafia: The Underworld and 'Bollywood'". *Frontline*, May 21, 1993.

Parent-Duchalet, Alexandre-Jean-Baptiste. *De la prostitution de la ville de Paris*. 2 vols. Paris: J.-B. Bailliere, 1836.

Parmar, Pratibha. "Black Feminism". In *Identity: Community, Culture, Difference*, edited by Jonathan Rutherford. London: Lawrence and Wishart, 1990.

Patel, Sujata. "The Urban Factor". *Seminar* 411 (November 1993): 27–30.

———. "Bombay's Urban Predicament". In *Bombay: Metaphor for Modern India*, edited by Sujata Patel and Alice Thorner. Bombay: Oxford University Press, 1995.

Phillips, Melanie. *Londonistan: How Britain Is Creating a Terror State Within*. London: Gibson Square Books, 2006.

Pike, David L. "Modernist Space and the Transformation of Underground London". In *Imagined Londons*, edited by Pamela Gilbert, 101–120. Albany: State University of New York Press, 2002.

Prakash, Gyan. "The Urban Turn". *Sarai Reader 02*: The Cities of Everyday Life: 2–7.

———. "Mumbai: the Modern City in Ruins". In *Other Cities, Other Worlds: Urban Imaginaries in a Globalizing Age*, edited by Andreas Huyssen, 181–203. Durham, N.C.: Duke University Press, 2008.

Pratt, Minnie Bruce. *Rebellion: Essays, 1980–1991*. New York: Firebrand Books, 1991. the

Premnath, Gautam. "Lonely Londoner: V. S. Naipaul and 'The God of the City'". In *Imagined Londons*, edited by Pamela Gilbert, 177–192. Albany: State University of New York Press, 2002.

Price-Chalita, Patricia. "Spatial Metaphor and the Politics of Empowerment: Mapping a Place for Feminism and Postmodernism in Geography?" *Antipode* 26, no. 3 (1994): 236–254.

Probst, Peter, Jan-Georg Deutsch, and Heike Schmidt. "Introduction: Cherished Visions and Entangled Meanings". In *African Modernities: Entangled Meanings in Current Debate*. Portsmouth, NH: Heinemann, 2002.

Punwani, Jyoti. "India: Searching for Answers in the Wake of Religious Violence". *Seminar*, 411 (November 1993).

Rabinow, Paul. *French Modern: Norms and Forms of the Social Environment*. Cambridge: MIT Press, 1989.

Rajan, Rajeswari Sundar. "The Feminist Plot and the Nationalist Allegory: Home and World in Two Indian Women's Novels in English". *Modern Fiction Studies* 39, no. 1 (Winter 1993): 71–92.

Ramchand, Kenneth. "Introduction". In *Lonely Londoners*, London: Longman Caribbean Series, 1986 [1956]. 3–21 by Sam Selvon.

———. The West Indian Novel and Its Background. London: Faber and Faber, 1970.

———. "Introduction". In *Minty Alley*, by C. L. R. James, London: New Beacon Books, 2nd ed. 1971.

———. "Introduction". In *Letters from London*, by C. L. R. James. Oxford: Signal Books, 2003.

Rao, R. Raj. "The Poetry of Bombay City". *The Journal of Commonwealth Literature* 31, no. 1 (1996): 63–70.

Rhys, Jean. *The Left Bank and Other Stories*. New York: Books for Libraries, 1927.

———. *Smile Please: An Unfinished Autobiography*. 1979; Harmondsworth: Penguin, 1981.

———. *Voyage in the Dark*. New York: W. W. Norton and Co., 1982.

———. *Good Morning Midnight*. New York: Penguin, 2000.

Rifkin, Adrian. *Street Noises: Parisian Pleasure–1900–1940*. Manchester: Manchester University Press, 1993.

Robins, K. "Tradition and Translation: National Culture in Its Global Context". In *Enterprise and Heritage: Cross-Currents in National Culture*, edited by J. Corner and S. Harvey, 21–44. New York: Routledge, 1991.

Rose, Gillian. *Feminism and Geography: The Limits of Geographical Knowledge*. Minneapolis: University of Minnesota Press, 1993.

Rushdie, Salman. *Imaginary Homelands*. New York: Viking, 1990.

———. *The Satanic Verses*. London: Penguin, 1989.

Sahgal, Gita. "Secular Spaces". In *Refusing Holy Orders: Women and Fundamentalism in Britain*, edited by Gita Sahgal and Nira Yuval-Davis. London: Virago Press, 1992.

Sahgal, Gita, and Nira Yuval-Davis, eds. *Refusing Holy Orders: Women and Fundamentalism in Britain.* London: Virago Press, 1992.

Said, Edward. *Culture and Imperialism.* New York: Vintage Books, 1994.

Sainath, P. "Mumbai: The Glory Days of the Raj?" *The Hindu,* February 13, 2008.

Sandhu, Sukhdev. *London Calling: How Black and Asian Writers Reimagined a City.* London: HarperCollins, 2003.

Sangari, Kumkum. "The Politics of the Possible". *Cultural Critique* 7 (Fall 1987). 157–186.

Sangari, Kumkum, and Sudesh Vaid, eds. *Recasting Women: Essays in Colonial History.* New Delhi: Kali for Women, 1989.

Sarkar, Tanika. "Women of the Hindutva Brigade". *Bulletin of Concerned Asian Scholars* 25, no. 4 (1993):16–24.

Sassen, Saskia. "The Global City: Strategic Site/New Frontier". In *Democracy, Citizenship, and the Global City,* edited by Engin Isin. London: Routledge, 2000.

———. *The Global City: New York, London, Tokyo.*2d ed. Princeton: Princeton University Press, 2001.

Scott, Bonnie Kime, ed. *The Gender of Modernism: A Critical Anthology.* Bloomington: Indiana University Press, 1990.

Scott, David. *Conscripts of Modernity: the Tragedy of Colonial Enlightenment.* Durham, N.C.: Duke University Press, 2004.

Schwarz, Bill. "Introduction". In *West Indian Intellectuals in Britain,* edited by Bill Schwarz. Manchester: Manchester University Press, 2003.

Self, Will. "The City That Forever Resists the Rational". *New Statesman,* July 7, 2003.

Sennett, Richard. *The Flesh and Stone: The Body and the City in Western Civilization.* New York: W. W. Norton, 1994.

Shahani, Roshan G. "Polyphonous Voices in the City: Bombay's Indian-English Fiction". *Economic and Political Weekly,* May 27, 1995: 1250–1254.

Shaw, Carolyn Martin. *Colonial Inscriptions: Race, Sex and Class in Kenya.* Minneapolis: University of Minneapolis Press, 1995.

Simmel, Georg. "The Metropolis and Mental Life" (1903). Reprinted in *The Sociology of Georg Simmel,* translated and edited by Kurt H. Wolff. New York:The Free Press, 1964.

Simon, David. "Rethinking Cities, Sustainability, and Development in Africa". In *Sacred Spaces and Public Quarrels: African Cultural and Economic Landscapes,* edited by Ezekiel Kalipeni and Paul T. Zeleza, 17–42. Trenton, N.J.: Africa World Press,, 1999.

Simone, AbdouMaliq. *For the City Yet to Come: Changing African Life in Four Cities.* Durham, N.C.: Duke University Press, 2004.

Sipe, Michelle. "Romancing the City: Arthur Symons and the Spatial Politics of Aesthetics in 1890s London". In *Imagined Londons,* edited by Pamela Gilbert, 69–84. Albany: State University of New York Press, 2002

Slaughter, Joseph R. "Master Plans: Designing (National) Allegories of Urban Space and Metropolitan Subjects for Postcolonial Kenya". *Research in African Literature* 35, no. 1 (Spring 2004): 30–42.

Smith, Anna Marie. *New Right Discourse on Race and Sexuality: Britain, 1968–1990.* Cambridge: Cambridge University Press, 1994.

Soja, Edward. *Postmodern Geographies: The Reassertion of Space and Critical Social Theory.* London: Verso, 1988.

Soman, D. S. "Tightening Mafia Grip—Choking Both Tinsel and Real Worlds". *Business Line,* February 1, 2001.

Sorkin, Michael. *Variations on a Theme Park: The New American City and the End of Public Space.* New York: Hill and Wang, 1992.

Soyinka, Wole. "The Writer in a Modern African State". *Transition* 6, no. 3 (1967): 11–13.

Srivastava, Sanjay. "Modernity and Post-coloniality: The Metropolis as Metaphor". *Economic and Political Weekly*, February 17, 1996: 403–412.

Swami, Praveen. "Mumbai's Mafia Wars". *Frontline*, March 27–April 6, 1999.

Tagore, Rabindranath. *The Home and the World*. Penguin, 2005.

Talal, Asad, ed. *Anthropology and the Colonial Encounter*. Atlantic Heights, N.J.: Humanities Press, 1973.

Tharu, Susie, and K. Lalita, eds. *Women Writing in India*, vol. II: *The Twentieth Century*. New York: The Feminist Press, 1993.

Thiong'o, Ngugi wa. *Writers in Politics*. London: Heinemann, 1981.

———. *Devil on the Cross*. London: Heinemann, 1987.

———. *Petals of Blood*. New York: Penguin, 1991.

Thomas, Sue. *The Worlding of Jean Rhys*. Westport, Conn.: Greenwood Press, 1999.

Triulzi, Alessandro. "African Cities, Historical Memory and Street Buzz". In *The Post-colonial Question: Common Skies, Divided Horizons*, edited by Iain Chambers and Lidia Curti. London: Routledge, 1996.

Umrigar, Thrity. *The Space between Us*. London: Fourth Estate, 2006.

UN Population Division, *World Urbanization Prospects: The 2003 Revision*. http://www.un.org/esa/population/publication/corp2002/WUP2003Report.

Vanaik, Achin. "Rendezvous at Mumbai". *New Left Review* 26 (March–April 2004): 53–65.

van Zwanenberg, R. "History and Theory of Urban Poverty in Nairobi: The Problem of Slum Development". *Journal of East African Research and Development* 2 (1972): 167–203.

Varma, Rashmi. "Provincializing the Global City: From Bombay to Mumbai". *Social Text 81* 22 (Winter 2004): 65–90.

———. "Bad Copy: The Indian City in Postcolonial Theory". Paper presented to the "Workshop on India's Global Cities", University of Warwick, May 2007.

Vassanji, M. G. *The In-Between World of Vikram Lall*. Edinburgh: Canongate, 2003.

Vidler, Anthony. *The Architectural Uncanny: Essays in the Modern Unhomely*. Cambridge: MIT Press, 1992.

Visram, Rozina. *Ayah, Lascars and Princes: The Stories of Indians in Britain, 1700–1947*. London: Pluto Press, 1986.

Viswanathan, Gauri. "Raymond Williams and British Colonialism: The Limits of Metropolitan Cultural Theory". In *Views Beyond the Border Country: Raymond Williams and Cultural Politics*, edited by in Dennis L. Dworkin and Leslie G. Roman, 217–220. New York: Routledge, 1993.

Walkowitz, Judith. *City of Dreadful Delight: Narratives of Sexual Danger in Late-Victorian London*. Chicago: University of Chicago Press, 1992.

Watson, Sophie, and Katherine Gibson. "Postmodern Cities, Spaces and Politics: An Introduction". In *Postmodern Cities and Spaces*, edited by Sophie Watson and Katherine Gibson, 1–12. Oxford: Blackwell, 1995.

White, Luise. *The Comforts of Home: Prostitution in Colonial Nairobi*. Chicago: University of Chicago Press, 1990.

Williams, Hywel. "Britain's Ruling Elites Now Exercise Power with a Shameless Rapacity". *The Guardian* April 11, 2006.

Williams, Patrick. "'Simultaneous Uncontemporaneities': Theorising Modernism and Empire". In *Modernism and Empire*, edited by Howard J. Booth and Nigel Rigby, 13–38. Manchester: Manchester University Press, 2000.

Williams, Raymond. *The Country and the City*. London: The Hogart Press, 1985.

Wilson, Amrit. *Finding a Voice–Asian Women in Britain*. London: Virago Press, 1978.

Wilson, Elizabeth. "The Invisible Flaneur". In *Postmodern Cities and Spaces*, edited by Sophie Watson and Katherine Gibson, 59–79. Oxford: Blackwell, 1995.

Wolff, Janet. *Feminine Sentences: Essays on Women and Culture*. Berkeley and Los Angeles: University of California Press, 1990.

Woolf, Virginia. *Mrs Dalloway* (1925). New York: Harcourt, Brace and Company, 1997.

Young, Iris Marion. "The Ideal of Community and the Politics of Difference". In *Feminism/Postmodernism*, edited by Linda Nicholson. New York: Routledge, 1990.

Index